Karl Marx's *Capital*
A Guide to Volumes I–III

Karl Marx's *Capital*
A Guide to Volumes I–III

Second Edition

Kenneth Smith

ANTHEM PRESS
LONDON · NEW YORK · DELHI

Anthem Press
An imprint of Wimbledon Publishing Company
www.anthempress.com

This edition first published in UK and USA 2021
by ANTHEM PRESS
75–76 Blackfriars Road, London SE1 8HA, UK
or PO Box 9779, London SW19 7ZG, UK
and
244 Madison Ave #116, New York, NY 10016, USA

First published in the UK and USA by Anthem Press in 2012

Cover design by Omid Asghari

British Library Cataloguing-in-Publication Data
A catalogue record for this book is available from the British Library.

Library of Congress Control Number: 2021933347

ISBN-13: 978-1-83998-000-8 (Pbk)
ISBN-10: 1-83998-000-1 (Pbk)

This title is also available as an e-book.

In a few days I shall be 50. As that Prussian lieutenant said to you: '20 years of service and still lieutenant', I can say: half a century on my shoulders, and still a pauper. How right my mother was: 'If only Karell had *made* capital instead of etc.'

(Marx to Engels, 30 April 1868; emphasis added)

This book is dedicated to my mother,
Mrs Alice Smith (née Flynn) 1926–2013

CONTENTS

PREFACE TO THE SECOND EDITION

The second edition of this book is substantially the same as the first except for a minor change in the title of the book (from 'A Guide to Marx's *Capital*, Vols. I–III' to 'Karl Marx's *Capital*: A Guide to Volumes I–III') and for the correction of a number of mostly minor typographical errors throughout the book. I would like to thank Professor David Ketterer of Liverpool University, UK for reading the first edition of this book for me and identifying these errors and Anthem Press for bringing out this corrected second edition of the book.

Kenneth Smith, March 2021

INTRODUCTION

Reading *Capital*

Marxists as divergent as Louis Althusser and Karl Korsch have recommended reading Volume I of Marx's *Capital* in a different order to that in which it is published.[1] Korsch (*Three Essays on Marxism*) suggests beginning with *Capital*, Vol. I, Part III, Chapter 7, on 'the labour-process and the process of producing surplus value' and then moving on more or less to the rest of Volume I; only then does he suggest the reader return to Parts I and II. Althusser (*Lenin and Philosophy and Other Essays*) suggests leaving aside Parts I and V, and reading first Parts II, III, IV, VI, VII and VIII, only then returning again to start at the beginning. Even Marx himself suggested a more comprehensible order of reading. In a letter dated 30 November 1867,[2] addressed to his good friend Dr Ludwig Kugelmann, shortly after the publication of the first German edition of *Capital*, Vol. I, Marx advises Kugelmann that he might tell his 'good wife' that the chapters 'Working Day' (Vol. I, Part III), 'Co-operation', 'The Division of Labour and Machinery' (Part IV) and 'Primitive Accumulation' (Part VI) were the most immediately readable – although he warns Kugelmann that it would still probably be necessary for him to explain to his wife some of the more 'incomprehensible terminology' in these sections (*MECW*, 1987, 42:490). While Marx gives slightly different advice to another woman, a Mrs Wollmann, in a letter dated 19 March 1877;[3] in which he advises her to start with the last section of the French edition of *Capital* (the last but one in the English translation), 'The Process of Accumulation of Capital'.

All of these suggestions seem to have been made with much the same intention; namely, to avoid the conceptually difficult Parts I and II of Vol. I, on the subject of commodities and money, including Marx's initial discussion of the general form of value and the section on commodity fetishism. However, this perfectly understandable intention leads to the peculiar result, in Korsch's case, of beginning *Capital* with the sections on the labour process and the process of producing surplus value *without* first having looked at Marx's preliminary discussion of value and the buying and selling of labour-power itself. While in Althusser's case, we find the even more peculiar suggestion that we should begin our reading of *Capital* with the rather dull and uninteresting sections on the various formulae for the circuit of money capital. Even Marx's own suggestions raise the interesting question why he chose to publish Vol. I beginning with the conceptually difficult Parts I and II if even *he* thought it might be better to start with the more descriptive historical material in Part III? In his letter to Mrs Wollman Marx gives some explanation of this. 'In the scientific exposition the arrangement is prescribed for the author, although some other arrangement might often be more convenient and more appropriate for the reader' (*MECW*, 1991, 45:212). This implies that the matter was out of his hands, but of course this was not the case.

Although I agree with Althusser and Korsch in wishing to avoid for the moment the conceptually difficult Part I of *Capital*, Vol. I, I do not agree that Part II, or even the first half of Part III, makes a suitable beginning for reading *Capital*. In what follows, I therefore adopt the procedure recommended by Marx himself in his letter to Kugelmann, and begin with the discussion of the lengthening of the working day and the distinction that Marx makes between absolute and relative surplus value.[4]

It is here, however, that my discussion of *Capital* departs dramatically from what has gone before in books which claim to provide a guide to reading Marx's *Capital*, but which in point of fact are nearly always restricted to discussions of *Capital*, Vol. I alone.[5] I believe that it is imperative at this point, if we are to gain a proper understanding of Marx's argument, to look at what Marx has to say on the subject of the accumulation of capital in *Capital*, Vol. II, and especially on the subject of merchant's capital, in *Capital*, Vols II and III, *before* we go back and gain a proper understanding of Marx's discussion of capitalist accumulation in Vol. I.

The reader who is new to *Capital* might well be surprised to learn that Marx did not publish either *Capital*, Vol. II or *Capital*, Vol. III during his own life time. Marx originally intended to publish *Capital*, Vols II and III as a single volume,[6] almost certainly of about the same length as the present Vol. I and therefore with much of the material included in the present Vols II and III left out. What we now call *Capital*, Vols II and III were edited by Marx's good friend Frederick Engels more or less as he found this material in Marx's notebooks, and were not published in their present form until after Marx's death in 1883: Vol. II appearing first in 1885 and Vol. III not until 1894, the year before Engels died. Just *why* Marx failed to publish this material during his own lifetime is likely to remain an enduring problem for Marxist scholarship, but is perhaps of little interest to anyone else. His health is usually given as one of the main reasons – never well, his health declined significantly during the later years of his life, during which time he spent much of his time convalescing at the seaside. This might well explain why he did little or no work on *Capital* from about 1880 onward, but it does not explain why he could not have done more during the thirteen years after the 1867 publication of *Capital*, Vol. I. In a letter to Kugelmann dated 18 May 1874 (*MECW*, 1991, 45:17–18), Marx cites his health as one of the main reasons why he could not continue further with *Capital*. He also mentions the considerable work he was doing at this time toward the publication of the first French edition of Vol. I, which appeared in instalments between 1872 and 1875 (*MECW*, 1991, 45:457, 17n). Marx and Engels also devoted a considerable effort during the period from 1864 to 1873 to the work they were doing for the First, or Communist, International, a loose association of workers movements throughout Europe and North America. However, an additional reason for the delay is given by Marx in a letter to Nikolai Danielson five years later (10 April 1879, *MECW*, 1991, 45:355–6). In it Marx again mentions his health – he jokes that his medical advisers had warned him to shorten considerably his 'working-day' if he did not wish to relapse into the poor state of health he was in 1874 – but goes on to say that '[t]he bulk of [new] materials I have received not only from Russia, but also from the United States, etc., make it pleasant for me to have a "pretext" of continuing my studies, instead of winding them up finally for the public.' For whatever reason then it seems that Marx simply did not *wish* to publish the second and third volumes of *Capital* during his own lifetime, but left this work to Engels.

Marx was a perfectionist as far as his work was concerned and simply could not bear to let it go until he was *entirely* satisfied with it. In a letter to Engels dated 31 July 1865, Marx says,

> But I cannot bring myself to send anything off until I have the whole thing in front of me. Whatever shortcomings they may have, the advantage of my writings is that they are an artistic whole, and this can only be achieved through my practice of never having things printed until I have them in front of me *in their entirety*. (*MECW*, 1987, 42:173; emphasis original)

Writing to Marx's wife Jenny in 1860, Engels says that 'there will be no one to blame but Mr Moor [Marx's nickname] himself' if there was a delay in publishing and refers to his 'thoroughness and his failure … to do anything about publishers himself' (15 August 1860, *MECW*, 1985, 41:179). While Marx himself, in a letter to Ferdinand Lassalle dated 28 April 1862, refers to 'that quirk I have of finding fault with anything that I have written and not looked at for a month, so that I have to revise it completely' (*MECW*, 1985, 41:356). Even during the period when Marx was writing up what eventually became the first (German) edition of *Capital*, Vol. I, although sympathetic to the problems caused by his health, Engels had to continually urge Marx to get on and publish something, even if this meant bringing out *Capital*, Vol. I before

Capital, Vol. II was ready for publication (10 February 1866; *MECW*, 1987, 42:225–6). This was the plan that Marx was eventually forced to adopt later that year (Marx to Kugelmann, 13 October 1866, *MECW*, 1987, 42:328).

Not only then was Marx a great perfectionist as far as his published work was concerned, but he was also a great procrastinator it seems, two things which of course often go together. Procrastinators are generally said to be extremely concerned about what other people think of them – the idea here seems to be that 'if I never finish I can never be judged' – and although Marx frequently claimed in his letters that he was not at all concerned what anyone said about him or about his legacy, this does not in fact seem to have been the case. According to David McLellan in his biography, *Karl Marx, His Life and Thought*, Marx and Dr Kugelmann had a friendship ending quarrel in 1874 over the issue of the publication of *Capital* while Marx was on a holiday in Carlesbad that had been arranged for him by Dr Kugelmann. According to McLellan, 'Marx and Kugelmann quarrelled violently during a long walk in which Kugelmann "tried to persuade Marx to refrain from all political propaganda and complete the third book of *Capital* before anything else", a subject on which', McLellan comments, 'Marx was always touchy' (McLellan 1973, 428). Elsewhere in his biography McLellan notes:

> A study of the evolution of agriculture in Russia was intended to illuminate Marx's ideas on ground rent in Volume Three of *Capital* in the same way as English industrial development provided the practical examples to the ideas expounded in Volume One. Marx had learnt Russian specifically to be able to study the original sources. As in the 1850s and 1860s, Marx amassed a huge amount of material but he now lacked the power of synthesis and the driving force to make something of it. After his death Engels was amazed to find among Marx's papers more than two cubic metres of documents containing nothing but Russia statistics. During these years Marx filled in his microscopic handwriting almost three thousand pages – these manuscripts comprising almost exclusively notes on his reading. In his later years this reading became almost obsessional: he no longer had the power to create but at least he could absorb. Thus the manuscripts for Volume Three of *Capital* remained virtually in the state in which they had been since 1864–65. Marx had rewritten almost half of Volume Two in 1870, but thereafter made only minor additions and revisions – realising as he said to [his daughter] Eleanor shortly before his death that it would be up to Engels 'to make something of it'. Marx kept the state of his manuscript a secret from everyone, including Engels, who wrote to [August] Bebel that 'if I had been aware of this I would not have let him rest day or night until everything had been finished and

> printed. Marx himself knew this better than anyone…' In fact, the state of the manuscript was so chaotic that Engels published Volume Three of *Capital* only eleven years after Marx's death. (McLellan 1973, 422)[7]

Following McLellan, I want to make a rather controversial claim in this book. I will argue that one of the main reasons Marx did not complete the publication of *Capital*, Vols II and III was not only because of his health etc., but because he was dissatisfied with his own account of reproduction on an extending scale in what we now know as *Capital*, Vol. II (the second volume to be published but actually the third to be written). Marx, I will argue, was concerned to find *a materially compelling* reason why capitalist accumulation took place on an extended scale and he was therefore not satisfied with an explanation that depended either on the inclinations of the capitalists – the lure of ever greater profit as it were – or on the supposed compulsion of capitalist competition to bring it about. Why, Marx wondered, should a capitalist, who might simply reproduce an existing process of production on the *same* unchanging scale (i.e. a successful capitalist enterprise perhaps which was already up and running), continually *extend* the scale of the process of production, with all the risks that this entailed for the process of production to become over-extended and then fail? The answer to this question could not be the one that is usually given (i.e. capitalist competition) because that is not a first order explanation: it does not explain why the *first* capitalist in any particular cycle of reproduction chooses to extend the scale of the process of production themselves, thereby forcing others to follow suit. Similarly, Marx could not rest easy with a more psychological explanation of the kind provided by Max Weber or Joseph Schumpeter, which relied on the entrepreneurial spirit of the capitalists or their desire for greater wealth. Such an explanation might well be the only one we have for this phenomenon, but it was not an explanation that satisfied Marx. Something so fundamental to the nature of capital as the colossal expansion of the capitalist mode of production on a continually expanding scale simply could not be due, Marx thought, to the will of the capitalist. There must then be some other, more fundamental, mechanism at work, embedded within the capitalist mode of production itself, that could account for reproduction on an extended scale and reproduction on a progressively extended scale *against* the natural inclination of capitalists to conserve what they already had. What then was this 'something else'? What was the explanation of this phenomenon?

Perhaps, as McLellan suggests, because of his failing powers of synthesis, or perhaps for some other reason, Marx simply could not find the answer to this question. However, in what follows, I will argue that the answer *is* contained in Marx's writings – it is in what is now known as *Capital*, Vol. II – and I suggest that the answer to this problem has something to do with what Marx himself referred to as the 'precipitation of fixed capital'. Marx spent a great deal of time considering this question and was convinced that the solution to the problem had something to do with the reproduction of fixed capital, but for some reason or other Marx just could not seem to see what the answer was for himself. The details of this argument – which have to do with why a capitalist should accumulate capital in its productive rather than in its money form – are explained in Part II, Chapter 9 of this book. In short though, I will argue that Marx simply became stuck at this point somewhere around 1870 – halfway through his rewrite of Vol. II, and at the point where we now know that he broke off his studies on the second volume of *Capital* altogether – and, being a perfectionist, felt that he simply could not complete this project, his life's work.

Once we have gained a thorough understanding of the process of capitalist accumulation in the second half of *Capital*, Vol. II – in Part II of the present book – we will then turn our attention, in Part III of this study, to what is now the first half of the present Vol. II, to look at Marx's discussion of the *circulation* of capital and the very important distinction that Marx makes here between the circuit of industrial capital and the circuit of merchant's capital. At this point we will then go on to look at Marx's further discussion of mercantilism and the circulation of money capital generally in the middle third of Vol. III and – following on from the argument presented in Part II of this study – I will present a second controversial argument; namely, that a proper understanding of this part of Vol. III is crucial for a correct understanding of why the capitalist mode of production did not develop as quickly or in the form that Marx seems to have expected it would. I argue that the pure, or fully developed, capitalist mode of production that Marx describes in detail in Vol. I became *underdeveloped* by the contact it had with the rest of the non-capitalist world at that time. It is simply not possible – it is not logical or dialectical, I think – to claim that the capitalist mode of production could have developed fully in isolation in Europe (or even in Europe and North America), and had the devastating effect on the rest of the non-capitalist world which Marx and Engels attribute to it in their writing on Ireland, India and China, without at the same time acknowledging that the underdevelopment of the rest of the non-capitalist world must also have had a devastating effect on the fullest possible (or as we might say, the pure) development of the capitalist mode of production itself in Europe. As Marx said on this point in a letter to Engels, dated 8 October 1858:

> There is no denying that bourgeois society has for the second time experienced its 16th century, a 16th century which, I hope, will sound its death knell just as the first ushered it into the world. The proper task of bourgeois society is the creation of the world market, at least in outline,

> and of the production based on that market. Since the world is round, the colonisation of California and Australia and the opening up of China and Japan would seem to have completed this process. For us, the difficult question is this: on the Continent the revolution is imminent and will, moreover, instantly assume a socialist character. Will it not necessarily be crushed in this little corner of the earth, since the movement of bourgeois society is still in the ascendant over a far greater area? (*MECW*, 1983, 40:346–7)

We now know that the answer to this question is 'yes'. The development of socialism in Europe, which Marx thought imminent in 1858, was crushed because the development of capitalism in the rest of the world was still taking place. This being the case, the relative underdevelopment of capitalism in the rest of the world at this time could not possibly fail to have an effect on the development of capitalism in Europe and hence on the development of socialism. As I will explain in Part III of this study, it is not only the development of socialism in Europe that was undermined by the underdevelopment of capitalism in the rest of the world at that time but also the character of the capitalist mode of production itself. In particular, this caused the CMP to change from the highly industrialized mode of production that Marx describes in *Capital*, Vol. I (one which is in fact premised on a closed economy model) to the more mercantile kind of capitalism that he describes in detail in Vols II and III and with which we are all too familiar today.

Finally, in Part IV of this book, once I have considered what Marx has to say in the first third of *Capital*, Vol. III, on the subject of the tendency of the rate of profit to fall, we will only then return to the first part of Vol. I and the question of the labour theory of value and the degree of exploitation of labour. And here I will present a third and probably even more controversial argument, since I will claim that Marx is not in fact especially interested in the question of the *nature* of value in the first part of Vol. I – he is not a supporter of a 'crude' labour theory of value, as developed by the English economist David Ricardo. Rather, much more important to Marx, and the basis of his own unique contribution to classical political economy, is the origin and nature of *surplus value* (what I will call 'the labour theory of surplus value' in order to distinguish it from Ricardo's theory), and this, I will argue, is the only reason we have for still being interested in what he has to say today. Extending the argument presented in Part III of this study, I will argue that it is only by looking at what Marx has to say on the subject of merchant's capital in Vol. II and on the subject of the rate of profit in Vol. III *before* we look at what Marx has to say on the nature and the substance of value generally at the beginning of Vol. I, that we can see what Marx meant when he famously claimed just 'how little the determination of value "directly" counts in bourgeois society' (Marx and Engels 1936, 239), and therefore just how much the fullest possible development of a purely capitalist mode of production has been undermined by the continuing vitality of a highly developed form of merchant's capital into the twenty-first century.

Of course, the reader who does not wish to follow this argument in the order that I present it here is perfectly at liberty to skip my account of the nature of the capitalist mode of production in Part II of this book and the underdevelopment of the CMP in Part III – Chapters 7–9 in particular are undoubtedly among the most difficult theoretically in the present study – and start by reading Part IV of this book. After all, this is the order of reading – the scientific presentation of the subject as Marx himself described this – that Marx claims he felt compelled to adopt. But if the reader does do this then they must not forget that Marx failed to publish *Capital*, Vols II and III during his own lifetime, with all the problems that this entails for a proper understanding of what he has to say in Vol. I, and they will then have to try to explain for themselves the reasons why this was the case.

A Note on Marx's Method

It might be helpful at the beginning of a book of this kind to say something about Marx's methodology or what is sometimes also known as 'dialectical' or 'historical' materialism. It has been suggested (see for example Harvey 2010, 12) that Marx did not provide us with any very clear statement of his views on this matter; however, the reader who is interested in this question only has to look at a section at the beginning of *Capital*, Vol. I (rather confusingly entitled an 'Afterword to the Second German Edition' in the Lawrence & Wishart/ Progress Press 1974 edition, but which was in fact included as a *preface* to the second German edition of *Capital* and which might therefore have been better described as a 'Postface to the Second German Edition', as was done in the 1976 Penguin edition) to see that this is not the case. In this section Marx gives us the first of what are in fact a number of reasonably clear accounts of his methodology which, taken together, do give us a fairly good idea of what he has to say on this subject:

> My dialectical method is not only different from the Hegelian, but is its direct opposite. To Hegel, the life-process of the human brain, i.e., the process of thinking, which, under the name of 'the Idea', he even transformed into an independent subject, is the demiurgos [the creator] of the real world, and the real world is only the external, phenomenal form of 'the Idea'. With me, on the contrary, the ideal is nothing else

> than the material world reflected by the human mind, and translated into forms of thought.
>
> The mystifying side of [the] Hegelian dialectic I criticized nearly thirty years ago, at a time when it was still the fashion. But just as I was working at the first volume of "Das Kapital", it was the good pleasure of the peevish, arrogant, mediocre [Epigones] who now talk large in cultured Germany, to treat Hegel in the same way as the brave Moses Mendelssohn in Lessing's time treated Spinoza, i.e., as a 'dead dog'. I therefore openly avowed myself the pupil of that mighty thinker [Hegel], and even here and there, in the chapter on the theory of value, coquetted with the modes of expression peculiar to him. The mystification which dialectics suffers in Hegel's hands, by no means prevents him from being the first to present its general form of working in a comprehensive and conscious manner. With him it is standing on its head. It must be turned right side up again, if you would discover the rational kernel within the mystical shell. (1974a, 29 [1976, 102–3])

Read in isolation this statement is rather hard to understand; what *exactly* is it that Marx means to say here? Fortunately for us, however, we do not need to rely on this explanation alone since Marx also gives us another account of Hegel's dialectical method, and also the way in which his own materialist method departed from this, in the section entitled 'The Method of Political Economy' in the preface to the notebooks, now known the *Grundrisse*, that Marx made before he began to write *Capital*, Vol. I. And since what Marx has to say about his method is much clearer here, I will once again quote him at length:

> The economists of the seventeenth century, e.g., always began with the living whole, with population, nation, state, several states, etc.; but they always conclude by discovering through analysis a small number of determinant, abstract, general relations such as division of labour, money, value, etc. As soon as these individual moments had been more or less firmly established and abstracted, there began the economic systems, which ascended from the simple relations, such as labour, division of labour, need, exchange value, to the level of the state, exchange between nations and the world market. The latter is obviously the scientifically correct method. The concrete is concrete because it is the concentration of many determinations, hence unity of the diverse. *It appears in the process of thinking*, therefore, as a process of concentration, *as a result, not as a point of departure*, even though it is the point of departure in reality and hence also the point of departure for observation [*Anschauung*] and conception.

> Along the first path the full conception was evaporated to yield an abstract determination; along the second, the abstract determinations led towards a reproduction of the concrete by way of thought. In this way *Hegel fell into the illusion of conceiving the real as the product of thought* concentrating itself, probing its own depths, and unfolding itself out of itself, by itself, whereas the method of rising from the abstract to the concrete is only the way in which thought appropriates the concrete, reproduces it as the concrete in the mind. (Marx 1973, 100–101; emphasis added)

The 'Afterword' to the second edition of *Capital* is the basis of the claim that is often made that Marx simply 'inverted' Hegel's dialectical method. However if we put this statement together with the above extract from the preface to the *Grundrisse*, I think we can see clearly enough that what Marx did was very much more than this and exactly how his own methodology differed from that of Hegel's.

According to Marx, Hegel came to believe – wrongly in Marx's view – that reality could only be properly understood through pure thought alone and that the real world was therefore, by contrast, merely the external form and reflection of this thought. For Marx the opposite is true: 'the ideal is nothing else than the material world reflected in the human mind, and translated into forms of thought' (1974a, 29 [1976 102–3]). However, in the *Grundrisse* Marx explains that, having reached this point in our understanding of the nature of reality, it is necessary to once again return to the concrete. In other words, although Hegel's thought represents an advance in this matter, he was wrong to let it rest at the level of thought alone. Hegel took the matter only so far but Marx went further. It is necessary *first* to rise up *inductively* from the concrete appearance of reality and to abstract from this *theories* about the nature of reality itself (Newton's theory of gravity would be a good case in point here) before once again returning to *apply* this theory to the real world. Marx then, as we can now see, does not so much turn Hegel's dialectic on its head, but *completes* it by filling in the other side of the project which had been left unexplained by Hegel. Hegel went so far with this project and made a good start but for some reason stopped short in his thinking about this matter. It is necessary, once having arrived at the *idea*, to bring this back down to reality. As Marx famously said in his eleventh and final theses on Feuerbach: 'The philosophers have only interpreted the world … the point is to change it' (*MESW*, 1968, 30).

Apart from these two reasonably clear statements of Marx's method, there are also three very good letters written by Engels during the 1890s to a young German correspondent of his, one Conrad Schmidt (Engels to Schmidt of 5 August 1890 and the 1 November 1891, and see also Engels to Schmidt of 12 March 1895). Here Engels not only compares Marx's exposition in *Capital*,

Vol. I from the commodity to capital (the order of presentation that Marx was so attached to) with the movement from Being to Essence in Hegelian thought; he also tries to explain to Schmidt the relationship between theory and reality. In the letter of 1890, Engels writes:

> In general the word 'materialistic' serves many of the younger writers in Germany as a mere phrase with which anything and everything is labelled without further study, that is, they stick on this label and then consider the matter disposed of. But our conception of history is above all a guide to study, [and] not a lever for construction after the manner of the Hegelians. All history must be studied afresh, the conditions of existence of the different forms of society must be examined individually before the attempt is made to deduce from them the political, civil-law, aesthetic, philosophic, religious etc. views corresponding to them ... But instead of this too many of the young Germans simply make use of the phrase historical materialism (and *everything* can be turned into a phrase) only in order to get their own relatively scanty historical knowledge – for economic history is still in its swaddling clothes! – constructed into a neat system as quickly as possible. (*MESC*, 1953, 497)

While in the letter of 1891, he writes:

> Hegel's dialectic is upside down because it is supposed to be the 'self-development of thought' of which the dialectics of facts therefore is only the reflection, whereas really the dialectics in our heads is only the reflection of the actual development going on in the world of nature and of human history in obedience to dialectical forms. (*MESC*, 1953, 520)

Finally, in addition to all of this, there are several very good explanations in the text of *Capital* itself, such as the footnote to 1974a, 352 [1976, 493–4] in which Marx argues that:

> Every history of religion, even, that fails to take account of this materialist basis, is uncritical. It is, in reality much easier to discover by analysis the earthly core of the misty creations of religion, than, conversely, it is to develop from the actual relations of life the corresponding celestialised forms of these relations. The latter method is the only materialistic and therefore the only scientific one.[8]

There are also a number of examples of Marx's use of the dialectical method, any one of which would show how Marx actually applied this method, and of which the best is probably in the famous chapter on credit in *Capital*, Vol. III (see Part III, Chapter 11 of the present study for a more detailed account of this point). Here, contrary to what is generally supposed to be the case, Marx explains that it is *not* his view that capitalism can bring about its own destruction, but only that it has a tendency to do this since, in bringing about its own destruction, it would of course destroy the very thing that is claimed was destroying it; namely, *itself*.

A Note on Social Class

Marx has surprisingly little to say on the subject of social class in the three volumes of *Capital* and, for this reason, it might be felt that there is no need to discuss this matter further in a book which is intended as a guide to the reader of *Capital*. However, looked at in another way, everything that Marx says in *Capital* is in one way or another concerned with the question of the relationship between the owners of land, the owners of capital and the owners of those who have nothing to sell but themselves. *Capital* itself was intended to provide a theoretical explanation to the working class of the reality of their class situation in a capitalist mode of production. The reason Marx does not discuss the concept of class explicitly in *Capital* – except for the famously incomplete chapter at the end of Vol. III, which is itself only a page and a half long – is clear enough. Simply put, it is because the major theoretical concept discussed in this book, which explains everything else, is capital, not class. If Marx had wanted to write a book on the subject of social class he would have done so and the fact that he did not must speak for itself.[9] Even so, I suspect that the reader who is new to *Capital* would expect to see more on the concept of class than there actually is and therefore I have decided to add a chapter on this subject as an appendix to this book. The reader who is only interested in what Marx has to say on the subject of class in *Capital* need only read the first two sections of this appendix while the reader who is interested in Marx's more general views on this question can read the whole thing.

A Note on the English Translations of *Capital*

At least two English language translations of Marx's *Capital* are currently in print – the Penguin 'Modern Classics' translation of 1976–81, by Ben Fowkes and David Fernbach, and the original English translation of 1887 by Samuel Moore and Edward Aveling (Lawrence & Wishart, 1974–7). If the more widely available Penguin translation is now threatening to take over from the original, and even to displace it, I regret the development. The language of the original translation, supervised by Engels, has more of the grandeur associated with the Victorian English of the 1880s than the more accurate but undeniably rather bland edition produced by the editors of the journal *New Left Review* nearly a century later. However, in order to overcome any problems that there might be with which translation is to be preferred, for the purposes of this guide to Marx's *Capital*, I provide the page numbers to *both* editions – with the original Moore/Aveling translation given first, followed immediately by the corresponding pages in the more recent Fowkes/Fernbach translation. The latter citation to the Penguin edition will be set off by square brackets. Thus the first page of *Capital*, Vol. I in the original Progress Press/Lawrence & Wishart edition of 1974, which begins on page 43 is therefore given as follows (1974a, 43), while the same page in the later 1976 Penguin edition, which begins on page 125, is therefore shown as [1976, 125]. Volumes II and III in Lawrence & Wishart/Progress Press edition were published in 1974 and 1977 and are hence are shown as 1974b and 1977, while Volumes II and III of the Penguin edition were first published in 1978 and 1981 and are therefore shown accordingly (see Table 1 below).

Table 1

Capital	Lawrence & Wishart/Progress Press edition	Penguin edition
Vol. I	1974a	1976
Vol. II	1974b	1978
Vol. III	1977	1981

The decision to give pages numbers to both editions of *Capital* has, however, created further problems of its own. The chapter numbers and the numbers of the various Parts into which Marx divided each volume of *Capital* remain largely the same from one edition of *Capital* to the next, except that these are given in roman numerals in the original and in arabic numbers in the more recent translation; I have therefore modernized these throughout in conformity with the Penguin edition. However this still leaves the problem which edition to refer to when a *direct* quotation is given from *Capital* itself since it would obviously be very awkward to give both translations on the same page. Fortunately, in what follows, direct quotations from *Capital* are rare – I generally prefer to summarize what Marx has to say and leave it to the reader, using the page numbers provided and the essential reading given at the end of each chapter, to follow up the details of each reference for themselves if they wish to do so. But where it seemed unavoidable to provide a direct quotation, or where this is done for the sake of clarity, I have always quoted from the *original* translation as supervised by Engels. This is not only because, for all its apparent inaccuracies, this is the translation that I still prefer, but also because I believe that most people today who wish to read *Capital* will almost certainly buy the more widely available Penguin edition, but might still like to see for themselves how Marx and Engels expressed the same point in the first English translation. Without needing to buy both translations of *Capital* then, the reader who has the Penguin edition will be able to see how the same point was expressed in the original translation and in the more recent one, while the reader who has the original Lawrence & Wishart/Progress Press edition will not see any difference between the two.

Finally, it is possible to read this book in one of three ways. It can either be read as a book in its own right, and without making any reference at all to the three volumes of Marx's *Capital*; it can be read in conjunction with Marx's *Capital*, checking what I say against the original and one's own understanding of what Marx says here; or it can be read individually or as part of a study group. It is for this reason that I have included 'points for further discussion' at the end of each chapter of this book as and when I thought these might be helpful.

Kenneth Smith
April 2012

Part I

THE DEVELOPMENT OF THE CAPITALIST MODE OF PRODUCTION

PREFACE TO PART I

Before we can begin to look at what the capitalist mode of production is like – its nature and form, etc. – we must first look at how this mode of production came into being. In the first part of this book, we will therefore look at the historical *development* of this mode of production and especially at the question, in Chapter 4, of the 'primitive', or non-capitalist, accumulation of wealth that Marx says was a necessary prerequisite before the development of the capitalist mode of production proper (CMP) could take place. We will also look at the development of machinery and modern industry, the transition from handicraft production in the Middle Ages through the period of manufacture (production by 'hands') up until about the 1750s and then onto the production of things by machines – or *machinofacture* as this is sometimes called – in Chapter 3. In Chapter 2, we will look at the development of cooperation and the division of labour in industry and society. We begin, however, in Chapter 1, by looking at the very important distinction that Marx makes between an increase in surplus value produced by an absolute lengthening of the working day, or 'absolute surplus value' as Marx calls this, and the parallel process of increasing surplus value by an increase in the intensification of labour – by causing the labourer to produce more in a shorter period of time – or 'relative surplus value' as Marx calls this.

1. ABSOLUTE AND RELATIVE SURPLUS VALUE IN *CAPITAL*, VOL. I, CH. 10 AND 12

It is obviously possible to extend the length of the working day from 7 or 8 hours, to 10, 12, 14, 16 or even 18 hours, and this was done as a matter of course at the beginning of the Industrial Revolution in Britain, and is still done to a greater or lesser extent in other parts of the world today in the form of so-called 'overtime' and 'over-working'. However, this process is not without its limits. Firstly, of course, there are only so many hours in the day; although on rare occasions a labourer might well be made to work for longer than 24 hours at one time, by definition the working day itself cannot be extended beyond 24 hours per day. Secondly, labourers must eat and rest in order to renew themselves and reproduce their capacity to labour, and it is not only in the interest of the labourers themselves that they should do this; it is also in the interests of the capitalists who employ them. A continuous supply of labour is just as essential to the capitalist mode of production as it is to any other and a labourer who has rested is likely to make fewer, less costly, mistakes than a labourer who is exhausted. Of course, although capital needs a continuous supply of labour generally speaking, where the supply of labour is plentiful, it is possible to work *individual* labourers to death and replace them with fresh labour in the form of entirely new labourers. This happened to some extent in the development of European capitalism (Urry 1981, 124); and the pattern of reproducing what Marx calls labour-power (as opposed to reproducing the labourers themselves) is characteristic of slave labour whenever the cost of such labour is sufficiently cheap.

When labour is scarce, however, labourers themselves become a valuable commodity. A slave becomes a valuable investment to a slave-owner when the slave costs more to buy than the value of the labour that can be extracted from the slave by working him or her to death. A slave might well cost more than the price of a horse or a cow, being able to provide a greater return for the owner than any other similar investment could, and this is the reason why slaves are often better looked after than other so-called 'free' labourers (whose 'freedom' might well consist of nothing more than the fact that they are free to starve unless they are willing to work on terms dictated by the capitalist). Even free labourers, however, are of value to capitalism where they possess certain skills that cannot easily be reproduced or when these skills are in short supply. Here again, it is the scarcity of a particular type of labour – of certain skills – that compels capitalism to allow the labourer to reproduce him or herself not only as a labourer, but also as a person. All of these factors then served to reduce the length of the working day from 24 hours to, say, 18 (in which the labourer is allowed to eat or sleep for 6 hours per day), or to 17 or even 16 (where the labourer is not compelled to eat on the job), while other moral objections, e.g. to the overworking of women and children or to working adult male labourers to an unnaturally early death, also served to further reduce the length of the normal working day from 16 hours to 14, 12 or 10 hours per day. (For more on all of this see Marx's extensive discussion of the history of the English Factory Acts; 1974a, 222–86 [1976, 340–416].)

On the other hand, however, when competition between capitalists makes it necessary to obtain a normal rate of profit or degree of exploitation of labour-power, or when the greed of the capitalists for surplus profits over and above what can be produced in a normal working day makes it desirable from the point of the capitalist to extend the length of the working day, the capitalist has an interest in increasing the length of that part of the working day that the labourers work for the capitalist over and above the hours the labourers work simply to reproduce their own wages. However, when the length of the working day is limited for some reason, e.g. by laws regulating the exploitation of labour, this becomes no longer possible. How then is the capitalist to extend his or her share of the working day without extending the actual length of the working day itself? Obviously this can only be done by shortening the number of hours that labourers spend simply in order to reproduce themselves and/or their families.

When the working day is 12 hours long and the labourers work to reproduce themselves for 6 hours and then work a further 6 hours for the capitalist, and when the length of the working day is unregulated in any way by law, the capitalist can extend the length of his or her share of the working day to 9 hours by simply extending the absolute length of the working day from 12 hours to 15. However, when the length of the working day is fixed at 12 hours, by law or for some other reason, the capitalists can only extend to 9 hours the period during which the labourer works for them by reducing to 3 hours the period during which the labourer works to reproduce him or herself. This can be done in one of the following three ways:

(i) The labourer's income (wages) can be reduced to a point below what is necessary to keep the labourer and/or his family alive. The labourer will starve, but in this case the reproduction of labour-power will not take place; labour will become scarce, and this scarcity will have the effect of once again pushing the price of labour back up to its value (the cost of reproducing the labourer).
(ii) When the labourers wages are measured in terms of a given number of commodities (so many loaves of bread for example), and when this figure remains constant despite the increase in the productivity of labour, new machinery may be introduced to improve the productivity of labour and so reduce the amount of time that the labourers need in order to reproduce themselves.
(iii) The actual value of labour-power itself can be reduced by shortening the time it takes to reproduce those items which directly enter into the cost of reproducing the labourer (such as food, clothing, housing, etc.). This can be done by increasing the productivity of labour in those industries that produce these items.

Marx refers to the work which the labourer performs during that part of the working day when the labourers reproduce themselves and/or their value or capacity to labour as *necessary labour*, and the labour performed during that part of the day when the labourer works solely for the capitalist's benefit as *surplus labour*. During the time that labourers work productively for the benefit of capitalists, they produce surplus value. Marx calls an increase in surplus value that is brought about by an *extension* of the working day beyond its normal limits *absolute surplus value* and an increase in surplus value that is brought about by shortening that part of the working day during which the labourer works to reproduce him or herself – whether this is done by means of an increase in the productivity of labour or by cheapening the value of labour-power or by increasing the *intensity* of labour by speeding up machinery, etc. – *relative surplus value*. This distinction can be expressed diagrammatically as follows:

Figure 1. Extension of the working day: Absolute surplus value

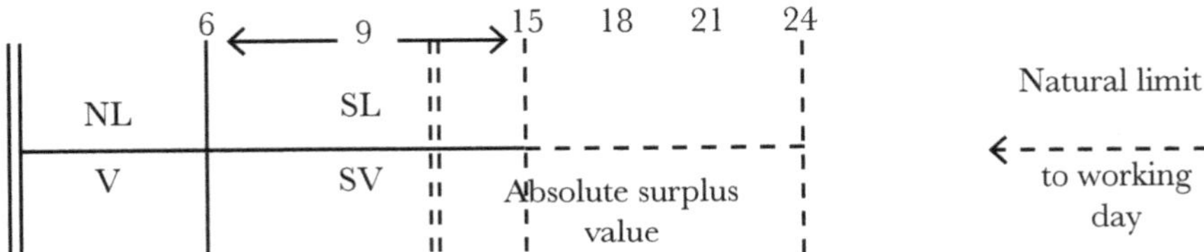

Figure 2. Intensification of working day increase in productivity

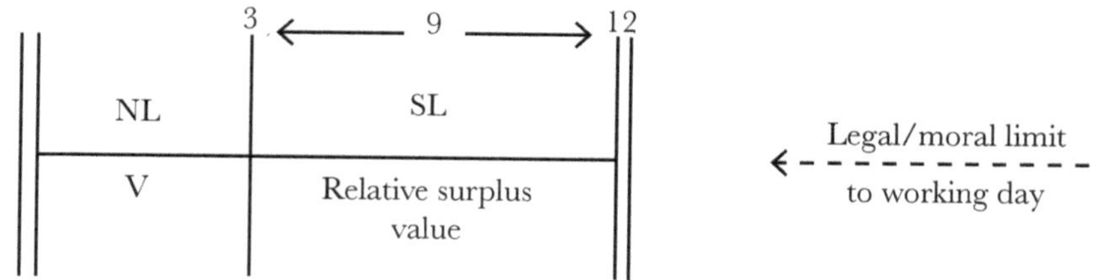

Points for Further Discussion

1. It is interesting to consider whether it is the case that the *whole* of the surplus value that the labourers produce for the benefit of the capitalist (the second six hours of a 'normal' twelve-hour day, and not just the surplus value produced during an abnormal extension of the working day) is *absolute* surplus value. Marx defines absolute surplus value as that which is produced by a prolongation of the working day but, from the point of view of the labourer, *all* surplus labour represents an unnecessary prolongation of the working day beyond what is strictly necessary to reproduce the labourer alone (see 1974a, 299 [1976, 432]). Why then is not this also absolute surplus value? Also, it is not clear that there really is a categorical distinction between the concepts of absolute and relative surplus value. See, for example, 1974a, 478–9 [1976, 645–7] where Marx argues that relative surplus value can appear absolute from the point of view of the labourer, since it compels an absolute prolongation of the working day beyond the time necessary for the existence of the labourers themselves, while absolute surplus value is relative since it requires a certain productivity of labour which will allow necessary labour to be restricted to only a part of the working day.
2. We might also consider the implications of the development of relative surplus value to the concept of what Marx sometimes refers to as the 'immiseration' of the working class (the eventual reduction of the working class to a state of wretchedness and misery). The development of relative surplus value means that it is no longer necessary to extend the length of the working day to an unendurable level. As such, it is therefore no longer necessary to reduce wages below the level of subsistence in order to increase the capitalist's share of the total surplus value produced during a normal working day. The capitalist can therefore pay the labourer the value of his or her labour-power, can allow the labourer to work for only a normal working day, and can still expect to increase his or her share of the total surplus value produced by intensifying the labour process and/or by increasing the

productiveness of labour. This being the case, we might ask: what necessity is there to reduce the working class to a state of immiseration? And, if it is no longer necessary to immiserate the working class, are the differences between the capitalists and the workers really irreconcilable? Finally, if the interests of capitalists and workers are not after all irreconcilable will class conflict develop to its fullest extent (in the form of what Marx calls class-warfare)? And, if there is no class warfare as such, what are the implications of all of this for the development of socialism? (On this point concerning the relationship between the development of relative surplus value and the fate of the working class, see also Marx on the existence of middle and intermediary classes in the Appendix to this book: pages 179–91.)

3. It seems inexplicable that a capitalist state (or even a state dominated by the interests of a capitalist class) should introduce legislation restricting the freedom of capitalists to exploit labour for longer than 10 or 12 hours per day. This has a number of implications for Marx and Engels' theory of the capitalist state as a committee for managing the common affairs of the bourgeoisie. An attempt has been made (for example, by Müller and Neusüss 1970) to argue that the capitalist state acted in the *general* interests of the capitalist class to prevent the particular excesses of individual capitalists from destroying one of the very foundations of the capitalist mode of production; namely, a plentiful and ready supply of labour-power. However, as we have already seen, where there is a plentiful supply of labour-power, capitalism can reproduce its conditions of existence without reproducing the particular person or the individual labourer. Therefore the above argument would only apply where there was a strong correlation between the introduction of the various Factory Acts and a *shortage* in the supply of labour. Failing this it would seem better to explain the introduction of the Factory Acts in terms of a committee for managing the common affairs, not merely of the capitalist class, but of capitalists and *landlords*. Rivalry between the interests of these two classes brought about an improvement in the conditions of labourers in Britain during the Industrial Revolution (see 1974a, 229, 258, 267 [1976, 348, 382–3, 393–4]).

Reading: Essential: *Capital*, Vol. I, Ch. 10, section 1, 'The Limits of the Working Day' (1974a, 222–5 [1976, 340–44]); Ch. 12, 'The Concept of Relative Surplus Value' (1974a, 296–304 [1976, 429–38]). Recommended: *Capital*, Vol. I (1974a, 226–86 [1976, 344–416]). Background: *Capital*, Vol. I, Ch. 17 (1974a, 486–96 [1976, 655–67]), on the possible variations of an increase in productivity, the intensity of labour and/or the length of the working day.

2. COOPERATION AND THE DIVISION OF LABOUR IN *CAPITAL*, VOL. 1, CH. 13–14

In this chapter we will look at two topics which at first sight seem to be quite different from, or even opposed to, one another: cooperation, i.e. the coming together of labour in the work place, and the division of labour, i.e. the separation of the various parts of the labour process into its constituent parts. However, in so far as manufacturing industry is concerned, Marx argues that these two processes are really just two sides of the same coin, and in fact, Marx actually defines manufacturing as cooperation based on the division of labour (1974a, 343 [1976, 485]).

In Chapter 13, Marx looks at various types of simple cooperation which do not involve a sophisticated division of labour; for example, when everyone helps to harvest a crop or dig a canal. This type of cooperation is necessary because there are certain things that one cannot usually do by oneself (such as lift a heavy rock, or tie a ribbon on a cake box). If one man can dig a canal or build the Great Wall of China in 14,000 years, 14,000 men can do this same thing in one year. Cooperation therefore makes possible the development of certain forms of agriculture and industry that would simply be impractical for an individual alone. However, this type of cooperation also imposes certain *communal* expectations and demands on the individual over and above those required in a typical nuclear family; where, for example, the help of many other individuals is required to harvest a particular crop within a given period of time – rice for example before it rots in the field – or where watering this crop requires the construction of large scale irrigation works (see 1974a, 481 [1976, 650] for more on this).

However, there are other forms of cooperation which involve a division of labour; for example, where some labourers harvest a crop, others thresh this, and still others make the crop or its waste product into bales for storage or transportation. This is the type of cooperation based on a division of labour characteristic to the manufacturing period of British industry which Marx argues, properly so called, extended from about 1550–1775 (1974a, 318 [1976,

455]). Manufacturing industry also arises in another way. Instead of a product passing through the hands of several skilled artisans during the process of production (such as a wheelwright, a harness maker, a tailor, a locksmith, an upholster, a turner, a painter and a polisher in the case of carriage making), in this second form of industry all the labourers in a particular workplace perform roughly the same type of labour where the process of production is reduced to its constituent parts. Instead of each worker being able to perform all the processes which go into making a wheel for example – e.g. cutting the length of the spokes, turning the wood, making the rim of the wheel, planing and polishing the finished product – now each labourer is restricted to the performance of only one of these tasks, and often to the performance of only one aspect of each task, until eventually whole factories develop to produce not carriages, and not even wheels, but only the spokes of wheels, or pins for these spokes. In these factories all the labourers perform more or less the same one- or two-detail functions of the process of production.

The division of labour in the workshop into its various detailed processes seemed to Adam Smith (*The Wealth of Nations*, Book 1, Ch. 1), to be a natural extension of the division of labour in society between the various branches of the process of production. Thus, the division of labour in a shoe making factory between the person who cuts the patterns for the shoes, the person who stitches them, and the person who makes only soles, seemed to Smith to be an extension of the division of labour between the cattle-breeder, the slaughterer of cattle, the tanner of leather, and the shoe-maker characteristic of the handicraft system of production which preceded the development of manufacturing. However, Marx argues that this is not the case, the difference between the division of labour in society and the division of labour within manufacturing industry being that while the cattle breeder, the tanner and the handicraft shoe-maker all produced a finished commodity – a use value which they exchanged with any other, or which, in the case of the cobbler, they sell to the ultimate consumer of the commodity – the detail labourer produces no commodities at all, but only a part of a finished commodity which is the collective product of all the detail labourers (1974a, 335 [1976, 475]).

In order to emphasize the differences between cooperation and the division of labour, Marx distinguishes between a *social* division of labour and a division of labour *in general* between the various branches of the process of production (agriculture, industry, commerce, finance, building, etc.), and the division of labour in *particular* within a given branch of production (e.g. in agriculture between dairy and arable farming, or within industry, between carriage making and ship-building) and the division labour within a particular workshop (i.e. within a particular factory, which Marx calls the division of labour in *singular*, or into its various detailed or distinct labour processes (1974a, 331–2 [1976, 471]). Marx also distinguishes between the divisions of labour and cooperation within a particular society and the *international* division of labour between largely industrial and largely agricultural economies (1974a, 425 [1976, 579–80]), and all of these distinctions can then be represented figuratively in the following way.

Figure 3. The division of labour in society

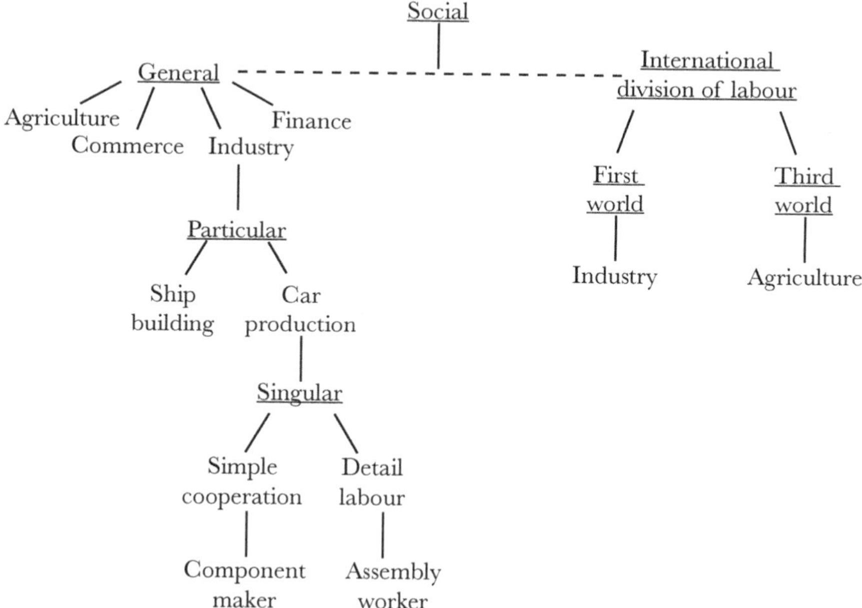

Points for Further Discussion

1. The concept of a 'collective labourer' (1974a, 307, 326, 329 [1976, 441, 464, 468]), and the related concept of a 'collective capitalist' (1974a, 3l6 [1976, 452]) – sometimes also referred to as the 'global capitalist' (Carchedi 1977) – is important when we come to look at the distinction Marx makes between productive and unproductive labour and the attempt made by some Marxists to differentiate between the working class and the petty bourgeoisie on the basis of this distinction (e.g. Poulantzas 1975). According to most commonsensical definitions, to be a productive worker one only has to produce some useful effect in order to labour productively. However, according to Marx, in capitalist society labour is only productive when it contributes towards the production of *surplus* value for the capitalist. Marx therefore repeatedly argues, especially in *Capital*, Vol. III, that commercial

labourers are not productive labourers because they do not produce surplus value for merchant capitalist but merely help their employers to increase their *relative* share of surplus value which has already been produced elsewhere (throughout *Capital*, Vol. III, but especially 1977, 297–300 [1981, 411–15]). However, as we have seen, in those cases in which a detail labourer produces only one part of a product in a process of production based on a developed division of labour, although they undoubtedly produce surplus value *collectively*, since they do not *individually* produce any commodities, it would seem that the detail labourer does not produce any surplus value for the capitalist since individually they do not produce commodities. This is correct but leads to the absurd conclusion that detail labourers are unproductive workers, while productive labour is identified either with the production of surplus labour or, more generally, with the production of something useful, and therefore Marx is forced to argue that the detail labourer is a productive labourer individually by virtue of his or her collective labour as a producer of surplus value.

The problem with this argument, however, is that if detail labourers are productive workers by virtue of their collective production of surplus value as opposed to the manual quality of the work they perform, so too must other non-manual workers (such as supervisors and managers) be productive where they produce surplus value for capital as a result of their individual contributions to the collective labour function. As Marx says: 'In order to labour productively it is no longer necessary for you to do manual work yourself; enough, if you are an organ of the collective labourer, and perform one of its subordinate functions' (1974a, 476 [1976, 643–4]). Therefore, since managers and even capitalists are productive where their labour of supervision or direction contributes to the collective labour function of producing surplus value, no very useful distinction can be made between the new petty bourgeoisie and the working class on this basis since we would have to include capitalists and managers, not in the petty bourgeoisie, but in the *working* class. See further on this point Marx's observation that shareholders in joint stock companies are part of the capitalist class by virtue of their performance of part of the collective capitalist function (1974a, 316 [1976, 455]).

Reading: Essential: *Capital*, Vol. I, Ch. 13–14, 1974a, 305–47 [1976, 439–91]. Background: *Capital*, Vol. I, Ch. 16, 1974a, 476–85 [1976, 643–54]. Additional: Ian Gough, 'Marx's Theory of Productive and Unproductive Labour', *New Left Review* no. 76, 1976.

3. MACHINERY AND MODERN INDUSTRY IN *CAPITAL*, VOL. I, CH. 15

Having looked in detail at the transition from handicraft production to manufacturing in the previous two chapters (on cooperation and the division of labour), in Chapter 15 of *Capital*, Vol. I, Marx turns his attention to the transition from manufacturing industry to the period of the production *of* machinery *by* machinery, the development of which is sometimes called *machino*facture in order to distinguish this from *manu*facture proper. If, as we have seen, the period of manufacturing industry can be said to extend from the middle of the seventeenth century to the beginning of the last quarter of the eighteenth century as Marx claims (1974a, 318 [1976, 492]), then the period of machinofacture may be said to start from the last quarter of the eighteenth century and extend to at least the early twentieth century. Just as manufacturing industry is distinguished from handicraft production by the deskilling of the labour process involved in manufacturing industry, machinofacture is distinguished from manufacture by the fact that in machinofacture machinery replaces not just a less sophisticated *tool* of production, but the human hand itself (1974a, 363 [1976, 506]).

The main theme of this very long chapter (1974a, 351–475 [1976, 492–639]) is that it is not machinery but its capitalist employment that has made the introduction of labour-saving machinery such a burden to mankind, and not the blessing it might otherwise have been in a socialist society. This point is neatly summarized by Marx as follows:

> It is an undoubted fact that machinery, as such, is not responsible for 'setting free' the workman from the means of subsistence. It cheapens and increases production in that branch which it seizes on, and at first makes no change in the mass of the means of subsistence produced in other branches. Hence, after its introduction, the society possesses as much, if not more, of the necessaries of life than before, for the labourers

> thrown out of work; and that quite apart from the enormous share of the annual produce wasted by the non-workers. And this is the point relied on by our apologists! The contradictions and antagonisms inseparable from the capitalist employment of machinery do not exist, they say, since they do not arise out of machinery as such, but out of its capitalist employment! Since therefore machinery, considered alone, shortens the hours of labour, but, when in the service of capital, lengthens them; since in itself it lightens labour, but when employed by capital, heightens the intensity of labour; since in itself it is a victory of man over the forces of Nature, but in the hands of capital, makes man the slave of those forces; since in itself it increases the wealth of the producers, but in the hands of capital makes them paupers – for all these reasons and others besides, says the bourgeois economist without more ado, it is as clear as noon-day that all these contradictions are a mere semblance of reality, and that, as a matter of fact, they have neither an actual nor a theoretical existence. (1974a, 415–16 [1976, 568–9])

Each of these points mentioned here are then discussed in detail in one or more of the ten sections of Chapter 15. In section l, Marx looks at the differences between a tool and a machine (1974a, 351–65 [1976, 492–508]). In section 2 (and see especially 1974a, 365–9 [1976, 508–13]), he considers the increase in the productivity of labour due to the introduction of machinery, as well as the increased intensity of production thereby made possible. In section 3b (especially, 1974a, 380–82 [1976, 526–8]), he looks at the lengthening of the working day brought about by the introduction of machinery (basically as a result of the necessity to recoup the value of the machine as quickly as possible). Even though the introduction of machinery shortens the working time necessary for the reproduction of the labourers themselves – the value of a machine being given, not by the cost of its production, but by the cost of its reproduction – it is necessary to recover its cost as quickly as possible before its value falls below a point at which it is uneconomical to continue to operate it if another machine is invented elsewhere which is either cheaper to make or more efficient to use. In section 3c (especially 1974a, 385–7 [1976, 533–5]), Marx turns his attention to the increase in the intensity of labour due to an increased familiarity in operating a given machine and at the fall in the value of a given commodity due to the increased production of commodities in a given time (see also 1974a, 398 [1976, 547]). While, in section 5 (especially 1974a, 404 [1976, 554–5]), he gives an account of the opposition directed against machinery by labour because machinery cheapened labour and reduced the number of hours in which the labourers needed to work to reproduce themselves and their families – something which should have been a blessing to the workers but which, because of its capitalist employment, threw many labourers out of work while increasing the intensity of the labour of those few workers who remained employed.

For the most part, however, Chapter 15 is extremely descriptive and therefore hardly worth reading at all except as an illustration of the detailed research Marx undertook before he began to write *Capital.* Chapter 15, section 4, for example, is a completely straightforward account of factory life in nineteenth-century Britain of the kind that any student of history would already be familiar with, although it may have had greater novelty at the time that Marx was writing and especially for his target audience in Germany. For example, 1974a, 428–32 [1976, 583–8] of section 7, is a short history of the development of the English Cotton Industry, while 1974a, 465–72 [1976, 627–35] of section 9 is entirely made up of extracts from English Factory Inspectors Reports. Unless therefore the reader wishes to read Vol. I from cover to cover, I would advise missing out the following pages of Chapter 15: 1974a, 372–9, 383–5, 388–95, 397–402, 405–75 [1976, 517–26, 530–33, 536–43, 546–53, 556–639]. Within these pages, however, there are a few passages of great interest which are worth noting here. These are, in particular: 1974a, 424–5 [1976, 579–80], in which Marx makes his very famous statement concerning the development of an international division of labour; 1974a, 372–3 [1976, 517–18], which contains Marx's equally famous statement that the value of labour-power is determined not only by the cost of reproducing the labourer but also his or her family; 1974a, 420–21 [1976, 574–5], in which Marx gives some still very interesting statistics on the very large size of the servant class in the nineteenth century, the growth of which Marx attributed to the cheapening of the cost of reproducing labour-power and the relatively larger share of surplus value this gave to the numerically small class of owners of capital; 1974a, 352, 2n [1976, 493–4, 4n], which contains a very interesting statement on historical materialism as a scientific method; and finally, a number of very amusing passages, especially, 1974a, 354, 2n [1976, 496, 8n], 1974a, 374, line 6 [1976, 519, line 19], which includes an advertisement in a local paper: 'Wanted 12 to 20 young persons, not younger than what can pass for 13 years', and 1974a, 377 [1976, 523], an extract from a factory inspectors report in which an inspector ask a manufacturer 'Pray, sir, can you read ... Aye Summat!' is the reply.

Points for Further Discussion

1. One sometimes wonders why Marx included this detailed historical material in *Capital* since it certainly gets in the way of the theoretical argument being presented. However, it is necessary to remember that although much

of what he describes was familiar to people in Britain at the time of the Industrial Revolution, the conditions he described were still almost entirely unheard of anywhere else in the world at this time.

Reading: Essential: *Capital,* Vol. I, Ch. 15 (1974a, 351–65, 365–9, 380–82, 385–7, 404 [1976, 492–514, 526–8, 533–4, 554]). Background: *Capital,* Vol. I, Ch. 15 (1974a, 405–75 [1976, 556–639]), if so inclined.

4. PRIMITIVE ACCUMULATION IN *CAPITAL*, VOL. I, PART VIII, CH. 26–33

The accumulation of capital, Marx argues, presupposes surplus value. We cannot accumulate unless we have something to accumulate with and this something must evidently be over and above (i.e. surplus to) what is necessary simply to reproduce the prevailing process of production on the same unchanging scale. However, the existence of surplus value *presupposes* the existence of capital, and the existence of capital presupposes accumulation. The whole thing, Marx argues, seems to turn in a vicious circle when viewed from the point of view of an already established capitalist mode of production (CMP) out of which we can only get by supposing some form of pre-capitalist or primitive accumulation ('previous accumulation' in Adam Smith's terminology), which takes place before the development of the CMP proper. As Marx says on this point:

> This primitive accumulation plays in Political Economy about the same part as original sin in theology. Adam bit the apple, and thereupon sin fell on the human race. Its origin is supposed to be explained when it is told as an anecdote of the past. In times long gone by there were two sorts of people; one, the diligent, intelligent, and, above all, frugal elite; the other, lazy rascals, spending their substance, and more, in riotous living. The legend of theological original sin tells us certainly how man came to be condemned to eat his bread in the sweat of his brow ; but the history of economic original sin reveals to us that there are people to whom this is by no means essential. Never mind! Thus it came to pass that the former sort accumulated wealth, and the latter sort had at last nothing to sell except their own skins. And from this original sin dates the poverty of the great majority that, despite all its labour, has up to now nothing to sell but itself, and the wealth of the few that increases constantly although they have long ceased to work. Such insipid childishness is every day preached to us in the defence of property. (1974a, 667 [1976, 873–4])

However, although Marx argues that the process of production undergoes a qualitative change in the transition from a pre-capitalist to the capitalist mode of production – which gives the capitalist mode of production a new character, or rather 'causes the disappearance of some of its previous characteristics' (1974a, 532 [1976, 712]) – once it is established, the CMP owes nothing at all to this pre-capitalist process of primitive accumulation, except in terms of its genealogy.[1] And although Marx has great fun ridiculing the classical economic concept of previous accumulation, he does in fact agree with it and accepts that capitalism *did* develop out of certain earlier modes of production – most directly, of course, the feudal mode (1974a, 668 [1976 874–5]). He therefore argues that certain pre-capitalist forms of accumulation *are* in fact a prerequisite of the establishment of the CMP, if not a condition of its continued existence, and he gives three examples of this previous or primitive accumulation.

The first example of primitive accumulation is of the kind usually put forward by the defenders of the capitalist system as the ideal type of pre-capitalist accumulation. In this model, an individual, by dint of hard work and their own labour, and by virtue of saving and frugality, builds up (i.e. accumulates) a sufficient surplus to set him- or herself up as a capitalist and thereby free themselves from the necessity to labour in future. If 8 hours of labour are sufficient to reproduce a single labourer's capacity to work for one day but under a capitalist process of production the labourer is made to work for 12 hours, then it is clear that our would-be capitalist can free him- or herself from the necessity to labour at all by employing *two* labourers for 12 hours a day providing only that he or she is prepared to live at a standard of living no better than that of a labourer. If, on the other hand, our would-be capitalist wants to live only twice as well as an ordinary labourer he or she must employ *four* labourers for 12 hours a day. If, in addition to this, the capitalist wants to make a profit or to set aside something to buy new machinery or new means of production, then it is clear that they can only do this by employing 8, 16 or 32 labourers, or more. The minimum cost of becoming a capitalist is therefore four times the cost of a day's labour plus the cost of any means of production necessary to establish the process of production itself. Marx gives an example of this kind of primitive accumulation in *Capital*, Vol. I (1974a, 291–2 [1976, 422–3]) and therefore concedes that this is sometimes how capitalist production began. As he later says on this point:

> But the process [of reproduction] must have had a beginning of some kind. From our present standpoint it therefore seems likely that the capitalist, once upon a time, became possessed of money by some accumulation that took place independently of the unpaid labour of others, and that this was, therefore, how he was enabled to frequent the market as a buyer of labour-power. (1974a, 534 [1976, 714])

And Marx gives a further example of primitive accumulation in Chapter 24, where he argues that:

> The original capital was formed by the advance of £10,000. How did the owner become possessed of it? 'By his own labour and that of his forefathers', answer unanimously the spokesmen of Political Economy. And, in fact, their supposition appears to be the only one consonant with the laws of the production of commodities. (1974a, 545–6 [1976, 728])

However, although Marx does admit that this type of primitive accumulation is possible and did in fact take place, he argues that the methods of primitive accumulation are usually anything but as idyllic as this. The second type of primitive accumulation that Marx mentions is that which is brought about by the forcible expropriation of the wealth of the developing world, initially that of South America:

> The discovery of gold and silver in America, the extirpation, enslavement and entombment in mines of the aboriginal population, the beginning of the conquest and looting of the East Indies, the turning of Africa into a warren for the commercial hunting of black-skins signalised the rosy dawn of the era of capitalist production. These idyllic proceedings are the chief momenta of primitive accumulation. (1974a, 703 [1976, 915])

And Marx further argues that in history 'it is notorious that conquest, enslavement, robbery, murder, briefly force, play the great part' in primitive accumulation (1974a, 668 [1976, 874]).

Even this type of primitive accumulation, however, does not exhaust all the avenues open to pre-capitalist entrepreneurs to centralize all of the already existing capital of society. The economic structure of capitalist society mainly grew out of the dissolution of the economic structure of feudal societies, and Marx argues that the third type of pre-capitalist accumulation arises from this development. Here, the essential thing as far as primitive accumulation is concerned is the forcible enclosure of the common lands and, what very often followed on from this, the separation of labour from the means of production. This was a crucial development in the pre-history of the capitalist mode of production and Marx gives any number of examples of this third type of accumulation in *Capital*, Vol. I, Chapter 27 (1974a, 671–85 [1976, 877–95]), where he argues that:

> The spoliation of the church's property, the fraudulent alienation of the State domains, the robbery of the common lands, the usurpation

> of feudal and clan property, and its transformation into modern private property under circumstances of reckless terrorism, were just so many idyllic methods of primitive accumulation. (1974a, 685 [1976, 895])

And further that:

> The so-called primitive accumulation, therefore, is nothing else than the historical process of divorcing the producer from the means of production. It appears as primitive, because it forms the pre-historic stage of capital and of the mode of production corresponding with it. (1974a, 668 [1976, 874–5])

This is all that Marx really has to say on the subject of primitive accumulation, at least in *Capital*, Vol. I, where he concedes this point to classical political economy, all the while making it seem as though he does not. However, since Marx claims that the final form of primitive accumulation mentioned above, the separation of labourers from the ownership of the means of production, is 'the real foundation in fact, and the starting point of capitalist production' (1974a, 535 [1976, 716]), it might be helpful to look at this third type of primitive accumulation in a little more detail here.

Instead of working 6 hours necessary labour for their own reproduction and 6 hours for the capitalist, as we assumed was the normal arrangement in a CMP in a working day of 12 hours, a labourer in a feudal society might work for three days on his or her own land using their own means of production, and for a further three days each week on land belonging to his or her feudal lord (with Sundays and holy days off for rest and regeneration). This arrangement, however, had at least three disadvantages for the feudal lord. In the first place, the labourer owned his or her own means of production – the means of reproduction of his or her own livelihood – and was to this extent independent of the landlord. Secondly, there was likely to be a considerable difference in the quality of the labour that the labourers performed for themselves and the quality of the labour that the labourer performed for the landlord, since the labourer could clearly distinguish between labour that they performed for themselves on their own land and the labour they performed for the benefit of the landlord. Thirdly, the labourers would have known exactly what it cost to reproduce themselves and/or their families and exactly which portion of the working week they worked for themselves and which portion they worked for the landlord. Therefore they also knew exactly what part of the working week was spent in necessary labour, reproducing themselves, and what part of the working week was spent in labour surplus to their own requirements. It was therefore principally owing to this – from the point of view of the landlord – injurious lack of mystification that the feudal landlord very often had to compel labourers to work for the landlord at all, and also usually to supervise their labour as well.

In the CMP, however, things are very different. The labourers neither own their own means of production, nor do they know when they are working for themselves and when they are working for the capitalist. Because they have been expropriated from the land the labourers have nothing to sell but themselves and as such are forced to go to the owners of the means of production simply in order to live, i.e. to reproduce themselves. Although nominally 'free' labourers, they are forced to work for the capitalist by economic necessity just as much as the labourer of feudal society was forced to work for the landlord. It is this type of force that Marx has in mind when he refers to 'the dull compulsion of economic relations [which] completes the subjection of the labourer to the capitalist' (1974a, 689 [1976, 899]) and which he argues arises directly from the separation of the labourer from the ownership of the means of reproduction even of their own lives. On this point see also the case of one Dr Hunter, who claimed that 'a few acres to the cottage would make the labourers too independent' (1974a: 674 [1976, 881]), and also that of a Mr Peel who took 3,000 labourers and means of subsistence to Swan River, Western Australia, only to find when he got there that the ungrateful labourers would not work for him at any price when they might just as easily work for themselves, even though he had paid for their passage from England (1974a, 717 [1976, 933]). 'So long, therefore, as the labourer can accumulate for himself – and this he can do so long as he remains possessor of his means of production' – Marx argues that, 'capitalist accumulation and the capitalist mode of production are impossible' (1974a, 718 [1976, 933]). As soon as this separation is complete, on the other hand, one of the main pre-conditions of the development of the CMP is present.

Points for Further Discussion

1. The separation of labour from the means of production can never be seen as a *condition* of the CMP itself, only as its *pre*-condition, since no mode of production of any kind, not even the most automated, is possible on the basis of the *continued* separation of labour from the means of production. Labour must in any event be reunited with the means of reproduction of life at some point for production to take place.
2. It is the relative *density* of population – the volume of land taken into private property compared to the mass of labour available to work this land or other means of production – that determines whether labour is legally 'free' from bondage or must be restricted in its movement in some

way in the form of slavery or serfdom. It is only then when flight is an absolute *impossibility*, due to geographical factors perhaps or to the volume of population having reached a relatively abundant level, that labour is set free (1974a, 333, 537–42 [1976, 472–3, 717–24]).

Reading: Essential: *Capital*, Vol. I, Part VIII, Ch. 26 (1974a; 667–70, Ch. 31, 702–12, Ch. 33, 716–24 [1976, 873–6, 914–26, 931–40]). Background: the remainder of *Capital*, Vol. I, Part VIII, i.e. Ch. 27–30 (1974a, 671–701, Ch. 32, 713–15 [1976, 877–913, 927–30]). Non-essential: *Capital*, Vol. I, Part VII, sections 4–5 (1974a, 600–66 [1976, 794–870]), an overwhelmingly descriptive account of the expropriation from the ownership of land of the agricultural populations of England and Ireland.

Part II

THE CAPITALIST MODE OF PRODUCTION

PREFACE TO PART II

Having considered in some detail in Part I of this book those more descriptive chapters in *Capital*, Vol. I concerned with the question of the *development* of the capitalist mode of production, we can now go on to look at the question of what it is that distinguishes the capitalist process of production proper from all previous modes of production.

In Part II of this book we will look at two major questions. Firstly, how is it possible that a single primitively accumulated investment and/or the hard work of a small master-capitalist *prior* to the development of a capitalist process of production proper is able to support the capitalist and his or her family (and all their descendants in perpetuity as it seems) without ever apparently becoming worn out or exhausted, even after the capitalist who made the original investment has long since ceased to work themselves and may in fact have died? Secondly, how is it possible that capitalists are apparently *compelled* to accumulate their surplus value without as it seems having any choice in the matter, and in what way this feature of the CMP distinguishes it from the type of accumulation that takes place in a highly developed mercantile process of production where the merchant capitalists can withdraw their surplus value from the process of production and realize its value in its money form?

We will begin therefore with the question of the apparent immortality of the capitalist's initial, primitively accumulated, investment.

INTRODUCTION TO PART II

Before we can distinguish the capitalist mode of production from its pre-capitalist forms there are one or two preliminary assumptions we need to make. First, as we have seen, each capitalist must be in possession of a primitively accumulated capital which is of a sufficient magnitude to allow the individual to enter into the process of production as a capitalist. Second, more controversially, we will assume that the capitalists themselves do not actually work in the enterprise they establish, not even to perform the labour of supervision, but employ other people to do this work for them in the capacity of overseers, foremen and managers. (A capitalist who works for himself when he might otherwise not do so – a guild master for example – being regarded by Marx as a hybrid, somewhere between a fully fledged capitalist and a labourer.) This second assumption seems odd at first. There were no doubt many manufacturers, especially at the beginning of the Industrial Revolution, who carefully managed the enterprises they had set up and jealously guarded their investments. However, this assumption is merely a simplifying abstraction that Marx makes in order to present his argument more clearly. What is more, although it was probably common for capitalists to work in the enterprises they owned during the manufacturing period proper (up until 1775 or so) this was not always the case during the period of machinofacture (from 1775 onward) that Marx is considering here. And today, of course, it would be a very odd thing indeed if everyone who has their savings in a bank or who has invested in a pension fund knew which companies their money was invested in, or still less took a hand in the day to day running of these enterprises. Marx gives the following illustration in Chapter 11, *Capital*, Vol. I (1974a, 291–2 [1976, 422–3]), on the 'Rate and Mass of Surplus Value', which incorporates both of these preliminary assumptions.

Before an individual can be transformed into a capitalist a certain sum of money must be assumed to be in the hands of our would-be-capitalist before such a transformation can take place. I call this individual a 'would-be capitalist' here because of course, at this stage, he or she has not yet actually become one. As we have already shown (see Part I, Ch. 4 of the present study) if a labourer can reproduce him- or herself (and/or his or her family) for one day by the performance of 8 hours labour and if, besides these 8 hours labour, a guild master/journeyman makes the labourer work an additional 4 hours, at the end of the working day of 12 hours the guild master/journeyman will be in possession of a value equivalent to half of what it takes to keep one labourer and/or his or her family for one day: 4 hours surplus labour. If the master-craftsman wishes to live *twice* as well as the labourers he employs he must then be in possession of a value equivalent to 16 hours surplus labour and he must therefore employ four labourers each working a 12-hour day. Finally, if he wants to accumulate as much surplus value as he himself consumes unproductively – in order, for example, to be able to renew the process of production in which the labourers he employs work – then he must employ a further 4 labourers, 8 in total, each working a 12-hour working day simultaneously before he can liberate himself from the necessity to work in order to live for one day (1974a, 291–2 [1976, 422–3]).

If we now further assume that the capitalist-to-be pays each individual labourer £5 per 12 hour working day, he must obviously pay these 8 labourers a total of £40 per day for one day's labour and £200 for five such days work (£240 if the labourers work a six day week). By convention this money is payable at the *end of the first week* of their employment – in effect the labourers work for a capitalist for nothing during the first week – but in all likelihood he will need to meet this payment before he is able to sell the product of the process of production. However, even this is not enough to turn the small master craftsman into a fully fledged capitalist employer since this sum of £200/£240 obviously only covers the would-be capitalist's costs in the form of wages, which Marx calls *variable capital* (or v) and it is still necessary to purchase raw materials, machinery, etc. and a factory in which to put all of these things. In other words, the additional cost of what Marx calls *constant capital* (or c) must also be taken into account before the capitalist process of production proper can get underway. If we then assume that one unit of variable capital (v) is capable in this case of setting in motion four units of constant capital (c), and that the ratio of variable to constant capital is therefore lv:4c, then, in addition to a variable capital of £200, our would be capitalist will also need to acquire £800 worth of machinery, raw materials, etc. before the process of production can begin on this basis. To free himself and his family from the necessity of work and to enter the process of production as a capitalist manufacturer rather than as a small master craftsman, the would-be capitalist must therefore be in possession of a capital of at least £1,000.

Having established then that the capitalist does not work himself, and that he or she is in possession of a primitively accumulated capital which is a sufficient sum to enter into the process of production as a capitalist producer, we can now turn our attention to Marx's discussion of simple reproduction in *Capital*, Vol. I, Chapter 23 (especially 1974a, 534–5 [1976, 714–15]). Here, in what may well be the most important chapter in Vol. I, we find a very good illustration indeed of how the capitalist process of production, simply by its mere continuity over time, undergoes a *qualitative* change from its pre-capitalist to its capitalist form and, as Marx says, 'brings about some wonderful changes' (1974a, 292 [1976, 423]) in the appearance of the actual relations between the owners of capital and the people who work for them.

5. SIMPLE REPRODUCTION IN *CAPITAL*, VOL. I, CH. 7, 11 AND 23

If the capitalist-to-be invests a primitively accumulated capital of £1,000, if this capital of £1,000 produces yearly a surplus value of £200, and if further this surplus value of £200 is consumed unproductively by the capitalist in order to reproduce him or herself and his family, then at the end of a period of 5 years the surplus value consumed unproductively (5 × £200 = £1,000) will be equal in value to the £1,000 originally invested and the original capital will in effect have been entirely used up and will exist no more. Similarly, if the capitalist-to-be consumes surplus value unproductively at only half the annual rate as that in the above example (i.e. at the rate of only £100 per year), it will take 10 years instead of 5 for the original investment to be consumed unproductively by the capitalist-to-be in the form of his profit on the enterprise. In both cases the result will be the same: if unproductive consumption takes place by the capitalist-to-be and his or her family in order to reproduce themselves and is not put back into the enterprise in some way, there must eventually come a point – whether it is in 5 years time, 10 years or even 50 years – when the original sum invested has been entirely used up during the process of production and is no more. Marx calls this period at the end of which the sum originally advanced has been consumed unproductively by the capitalist-to-be the *reproduction period* of the original sum invested and he argues that the would-be capitalist, having received back a sum equivalent in value to his or her original investment, has no further interest in the value embodied in the process of production that still exists on the same site and in the same place as his or her original investment. On the contrary, Marx argues that these means of production – the factory, the machinery, the raw materials, etc. – which are equivalent in value to the would-be capitalist's original investment belong to all the people employed in the process of production during the previous 5, 10, 50 years, or however long the reproduction of the original primitively accumulated capital has taken.

'But, hang on a minute! Just wait just a moment!' our would-be capitalist says (1974a, 185–9 [1976, 297–303]). 'Did I not work hard and save up my money, frugally, and by virtue of my own labour, to set up this process of production? Do I then deserve nothing for all my hard work prior to the process of production even though I have not myself worked in the enterprise for the last 5 or 10 years?' Well of course he *does* deserve something for this, Marx says, and this is the £1,000 he originally invested in the process of production and which has been returned to him in full at the rate of £200, £100, £10 per year during the previous 5, 10, 50 or so years. 'But,' objects the capitalist, 'I did not advance my money merely in order to have it returned to me gradually over a period of 5 or 10 years! I advanced my money for the express purpose of making *more* money.' Well, says Marx, 'the way to Hell is paved with good intentions, and he might just as easily have intended to make money without producing anything at all' (1974a, 186 [1976, 298]), as he intended to make *more* money without himself doing any work. But now the would-be capitalist becomes obdurate: he knows when he is being cheated. 'These are *my* machines. This is *my* factory. I paid for them out of my original investment of £1,000. They occupy the same space and have much the same form as the machines and factory I established 5 or 10 years ago' (he ignores for the moment the fact that the raw material consumed by the process of production, and even much of the machinery, have changed their form any number of times during the previous five or ten years and been continually replaced and renewed). 'These are my machines and I *own* them', he says. Very well, says Marx, these *are* your machines and this *is* your factory. You did indeed invest a capital of £1,000 and these machines and this factory are in point of fact worth exactly £1,000 (Marx ignores for the moment the fact that the value of these things might well have been increased). These machines and this factory undoubtedly belong to you. But what, in that case, Marx asks, did the capitalist live off during the previous 5 or 10 years?

The capitalist-to-be cannot have it both ways, Marx argues. *Either* the £1,000 he withdrew from the process of production over the period of 5 or 10 years *was* the equivalent of his original investment, in which case of course he is perfectly entitled to get this money back, but then he is no longer entitled to claim to be the owner of the process of production now occupying the same site as, and equivalent in value to, his original investment. *Or* the value of the factory and machinery up to £1,000 is the equivalent of his £1,000 originally invested and he *is* therefore still entitled to claim to be the owner of the factory and the machinery, etc. that still exist on this site, but he cannot have been entitled to withdraw £1,000 surplus value from the enterprise at the rate of £200 or £100 per year during the previous 5 to 10 years when he did not work himself. Now, in point of fact, the capitalist-to-be *does* have it both ways and it is of course the entire rhyme and reason and the very essence of the capitalist mode of production that he should do so. The capitalist not only wants to have his cake and eat it, but he does in fact do so, and it is at this point therefore, and this point only, that he becomes a capitalist proper. But this, Marx insists, does not alter the facts of the matter. Either the capitalist, in keeping intact his original investment and thereby claiming to be the rightful owner of the capitalist enterprise (as it has now become), must admit that he has been consuming unproductively surplus value produced by the unpaid labour of others who worked for him during the previous 5 to 10 years, or, if, as seems likely, he is unwilling to concede this point, he must agree that the money he has been living off during the previous 5 to 10 years (or whatever), that he has consumed unproductively in order to reproduce himself and his family, was a return to him of a sum equivalent in value to his original investment, in which case it is hard to see on what basis he can continue to claim to be the *legitimate* owner of the process of production in question.

In claiming to be *both* the legitimate owner of the enterprise *and* to have lived off the product of his own hard work and effort during the period in which the original sum invested has been consumed and reproduced anew during the capitalist process of production, the capitalist – in so far as he thinks about these matters at all – is forced to claim that his capital can somehow (a) reproduce itself anew, and (b) reproduce the capitalist and/or his family *without ever becoming worn out or needing to be renewed again*. In other words, he is forced to claim – and probably really does believe himself – that his capital has developed almost magical and certainly entirely fantastic properties against which the goose that laid the golden egg and Aladdin's lamp have nothing to compare: namely, that the original investment, once made, will be enough *by itself* to reproduce the capitalist and his family without the need for them ever to work again. The capitalist *hopes* he can live off his original investment in perpetuity. He *thinks* he is entitled to the surplus value produced by the process of production and to continue to claim to be the owner of the enterprise in question. He *wishes* that this state of affairs was in fact the case and will continue. But, as Marx says, what the capitalist wishes cannot alter the facts of the matter.

What then is really going on here and what are the actual facts of the matter? There are of course *two* lots of value here, both worth exactly £1,000 each. One was primitively accumulated by the capitalist-to-be and invested by him in the process of production. The other is the product of this process of production, which has been produced anew by all the labourers who work in this enterprise during the reproduction period of the initial sum invested, and which has then been used to establish the *second round* in the production process. During the first cycle of this process of production, the capitalist-to-be believes that he is living off the unpaid labour of others and is renewing his primitively accumulated capital in the process of production, but for this one cycle only Marx argues that this is *not* in fact the case. During this first reproduction period there is a capital of £1,000 which has been primitively accumulated by the capitalist-to-be and to which, however it was come by, he does seem to be entitled to have returned to him. Marx therefore claims that during this period *alone* the capitalist lives off his original investment and does *not* in point of fact consume unproductively the surplus value being produced by the labour of others (which is in fact reinvested in the process of production itself). At the end of the first reproduction period, however, the capitalist's original primitively accumulated capital has been entirely used up and a sum equivalent has been returned to the capitalist for his own unproductive consumption. The original sum invested by the-would-be capitalist is therefore no more and, Marx claims, not a single atom of the value of this continues to exist in the capitalist enterprise (1974a, 535 [1976, 715]). It is at this point then that merely quantitative changes in the process of production become qualitative changes and that the capitalist-to-be, by continuing to claim to be the owner of the enterprise, becomes a capitalist proper.

Because the capitalist at the end of the first reproduction cycle *still* has in his possession a means of production to the value of £1,000, because this means of production occupies the same physical space and may even have much the same material form as the means of production bought with his original investment, and because at the end of a second, third, or even the tenth cycle of this process of production the capitalist will in all probability *still* have in his possession the means of production to the value of £1,000 as originally invested, *then* the capitalist comes to believe that he is living off not the surplus product produced by the unpaid labour of others, but his original investment, which therefore appears to him to have developed the fantastic property of never needing to be reproduced or renewed. Unless it has been expanded or extended in some way, the factory, and in all likelihood everything in it, will look much the same as it ever did and it is due to the fact that an entirely *new* capital of £1,000 has much the same physical form and occupies the same physical space as the original sum invested that the capitalist is able to continue to claim to be the legitimate owner of the enterprise in question. In fact though, Marx argues, once the capitalist has consumed unproductively a surplus value which is equivalent to the original sum invested (i.e. once the second round of the process of production begins), from this point onwards the capitalist does not live off his investment as he supposes (and as was in fact the case during the first reproduction cycle of his original capital), but does now live off the unpaid labour of others and thus is no longer the owner of the enterprise in question (the thing he is entitled to claim to be the owner of having been used up and consumed unproductively by him during the first cycle of production). Only once this point has been reached (i.e. at the end of the reproduction period of the original, primitively accumulated, sum invested and the beginning of the second period in this process of production) can a fully fledged capitalist process of production be said to have come into existence and capitalist production proper begins to take place. A trick has been played, as Marx says (1974a, 189 [1976, 301]) and a sleight of hand performed. The original sum invested has been converted into capital and the would-be capitalist has been converted into a capitalist. And not the least interesting thing about this whole process is that the capitalist fools himself by the trick performed just as much, if not even more so, than he does everyone else concerned.

Points for Further Discussion

1. Labourers too withdraw value from the process of production during the reproduction cycle of the original capital in the form of wages in order to reproduce themselves and their families; therefore do not labourers consume surplus value unproductively too? No, because although they do consume part of the product of the process of production in the form of wages in order to reproduce themselves and their families, they work in order to do this and in fact produce more value than it costs to reproduce themselves. Their own reproduction in this case is therefore properly considered to be part of the reproduction of the process of production as a whole. The basic argument that Marx is advocating here is – and it is in fact the basis of everything that he says above – is that no one can appropriate wealth to themselves except by their own labour and that it is a pure fantasy to think otherwise. Therefore, if someone does not themselves work, they *must* be exploiting the labour of others.
2. But what then – and this is of course the obvious objection to the entire argument presented above – if the capitalist *also* works in the enterprise he or she set up, e.g. to perform the important labour of supervision; might not the capitalist by his or her own hard work and labour earn the money he or she withdraws from the process of production each year in order to reproduce him- or herself just as it is claimed his or her labourers do? Well, he or she might, but then in this case, just like any other labourer, he or she would be entitled in the form of a wage to the value of that part of the process of production he or she had him- or herself produced anew. But Marx, as we have already seen, covers this possibility in his discussion of the collective labourer and the collective capitalist (*Capital*, Vol. I, 1974a 316, 321, 329–30 and 476 [1976, 452, 458, 468–9 and 643–44]).

The capitalist is entitled to the value of the product of the process of production which he or she produces as part of the collective labour of the enterprise, and where this labour is exceptionally skilled or of a greater intensity than the labour performed by the average worker (as we might well imagine the capitalist to argue that the labour of supervision is) Marx is prepared to admit that the capitalist might well be paid more than the average worker in the enterprise due to the greater cost of reproducing his labour. (For a more detailed discussion of this point see Marx's 'Marginal Notes on the Programme of the German Worker's Party', now more usually known as the *Critique of the Gotha Programme*.) But the key point to understand here is that, even if the capitalist actually works in the enterprise in question and withdraws let us say £100 per year in the form of a wage for the labour of supervision and another £100 per year as the return to him or her of his or her original investment, it will simply take *longer* to reach that point at the end of the reproduction cycle of the original primitively accumulated capital when the capitalist has eventually used up and consumed unproductively his or her entire original investment. It is therefore only if the capitalist *never* takes back a sum equivalent to that originally invested, but simply consumes what he or she adds to the process of production by virtue of his or her own labour, that the end of the reproduction period of the original sum invested would never be reached. However, this in effect means that the would-be capitalist never becomes a capitalist at all but continues to live and work alongside his labourer much as small master-capitalists did during the period before the development of the capitalist mode of production.

3. This is also the case if we say that the would-be capitalists are entitled to something more – let us say five or ten per cent more – over and above the sum they originally invested, for example, as a return to them for the risk they take in investing their money to start up a capitalist enterprise which they might otherwise have consumed unproductively for themselves. All that will happen in this case is that it will take one or two years longer to reach that point at which the £1,000 the capitalist originally invested has been returned, plus interest of £50 or £100. It is only if the would-be capitalist demands interest at the rate, not of five to ten per cent of the entire sum advanced (five to ten per cent of £1,000 over a period of five to fifty years say) but rather five or ten per cent *per year* – i.e. £50 or £100 *per year* as what would then in effect be the interest repaid on a loan rather than an investment made by the capitalist him- or herself in an enterprise he or she claims to own – that the situation seems to be different until we realize that all that we are considering here is the difference between interest-bearing capital and capital invested productively in a capitalist enterprise.

Then we can see that the way in which the owners of interest capital claim to be entitled to a return on their investment at this extraordinarily high rate of interest is in fact no different – and in point of fact no more legitimate – than the would-be capitalist's claim to be the legitimate owner of a capitalist enterprise that he or she has invested in directly.

4. Finally, it makes no difference at all to the above argument whether any part of the value entering into the second, third or fourth cycles of the process of production, or any other cycle after that, has the same physical or material form as part of the capital which formed the original process of production. That is to say, it does not matter whether or not this value is in fact in part embodied in the *same* means of production (i.e. the *same* machines and the *same* factory) as the means of production that existed during the first reproduction cycle of the process of production in question. It might take 20 years for the full value of a particular machine to be entirely used up or 50 or 100 years before the bricks of which the factory is composed need repairing or replacing, but this will not alter the length of the reproduction period of the original sum invested since this is determined by the point at which a value *equivalent* to that which was originally invested has been withdrawn by the capitalist from the process of production and consumed unproductively by him. It does not matter at all what form this value withdrawn takes. All that would happen in a case such as this is that the value of some part of the process of production – the raw materials, for example – might have been worn out and replaced several hundred times over while the reproduction of other parts of the factory or machinery take much longer than this. But this will not alter the fact that the reproduction period of the original sum invested has been reached once a value equivalent to this has been returned to the capitalist and what is in effect an entirely new process of production has been established in its place.

Reading: Essential: *Capital*, Vol. I, Ch. 23 (1974a, 531–7 [1976, 711–18]). Background: the remainder of Chapter 23 (1974a, 538–42 [1976, 719–24]), which is a continuation of the discussion of the separation of labour from the ownership of the means of production and the way in which the labourer is still held in bondage even in capitalist society, which I looked at in some detail in Part I of this study; *The Critique of the Gotha Programme* (*MESW*, 1968, 315–31). Finally, see also *Capital*, Vol. I, Ch. 7, section 2, (1974a, 181–92 [1976, 293–306]) for a less technical discussion of the above argument but also some further possible objections to this account of simple reproduction in a capitalist process of production.

6. EXTENDED REPRODUCTION IN *CAPITAL*, VOL. I, CH. 24

Marx's discussion of extended reproduction, in *Capital*, Vol. I, Chapter 24, really only reiterates what he has already said on the subject of simple reproduction in Chapter 23, with however one very important difference. Instead of supposing that capitalists consume unproductively the entire surplus value produced by the process of production in order to reproduce themselves and their families, he now assumes that they reinvest a part of the surplus in order not only to simply reproduce themselves, but to *extend* the scale of the process of production.

In the main example he gives of this (1974a, 543–9 [1976, 725–33]), Marx supposes that the capitalist has advanced to the process of production a capital, not of £1,000 this time, but £10,000, of which four-fifths (£8,000) is spent on constant capital (means of production, raw materials, etc.), and one-fifth (£2,000) is spent on variable capital (wages). Assuming a rate of surplus value (the ratio of variable capital advanced as wages to the total surplus value produced) of 1:1, or 100%, where the variable capital is £2,000, the surplus value produced by this process of production will also be £2,000, since r = s/v. Up to this point, this illustration is the same as the one we looked at in the previous chapter. The only difference is that, in this case, the magnitude of the original capital and the surplus value it produces have been multiplied by 10: instead of a capital of £1,000 producing a surplus value of £200, we now have a capital of £10,000 which produces a surplus value of £2,000.[1] Now, however, instead of allowing the capitalist to consume this surplus value of £2,000 unproductively, Marx assumes that the capitalist not only continues to reproduce his or her original capital of £10,000 at the same rate, but *also* that he or she capitalizes the additional surplus of £2,000 and uses this to create an additional process of production which may or may not remain united with the original process of production.

In order to capitalize the surplus value of £2,000, all other circumstances remaining as before, the capitalist must advance four-fifths of this £2,000 (or £1,600) to be converted into constant capital and one-fifth (or £400) to be converted into variable capital, thereby producing a further surplus value of £400 in this new process of production assuming, as before, a rate of surplus value of 100%. There are now therefore *two* capitalist processes of production at work here, which may or may not be united or which might well exist independently of one another. In one of these scenarios, the capitalist's original investment of £10,000 continues to reproduce itself at the same unchanging rate and therefore continues to produce a surplus value of £2,000 at the end of each reproduction cycle of this capital. In the other, with a value of £2,000, a new surplus value of £400 will be produced by the end of its initial reproduction cycle and will continue to reproduce *successive* capitals of £400 for as long as it continues to be reinvested. If the capitalist, instead of consuming unproductively the surplus value of *either* of these capitals, now reinvests both the original capital and its surplus product, there will be not one or two but four capitals in existence simultaneously: the original capital of £10,000, the first capital of £2,000, the £400 surplus value this produced, and, in addition to this, a second surplus value of £2,000 produced by the second cycle of the original capital of £10,000. Furthermore, other things being equal, this process will obviously continue to expand itself as follows:

Figure 4. Reproduction on a *progressively* extending scale

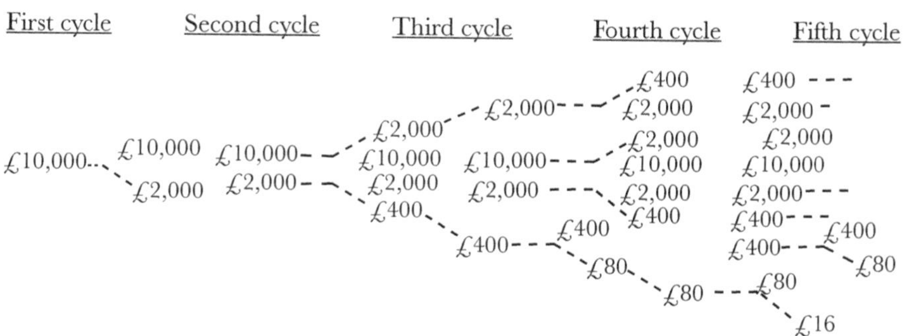

Thus, as Marx says, there develops a process, not of simple reproduction, but of reproduction on an extended scale and then of reproduction on a progressively extending scale. 'The circle in which simple reproduction moves, alters its form, and, to use Sismondi's expression, changes into a spiral' (1974a, 545 [1976, 727]).

If it is now asked what the capitalist is supposed to live on if he or she accumulates the *entire* surplus value produced by the capitalist process of production – i.e. what part of this surplus is used to reproduce the capitalist and his or her family – this apparent objection can easily be overcome if we assume that, in addition to the above capital of £10,000 the capitalist has all along a *further* capital of £1,000 or so (or whatever is required in order to reproduce the capitalist and his or her family at a standard which makes it unnecessary for them to actually do any work themselves), which he or she simply reproduces on the *same* unchanging scale as in the example previously given, and where the surplus value of *this* capital is consumed unproductively.

The question then arises why capitalists should choose to do any of this. Why do they accumulate their capital on an extended scale, and still less on a progressively extending scale (with all the risks this involves of the existing process of production becoming over-extended and the capitalist becoming bankrupt), when they might otherwise simply reproduce the existing process of production on the same unchanging scale? Why, in other words, don't they simply reproduce their entire capital (£10,000 + £2,000 + £400 etc.) on the *same* unchanging scale and consume unproductively the entire surplus value that this produces? After all, they would seem to have a much better standard of living if they did do this. This is the question we will consider in detail in the remaining three sections of this study, where we will look at Marx's attempt in *Capital*, Vol. II to elaborate a set of conditions under which capitalists might be said to be materially compelled to accumulate their surplus product on a progressively extending scale. But for now we will restrict our discussion to the preliminary answer Marx gives to this question in his discussion of extended reproduction alone in Vol. I.

The usual Marxist explanation of extended reproduction in the capitalist mode of production is in terms of competition between capitalists, and Marx gives a very good illustration of this argument in Chapter 24. According to Marx,

> the development of capitalist production makes it constantly necessary to keep increasing the amount of capital laid out in a given industrial undertaking, and competition makes the immanent laws of capitalist production to be felt by each individual capitalist, as external coercive laws. It compels him *to keep constantly extending his capital, in order to preserve it*, but extend it he cannot, except by means of progressive accumulation. (1974a, 555 [1976, 739]; emphasis added)

The argument here is that if one capitalist invests in new machinery and thereby cheapens the cost of production of a certain commodity, another capitalist, producing the same commodity, will also be forced to invest in the same or better machinery in order simply to compete. Taken by itself, however, all an explanation in terms of capitalist competition does is to move the problem we are considering one stage further back, since we would still require an explanation of what motivated the *first* capitalist to invest in new machinery which then put the *second* capitalist under pressure to compete. In short, competition between capitalists does not provide us with what is known as a 'first-order explanation' but only allows us to explain something once this process is underway.

Clearly something *else* is required over and above the individual will – or, as we might say, the spirit – of the capitalist to accumulate in order to explain the transition from simple reproduction to extended reproduction in a more *materially* compelling way, and this something else would seem to be provided by what Marx has to say about the *material form* of the surplus product of the capitalist process of production itself. 'Surplus value is convertible into capital,' Marx claims, 'solely because the surplus-product whose value it is, *already* comprises the material elements of new capital' (1974a, 544–5 [1976, 727]; emphasis added).

> The annual production must in the first place furnish all those objects (use-values) from which the material components of capital, used up in the course of the year, have to be replaced. Deducting these there remains the net or surplus-product, in which the surplus value lies. And of what does this surplus product consist? Only of things destined to satisfy the wants and desires of the capitalist class, things which, consequently, enter into the consumption-fund of the capitalists? Were that the case, the cup of surplus value would be drained to the very dregs and nothing but simple reproduction would ever take place. (1974a, 544 [1976, 726])

By itself, however, there is nothing in the fact that surplus value is produced in a material form in which it cannot be consumed *unproductively* that compels it to be consumed *productively* – its value might simply be wasted after all – while even if the surplus product is produced in a material form in which it is only suited for productive consumption, nothing will be altered in this case if this surplus product can be exchanged for something else which can be consumed unproductively. For this reason, Marx is forced to introduce a *further* limiting condition before the transition from simple to extended reproduction can be explained in terms of anything more than the will of the individual capitalist to accumulte: the assumption of a closed economy model. In a footnote to Chapter 24, Marx says:

> We here take no account of the export trade, by means of which a nation can change articles of luxury either into means of production or means of subsistence, and *vice versa*. In order to examine the object of our investigation in its integrity, free from all disturbing subsidiary

circumstances, we must treat the whole world as one nation, and assume that capitalist production is everywhere established and has possessed itself of every branch of industry. (1974a, 545, 1n [1976, 727, 2n])

Points for Further Discussion

Taken together these three conditions seem to provide a sufficient set of causes adequate to explain the transition from simple to extended reproduction. The capitalist must consume the surplus productively because (a) he cannot consume it unproductively (its material form simply will not permit this); (b) it cannot be exchanged for something else which can be consumed unproductively; and (c) for some as yet unexplained reason, he or she cannot simply waste it. However, as we have seen, competition by itself can only properly be considered as an *effect* of a round of previously existing capitalist accumulation, and it is an interesting point to note that in his much more detailed study of simple and extended reproduction in Part III of *Capital*, Vol. II (see Chapter 7 below) Marx makes no mention of competition as a materially compelling motive for the transition from simple to extended reproduction. Competition *does* compel capitalist accumulation of course – we know this happens all the time – and such competition is undoubtedly a material cause for the continuation of the process of reproduction on a progressively extending scale *once this process is under way*. But by itself it cannot be used to explain the initial transition from simple to extended reproduction and therefore, in the remaining chapters of Part II of this study, we will look at Marx's detailed attempt in the last third of *Capital*, Vol. II to explain the mechanism of this transition in terms of a slightly different set of conditions: (i) a closed economy model, (ii) the material form of the product of the capitalist process of production, and (iii) the accumulation of the capitalists' fixed capital before such time – or in other words 'precipitously' – as it is needed simply to reproduce the mode of production on the same unchanging scale. Once again however, as we shall see, Marx's attempt to explain extended reproduction in terms of what he refers to as the precipitation of fixed capital is in fact unsuccessful.

Reading: Essential: *Capital*, Vol. I, Ch. 24 (1974a, 543–6 [1976, 725–9]). Background: the remainder of Ch. 24, 1974a (547–73 [1976, 730–61]). It is not necessary to go on to look at Ch. 25 yet as I consider this in detail later when I review what Marx has to say on the subject of the concentration and centralization of capital in Part III of this study.

7. SIMPLE REPRODUCTION IN *CAPITAL*, VOL. II, SECTIONS 1–8

Marx's discussion of simple and extended reproduction in *Capital*, Vol. II begins with a rather long-winded discussion of simple reproduction and circulation in Chapter 17 (1974b, 329–48 [1978, 399–418]) and then a very brief discussion of extended reproduction (1974b, 348–54 [1978, 418–24]). However, this discussion (which basically focuses on the question of the money-supply necessary for circulation to take place) is of very limited interest to us here, and really only needs to be studied in any detail at all if one is interested in Rosa Luxemburg's claim that a *third* department of production is required to produce the means of exchange (Luxemburg 1963, 99–103).

Of much greater interest to us here is Marx's discussion of simple and extended reproduction in Chapters 20 and 21 of Vol. II. This is the famous Department I (DI) and Department II (DII) discussion of the reproduction of the total *social* capital of society, rather than of any individual or particular capital, as was the case with Marx's discussion of simple and extended reproduction in *Capital*, Vol. I. Once again these two chapters are composed of a very long discussion of simple reproduction (in Chapter 20) and a very much shorter and rather more to the point discussion of extended reproduction (in Chapter 21). Fortunately it is not necessary for our purposes to look at both of these chapters in detail here. We will look at Chapter 21 (1974b, 493–527 [1978, 565–99]) in some detail in Chapter 8 of this study, but even then it is not necessary to read it all. While Chapter 20, section 13 (1974b, 484–92 [1978, 556–64]) is a completely uninteresting discussion of Destutt de Tracy's theory of reproduction which, in my opinion, might well have been included by Engels in the book which is now know as *Theories of Surplus Value* – sometimes also called the fourth volume of *Capital* – without losing anything from Marx's discussion of simple reproduction in Vol. II. It would also be possible to omit without losing anything from Marx's discussion of simple reproduction in Vol. II Marx's equally uninteresting discussion of the Physiocrats and Adam Smith in *Capital*, Vol. II, Chapter 19, entitled 'Former Presentations of the Subject' (1974b, 363–95 [1978, 435–67]). Chapter 20, section 12, on the reproduction of the material form of money (i.e. as gold, silver, paper, etc.) is again only of limited interest in the context of Rosa Luxemburg's discussion of the necessity for a third department for the production of the means of exchange. While Chapter 20, sections 10 and especially section 11, on the replacement of fixed capital, are of very great interest to the question of the precipitation of fixed capital, but here again, I discuss this question in great detail later, in the final chapter of this part of this book. Finally, Chapter 20, section 9, 'A Retrospect to Adam Smith, Storch and Ramsey', could also have easily been left out of *Capital*, Vol. II altogether without any loss to Marx's discussion of simple reproduction and will therefore not be discussed here.

This just leaves Chapter 20, sections 1–8 (1974b, 396–437 [1978, 468–509]) on simple reproduction which we will look at in detail in what follows. Before we do this, however, there are once again one or two simplifying conditions we must note before we can situate this discussion of simple and extended reproduction in relation to Marx's discussion of these matters in *Capital*, Vol. I. Firstly, as in the case of Marx's discussion of extended reproduction in *Capital*, Vol. I, this whole discussion of the DI–DII model takes place within the assumption of a closed-economy model. Thus, for example, in the otherwise relatively uninteresting section 12 of *Capital*, Vol. II on the reproduction of the material form of the money Marx claims that:

> Capitalist production does not exist at all without foreign commerce. But when one assumes normal annual reproduction on a given scale one also assumes that foreign commerce only replaces home products by articles of other use or bodily form, without affecting value-relations … The involvement of foreign commerce in analysing the annually reproduced value of products can therefore only confuse without contributing any new element of the problem, or of its solution. For this reason it must be entirely discarded. (1974b, 474 [1978, 546])[2]

Secondly, and somewhat paradoxically given the above closed economy assumption, Marx points out that what we are concerned with here (as opposed to the discussion in *Capital*, Vol. I) is precisely the replacement of the *material* form of capital (albeit within the capitalist mode of production), rather than with the mere value form in which capital is exchanged. As Marx says in the section which introduces his discussion of the two departments of social production:

> So long as we looked upon the production of value and the value of the product of capital individually, the bodily form of the commodities produced was wholly immaterial for the analysis, whether it was machines,

for instance, corn, or looking glasses. It was always but a matter of illustration, and any branch of production could have served that purpose equally well. What we dealt with was the immediate process of production itself, which presents itself at every point as the process of some individual capital. So far as the reproduction of capital was concerned, it was sufficient to assume that that portion of the product in commodities which represents capital-value finds an opportunity in the sphere of circulation to reconvert itself into the elements of production and thus into its form of productive capital … This merely formal manner of presentation is no longer adequate in the study of the total social capital and of the value of its products. The reconversion of one portion of the value of the product into capital and the passing of another portion into the individual consumption of the capitalist as well as the working-class form a movement within the value of the product itself in which the result of the aggregate capital finds expression; and this movement is not only a replacement of value, but also a replacement in *material* and is therefore as much bound up with the relative proportions of the value-components of the total social product, as with their use-value, their material shape. (1974b, 398 [1978, 470]; emphasis added)

Finally, as the above quotation makes clear and as we have already seen in the introduction to this section, what Marx is concerned to analyse in *Capital*, Vol. II is not only the material form of the exchange of capital within a closed economy model, but also the movement of the total social capital of a given society rather than, as in the previous case, the behaviour of any given individual capitalist. 'The circuits of individual capitals intertwine,' Marx argues, 'presuppose and necessitate one another, and form, precisely in this interlacing, the movement of total social capital' (1974b, 357 [1978, 429]). It is precisely this interrelation of capital then that we are now going on to look at in detail.

Bearing the above points in mind, what then does Marx have to say on the subject of simple reproduction in *Capital*, Vol. II, Chapter 20, sections 1–8? Well, not much actually: beyond what he has to say in section 2 alone, the other seven sections being little more than a detailed elaboration of the points outlined in section 2. The only absolutely essential part of *Capital*, Vol. II which must be read here therefore is Chapter 20, section 2 (1974a, 399–402 [1978, 471–4]). According to the model Marx elaborates here, the total production of a given society may be divided between two major sectors or 'departments'. Department I which produces means of production; that is to say, commodities which have a material form 'in which they *must*, or at least may, pass into productive consumption' (1974b, 399 [1978, 471]).[3] And Department II, which produces means of consumption; that is, commodities which have a certain material form which determines that they must pass into the individual consumption of the capitalist or the working class. DI and DII are then both departments of production, and not, as is sometimes mistakenly suggested, a department of production (DI) and the department of consumption (DII). DI is the department for the production of means of production and DII is the department for the *production* of means of consumption. DI and DII are then divided between constant and variable capital in the normal way. However, here variable capital is defined as the value of the social or aggregate labour power (the *total* cost in the form of wages of necessary labour), while constant capital is defined as the aggregate value of the total means of production of DI and DII. Marx then gives the following example of simple reproduction in which the rate of surplus value (the ratio of surplus value to variable capital) is, as usual, assumed to be 1:1, or 100 per cent:

Figure 5. Simple reproduction

DI	4,000c	+	1,000v	+	1,000s	=	6,000	means of production
DII	2,000c	+	500v	+	500s	=	3,000	means of consumption
	6,000c	+	1,500v	+	1,500s	=	9,000	total annual production

Simple reproduction is said to take place when the total annual production of means of production produced in DI is equal to the annual requirement of DI and DII for means of production (these means of production being purchased with constant capital), and when the total production of means of consumption is equal in one year to the annual requirement for means of consumption of DI and DII in the following year. In this example, this is shown in the case of DI producing 6,000 units of means of production for DI and DII to purchase in the following year (or reproduction period) with 6,000 units of constant capital, and DII producing 3,000 units of means of consumption in a given reproduction period, equal to the demand of DI and DII for 3,000 units of means of subsistence (1,500v) and articles of luxury (1,500s) in the following reproduction period. The key point here is that Marx argues that there must be *an equilibrium* between the production of means of production and means of consumption in DI and DII and the requirements of DI and DII for these things. In the next chapter I explore what happens when such an equilibrium *fails* to occur.

Points for Further Discussion

1. Where accumulation takes place, Marx argues that simple reproduction is *always* a necessary and unavoidable part of this, and even that it is the most

important part of reproduction on an *extended* scale (1974b, 399, 415 [1978, 471, 487]). Where this is the case, simple reproduction can never be said to be a pre-capitalist or 'primitive' form of accumulation, but is in fact a precondition of extended reproduction itself. Simple reproduction has to be satisfied *first of all* therefore before any extension of the scale of the process of production can take place.

2. Apart from being distinguished from DI by the fact that it produces means of consumption rather than means of production, DII is further distinguished between two great subdivisions: subsection i, which produces means of subsistence, and subsection ii, which produces articles of luxury. In practice, however, it is difficult to distinguish between means of consumption that are necessities and means of consumption that are articles of luxury. In point of fact Marx – a heavy smoker himself – even goes so far as to argue that *tobacco* may be counted as a consumer necessity, even though it does not enter into the physiological reproduction of labour-power (and as we now know is in fact detrimental to this), his argument being that tobacco has habitually been treated as such (1974b, 407 [1978, 479]).
3. It is *not* necessary to this model to always assume that the proportion of constant to variable capital will be the same in DI as it is in DII, or even that it will be the same within DI and DII. This assumption is made by Marx here purely as a simplifying abstraction (1974b, 410 [1978, 482).
4. Finally, while simple reproduction indisputably does involve the accumulation of capital, it is interesting to note that Marx refers to reproduction on an extended scale alone as 'accumulation proper' (1974b, 477 [1978, 548]).

Reading: Essential: *Capital*, Vol. II, Ch. 20 sections 1–2 (1974b, 396–402 [1978, 468–74]). Background: *Capital*, Vol. II, Ch. 20, sections 3–8 (1974b, 402–37 [1978, 474–509]). Non-essential: *Capital*, Vol. II, Ch. 17–19 (1974b, 323–95 [1978, 394–467]).

8. EXTENDED REPRODUCTION IN *CAPITAL*, VOL. II, CH. 21, SECTION 3

In this chapter we will consider Marx's detailed discussion of extended reproduction in the case of the DI–DII model from what is in fact the last chapter of *Capital*, Vol. II (Ch. 21, 1974b, 493–527 [1978, 565–99]). However, as before, we are here really only concerned with a very small part of this already short chapter, namely section 3 (1974b, 510–26 [1978, 581–97]), and even then only with the second illustration of his argument (1974b, 518–26 [1978, 589–97]). This is because we will look at Marx's discussion of the precipitation of fixed capital in the first part of Vol. II, Chapter 21 (1974b, 493–509 [1978, 565–81]) in detail in the following chapter, but also because Marx makes a number of false starts in his first attempt to express the essential relations of extended reproduction, all of which were nevertheless included by Engels in Chapter 21, presumably in order to show the stages by which Marx arrived at his first successful formulation of the model for extended reproduction. In this chapter Marx is once again particularly concerned with the *material* form of the exchanges that take place between DI and DII, and he continues to assume a closed economy model exists and to consider the question of accumulation from the point of view of the total social capital. He is also concerned to effect the transition from simple to extended reproduction merely by a qualitative alteration of the elements of constant and variable capital, surplus value, and means of production and means of consumption, which are already given in the case of simple reproduction shown in Fig. 5. Now, however, he varies one of the conditions he previously posited as being essential for simple reproduction: if simple reproduction can only take place on the basis of a strict equilibrium between production and demand of DI and DII, it is reasonable to suppose that an essential condition of extended reproduction must be that there is some form of *disequilibrium* between DI and DII.

Marx's discussion of extended reproduction therefore begins with what appear to be a number of *failed* attempts to formulate a model in which there is a disequilibrium between DI and DII. The first of these is shown *Capital*,

Vol. II, Chapter 21, section 3 (1974b, 510–13 [1978, 581–5]), and is as follows:

Figure 6. First unsuccessful attempt

DI 4,000c	+	1,000v	+	1,000s	=	6,000MP
DII 1,500c	+	376v	+	376s	=	2,252MC
5,500c	+	1,376v	+	1,376s	=	8,252TCP
		2,752v + s				

Here a surplus of 500 units of means of production has been produced by DI over and above the combined requirement of DI and DII for such means of production in the next cycle of the process of production represented by the 5,500 units of constant capital in DI and DII, and it seems to be essential that a surplus of this kind should exist if extended reproduction is to take place. The ratio of constant to variable capital, at 4c:1v, is also approximately the same in DI as it is in DII,[4] and this is the same ratio of constant to variable capital found in the previous illustration of simple reproduction. Only now, however, the total production of means of production in DII is insufficient to meet the combined demand of DI and DII for 2,752 units of means of subsistence and articles of luxury, and the total commodity production of 8,252 units of means of production and means of consumption has *fallen* from the 9,000 units found in the case of the previous illustration of simple reproduction to only 8,252 units. Under these circumstances, where the total social production has not managed to produce even the same amount of commodities found in the previous cycle of production, Marx argues that there is no possibility of even simply reproducing the existing process of production on the same unchanging scale, let alone extending this, and he therefore abandons this attempt to formulate the conditions of extended reproduction.

Marx tries again in the next illustration of his argument (1974b, 514–17 [1978, 586–9]), with another example in which the total commodity production stays the same as it was in the case of simple reproduction (i.e. 9,000 TCP) but where there is nevertheless a surplus of 500 units of means of production over and above the combined requirement of DI and DII for 5,500c. This illustration is as follows:

Figure 7. Second unsuccessful attempt

DI 4,000c	+	1,000v	+	1,000s	=	6,000MP
DII 1,500c	+	750v	+	750s	=	3,000MC
5,500c	+	1,750v	+	1,750s	=	9,000TCP
		3,500v + s				

However, there seems to be another problem here. The ratio of constant to variable capital in DII is very much higher at 2c:1v than the ratio of constant to variable capital is in DI at 4c:1v. This is not necessarily a problem as Marx argues (in the chapter on simple reproduction that we have already looked at in *Capital*, Vol. II; see 1974b, 410 [1978, 482]) that it is not at all necessary to assume that the ratio of constant to variable capital is always the same in different branches of industry or different spheres of production, but that this assumption is only made for the sake of simplicity. However, as Rosa Luxemburg argues (1963, 99–103), in order to avoid any suspicion that the conditions of extended reproduction have been achieved by violating those precise logical rules which lay down the proportion of constant to variable capital in DI, Marx rejects this model yet again.

In his third attempt to illustrate the conditions of extended reproduction (1974b, 518–19 [1978, 589–91]) Marx presents us with a slightly different formula. Here the total commodity production is still 9,000 units, there is a surplus of means of production produced in DI over and above DI and DII's combined demand for these commodities, and the ratio of constant to variable capital is the same in DI as it is in DII, only now, however, the ratio of constant to variable capital has gone up from 4c:1v to 5c:1v, as follows:

Figure 8. Conditions of extended reproduction

DI	5,000c	+	1,000v	+	1,000s	=	7,000MP
DII	1,430c	+	285v	+	285s	=	2,000MC
	6,430c	+	1,285v	+	1,285s	=	9,000TCP
			2,570v + s				

In this case all the above conditions of extended reproduction have been satisfied. The ratio of constant to variable capital is the same in DI and DII, the total commodity product is the same as it was in the case of simple reproduction, and there is now a surplus of 570 units of means of production in DI over and above the combined requirements of DI and DII for commodities of this type. However, the fact that there is a surplus of means of production in DI and that this creates a disequilibrium between DI and DII is not by itself sufficient to bring about an actual expansion of production in society. The 570 units of means of production in DI must themselves be capitalized in the ratio of 5c:1v if they are to be employed productively, while the demand of DI and DII for means of consumption must be reduced by exactly this same amount of units of means of consumption. How is this done?

If the capitalists of DI are to not waste their surplus 570 units of means of production (and we have not yet seen any good reason why they should not do just this and continue to simply reproduce the capital they had in their possession before this surplus was produced on the same unchanging scale), then Marx argues that they must accumulate it. He therefore assumes that the capitalists of DI decide to forgo the unproductive consumption of 500 of the 1,000 units of surplus value they have in their possession, and to spend them instead on 500 of the 570 units of surplus means of production which are also in DI. DI is now increased from 5,000c to 5,000c plus the 500 units of means of production still to be capitalized, plus 1,000v as before in Fig. 8, plus the 500s remaining from the 1,000s in Fig. 8. This still leaves 70 units of means of production in DI since, if DI accumulated its entire surplus of means of production itself, it would have nothing left to exchange with DII for means of consumption with which to set in motion the 500 units of means of production still remaining to be capitalized in DI. Marx therefore argues that DII must take up this remaining 70 units of means of production in DI (although, once again, it is by no means clear why the capitalists of DI *should* do this since they have already satisfied their demand for 1,430 units of means of production from DI and already have in their own possession more than enough means of consumption with which to capitalize these 1,430 units of means of production on the basis of simple reproduction). The capitalists of DII therefore reduce their unproductive consumption of 285s to 215s in order to take up the 70 units of means of production in DI. Once this exchange has taken place the 70 units of means of production are added to DII since, due to their material form as means of production, they can only function as part of the constant capital of DII. DII is now therefore increased from the 1,430c found in Fig. 8, to 1,430c plus 70 units of means of production which have still to be capitalized (bringing DIIc up to a potential 1,500c), plus the 285v found in Fig. 8, plus the 215s remaining from the previous 285s found in Fig. 8. After all these qualitative alterations in the functioning of the capitals of DI and DII have taken place we have the following formula for the combined capitals of DI and DII:

Figure 9. Qualitative alteration in the capital of DI and DII

	+ 500MP (still to be capitalized)			70s
DI	5,000c +	1,000v +	1,000s =	7,000MP
DII	1,430c +	285v +	285s =	2,000MC
	+ 70 MP (still to be capitalized)			– 70s 215s
	7,000c +	1,285s +	715s =	9,000TCP

The total capital of DI and DII has now been brought back into a rough equilibrium. The combined demand of DI and DII for 7,000 units of means of production is exactly equal to the production of DI of articles of this kind, while the combined demand of DI and DII for articles of luxury and means of subsistence is exactly equal to the 2,000 units of means of consumption produced by DII. However, there is still the matter of the 500 units of means of production in DI and the 70 units of means of production in DII that have still to be capitalized (i.e. have still to be set in motion by labour). How is this to be done? Assuming the same ratio of constant to variable capital as in the previous cases above (5c:lv), if the 70 units of means of production in DII are to be set in motion as constant capital they must be acted upon by 14 units of variable capital. Since this 14v can only be withdrawn from DIIs without further upsetting the equilibrium between DI and DII, Marx is forced to argue that the capitalists of DII must reduce their expenditure of surplus value and their demand for articles of luxury by a further 14s in addition to having already reduced their demand for items of luxury by the 70s they had already exchanged with DI for the 70 units of means of production in the first place. DII is now therefore increased from 1,430c, to 1,500c (i.e. 1,430c + 70c). DIIv is increased from 285v to 299v (i.e. 285v + 14v), while DIIs is reduced from 285s to 201s (i.e. 285 – 70 – 14). We then have the following equation for DII as a whole:

Figure 10. Capitalization of 70MP as DIIc

	1,430c	+	285v	+	215s	=	1,930
DII	70c	+	14v	+	–14s	=	70
	1,500c	+	299v	+	201s	=	2,000MC

There is still the matter of the capitalization of the 500 units of means of production in DI. This is carried out in much the same way as the capitalization of the 70 units of means of production in DII, except that here, instead of making the capitalists of DI reduce their expenditure of surplus value and their demand for articles of luxury by 100s in order to capitalize the 500 units of means of production in DI in the ratio of 500c:100v, Marx does a rather peculiar thing and argues instead that the capitalists of DI *divide* the 500 units of means of production in DI between one part which will function as additional constant capital and another part which will be exchanged with DII in order to function as additional variable capital in DI. Assuming the same ratio of constant to variable capital as before, Marx therefore argues that the capitalists of DI decide to capitalize 417 of the 500 units of means of production as constant capital and to exchange the remaining one-sixth (or 83) units of means of production for means consumption with DII. This means that once again the capitalists of DII must reduce their expenditure of surplus value and their demand for articles of luxury by a *further* 83s in order to buy the 83 units of means of production from DI (and this all because the capitalists of DI do not want to reduce *their* consumption of articles of luxury by 100s). After this exchange we have the following equations for DI and DII:

Figure 11. Capitalization of 500MP as DI

	5,000c	+	1,000v	+	500s		
		500 MP (to be capitalized)					
DI	417c	+	83v	+	500s		
	5,417c	+	1,083v	+	500s	=	7,000MP

Figure 12. Exchange of 83s for 83MP in DII

	1,500c	+	299v	+	201s		
DII	83MP (still to be capitalized)				–83s		
	1,583MP	+	299v	+	118s	=	2,000MC

After this exchange has taken place there is now only the 83 units of means of production in DII still to be capitalized. This is done in the same way as the capitalization of the 70 units of means of production in Fig. 10, only here the capitalists of DII are required to reduce their expenditure of surplus value and their demand for articles of luxury by 17v not 14s (as was the case in Fig. 10), since it obviously requires 17v to set 83 units of means of production in motion as constant capital given a ratio of 5c:1v. DIIs is now therefore further reduced from 118 to 101s, and DIIv is correspondingly increased from 299v, as follows:

Figure 13. Capitalization of 83MP in DII

	1,583MP	+	299v	+	118s		
	1,500c	+	299v	+	17s		
DII	83c	+	17v	+	101s		
	1,583c	+	316v	+	101s	=	7,000MC

If we now take the last line of Fig. 11 and Fig. 12, the final result of the capitalization of the surplus product of DI for this particular circuit of this capital is as follows:

Figure 14. Simple reproduction on an extended scale

DI	5,417c	+	1,083v	+	501s	=	7,000MP
DII	1,583c	+	316v	+	101s	=	2,000MC
	7,000c	+	1,399v	+	601s	=	9,000TCP
			2,000v + s				

The supply of means of production and means of consumption in DI and DII now exactly equals the combined demand of DI and DII for these kinds of commodities during the next cycle of the process of production. The surplus product of 570 units of means of production in DI in Fig. 8, has now been entirely used up productively in the process of production, partly in DI and partly in DII. Similarly, the combined demand of DI and DII for means of consumption has been reduced from 2,570 units to only 2,000 units, which is once again exactly the number of this kind of commodity that DII has in hand to dispose of during the next cycle of the process of production. *Simple reproduction* can therefore take place once again, only now the scale of the process of production has been considerably expanded, with the capital of DI having been increased from 6,000c + v in Fig. 8, to 6,500c + v above (i.e. 5,417c + 1,083v), while the capital of DII has likewise been increased from 1,715c + v in Fig. 8, to 1,899c + v in Fig. 14.

No *actual* expansion in the product of this process of production has taken place as yet. The total commodity product of DI and DII is still 9, 000 units of means of production and means of consumption as it was in Fig. 8. However, if we continue to assume a rate of surplus value of 100% (i.e. a ratio of ls:lv), we get the following result when we set the above expanded capitals in motion.

Figure 15. Reproduction on an extended scale

DI	5,417c	+	1,083v	+	1,083s	=	7,583MP
DII	1,583c	+	316v	+	316s	=	2,215MC
	7,000c	+	1,399v	+	1,399s	=	9,798TCP
			2,798v + s				

The 601s units of surplus value in DI and DII in Fig. 14 have been spent on 601 units of means of consumption, consumed unproductively, and have therefore been lost to the process of production. Meanwhile, the 1,399 units of variable capital have been set to work in the form of labour and have acted upon the 7,000 units of constant capital in the form of means of production to produce a new surplus value of 1,399s. An actual expansion of the scale of the process of production – as opposed to the merely potential expansion which was immanent in Fig. 14 – has thus taken place. The total commodity product of DI and DII has been increased from 9,000 to 9,798 units of means of production and means of consumption. However, in effecting this increase, a *further* disequilibrium has been brought about between DI and DII. There are now 7,583 units of means of production in DI, while DI and DII together only have 7,000 units of constant capital to spend on means of production in the next cycle of the process of production. Similarly, DI and DII together have 2,798 units of variable capital and surplus value to spend during the next cycle of the process of production, while DII has in its possession only 2,215 units of means of consumption to satisfy this demand.

If the capitalists of DI and DII are not to waste that part of their surplus value which they might otherwise have spent on articles of luxury, and if the capitalists of DI are not to waste 583 units of means of production for which there is no demand in either DI or DII, then the proportions of constant and variable capital to surplus value must once again be altered in a manner very similar to the alterations of the capital of DI and DII in Figs 8–14. If this is done the process of production will once again be brought back into equilibrium and the effect of this alteration will be to have once again extended the scale of the process of production further. When this enlarged capital is set in motion, an even greater disequilibrium will be created, and the adjustment of the capital of this process of production will further enlarge the scale of this process of production. Reproduction on a *progressively* extending scale takes place then as successive enlargements of the total social capital create successive disequilibriums in this process, and as the necessity to re-establish the conditions of an equilibrium brings about successive enlargements in the scale of the process of production itself (1974b, 523 [1978, 595]).

Points for Further Discussion

The key question we have to consider here, as I said before, is why the capitalists of DI and DII should continually extend the scale of the process of production in the above way as described by Marx when they can apparently continue to *simply* reproduce the process of production on the same unchanging scale (there being more than enough means of production and means of consumption for simple reproduction to take place). In a *planned* economy, officials of the state might well do this for the greater good of society as it were;[5] but why should individual capitalists, or even capitalists collectively, do this when they might apparently consume unproductively any surplus left over if it was produced in a material form which would permit this or waste the surplus product if it was produced in a form that could only be consumed productively? Specifically, this point can be expressed as follows: (i) why cannot the capitalists of DI simply waste their surplus production of means of production, and (ii) why should the capitalists of DI and more especially DII, continually *reduce* their spending on articles of luxury in order to effect an expansion of the capital of DI when (a) DI has already satisfied DII's demand for means of production and when (b) DII already has in its possession more than enough means of consumption for its own simple reproduction?

Capital, Vol. II ends with the above discussion of extended reproduction – and this is the point at which Marx apparently gave up the attempt to publish *Capital*, Vols II and III during his own life time – but unless we can find a materially compelling explanation for reproduction on an extending scale we will be back to where Marx left this problem in *Capital*, Vol. I, with no explanation of why capitalists (in this case the capitalists of DII) should forgo luxury consumption in order to expand the scale of the capitalist process of production. In the next chapter of this study I therefore look at what Marx has to say on the subject of the precipitation of fixed capital in an earlier part of Vol. II to see if this can provide us with any solution to the above problem.

Reading: Essential: *Capital*, Vol. II, Ch. 21, section 3 (1974b, 518–23 [1978, 589–95]). Background: *Capital*, Vol. II, Ch. 21, section 3 (1974b, 510–17, 524–6 [1978, 581–9, 595–7]).

9. THE PRECIPITATION OF FIXED CAPITAL IN *CAPITAL*, VOL. II, CH. 21, SECTIONS 1–2; CH. 20, SECTION 11

At this stage, and taking into account the *highly* abstract nature of Marx's discussion of reproduction and accumulation in *Capital*, Vol. II, it may seem that we do not know very much more about the material conditions which are said to compel capitalist accumulation than we already knew following Marx's discussion of this in Vol. I. However, I want to suggest that this is not the case and that, in point of fact, we actually do know quite a bit more than we did before, of which the following may be said to be the most important points:

(i) There must be an *equilibrium* between the supply and demand of DI and DII for means of production and means of consumption if *simple* reproduction is to take place.
(ii) There must nevertheless be a *disequilibrium* of some kind within the system of production if reproduction on an *extended* scale is to take place.
(iii) *Simple* reproduction is always a part (and Marx says the most important part at that) of all annual reproduction on an *extended* scale.
(iv) That therefore, the disequilibrium necessary for reproduction on an extended scale to take place must always be brought back into equilibrium before simple reproduction on an extended scale can take place.
(v) That this disequilibrium cannot simply be of such a kind as to create an *over*-production in society since, where this is the case, there would seem to be no reason why this over-production cannot simply be *wasted* if, by definition, it is surplus to the requirements of simple reproduction.
(vi) That, on the other hand, this disequilibrium cannot be of such a kind as to be brought about by a *shortfall* in production since in this case not even simple reproduction will take place.
(vii) That there must nevertheless be a surplus *of some kind* on the material basis of which the scale of the process of production can be extended, since otherwise reproduction on a extending scale would never take place.

(viii) That it seems somehow unsatisfactory to suggest that this surplus can be achieved by the capitalists of either DI or DII *reducing* their consumption of articles of luxury when there does nor seem to be any motive for them to do this.

(ix) That it is the capitalists of DII in particular (who produce their surplus product in a material form in which it can immediately be consumed unproductively), who seem to lack any materially compelling motive to expand the scale of the process of production, rather than the capitalists of DI (who produce their surplus product in a form in which it can only be consumed productively).

(x) And finally that the only *materially compelling* reason why the capitalists of DI and/or DII should *extend* the scale of the process of production is if, paradoxically, they must do this because they are *unable to reproduce the existing mode of production on even the same unchanging scale* without first having to extend the scale of this mode of production.

If these ten points are taken together we can see that they can be reduced to two major propositions. First, what we are looking for is some sort of a surplus which is not surplus to the requirements of simple reproduction – a surplus which is *not* a surplus as far as *simple* reproduction is concerned, but which may well be as far as extended reproduction is concerned – and the only thing that fits the description of such a surplus is some kind of a *slack* within the system. But we must remember that this slack cannot be of such a kind as to bring about a shortfall in the system of production, since in this case not even simple reproduction will take place. Second, we are looking for something which is essential for *simple* reproduction – something without which not even simple reproduction could take place and where therefore production of any kind would be impossible – and that this something would probably be of such a kind that it could bring about disequilibrium within or between DI or DII. What then is the mysterious element which satisfies all of these conditions, and how does its reproduction bring about an expansion in the scale of the capitalist process of production? The answer to this question is that this element is *potential fixed capital* – capital which (a) *will* be needed shortly for even *simple* reproduction to take place but which crucially is not needed *yet* for this purpose, but which (b) due to its material form, will deteriorate in value if it is not made use of immediately and therefore the preservation of which requires that the capitalist *must* extend the scale of the process of production immediately in order simply to reproduce or preserve the value of this capital for its use as fixed capital at a *later* date.

What then does Marx mean by 'fixed capital'? Marx defines fixed capital somewhat loosely at the beginning of *Capital*, Vol. II, Chapter 20, section 2 (1974b, 400 [1978, 472]) as 'machines, instruments of labour, buildings, labouring animals, etc.', and he distinguishes this from circulating capital, which he defines as 'materials of production: raw and auxiliary materials, semi-finished products, etc.' However, Marx provides us with a much better definition of fixed capital in Vol. II, Part II (1974b, 156–354 [1978, 233–424]) in the section entitled 'Fixed Capital and Circulating Capital' (see especially 1974b, 160–65 [1978, 237–41]). Here Marx explains that the fixity of capital has nothing whatsoever to do with its immobility as such (a ship, for example, may be fixed capital). Nor does this fixity have anything to do with the material form of the capital in question; although fixed capital usually takes the form of machinery or instruments of labour, and rarely, if ever, takes the form of raw materials (which enter bodily into the product of the process of production) or of variable capital. Rather it is the peculiar manner in which fixed capital *circulates* that defines it as such:

> What determines that a portion of the capital-value invested in means of production is endowed with the character of fixed capital is *exclusively* the peculiar manner in which this value circulates. This specific manner of circulation arises from the specific manner in which the instrument of labour transmits its value to the product, or in which it behaves as a creator of values during the process of production. This manner again arises from the special way in which the instruments of labour function in the labour process (1974b, 163 [1978, 239–40]; emphasis added).

The 'specific manner' in question is the way in which fixed capital transfers its value gradually during the process of production to the product of this process until such time that its full value has been entirely used up, while *at the same time* continuing to function at its full value as fixed capital in the process of production. For a certain period of time then, during which the existing fixed capital continues to function at its full capacity and before it needs to be replaced in its entirety, the value of the fixed capital has a *dual existence*. There are in existence two commodities which represent the *same* value: one in the form of the already functioning machinery and instruments of labour, etc., the other in the form of potential fixed capital in the hands of the capitalist which will eventually be required to replace the actually functioning fixed capital when this eventually wears out. As Marx says on this point, in the famous letter to Engels of 24 August 1867 in which he announced that he had finished writing *Capital* Vol. I:

> The concluding part of the second book (*Process of Circulation*), the part I am now writing, contains a point concerning which I must once more apply to you for help, as I did many years ago.

> Fixed capital has to be replaced in its natural form only after, say, 10 years. In the meantime its value returns partially and gradually as the commodities produced by it are sold. This progressive return is not needed for the replacement of the fixed capital (leaving repairs and the like out of consideration) until it has ceased to exist in its material form, for instance that of a machine. *In the interval* the capitalist has these successive returns on hand.
>
> Many years ago I wrote you that thus apparently such an *accumulation fund* was forming, for the capitalist was naturally *employing* the returned money *in the interval* elapsing before he replaced the fixed capital with it. In one letter you argued somewhat superficially against this. *Later* I found that McCulloch represented this *sinking fund* as an *accumulation fund.* Convinced that no idea of McCulloch's could ever be right I dropped the matter. The *apologetic* purposes he pursued in this connection have already been crossed by the Malthusians, but *they* too admit the fact.
>
> You as a manufacturer must know what you do with the returns intended for the fixed capital *before* it has to be replaced in *its natural form.* And you must give me an answer on this point (without theory, *purely* as a matter of *practice*). (*MESC*, 1953, 232–3; emphasis original)

Thus, according to Marx there exists within the process of simple reproduction a slack or surplus capacity in the system of production in the form of the potential fixed capital, which the capitalist has to hand *sooner* than it is actually needed to replace the functioning fixed capital whose value it represents (the reproduction period of fixed capital being defined by Marx precisely by the fact that fixed capital does not need replacing as soon as its value has been returned to the capitalist in the form of money). While no part of *surplus value* can function simultaneously as both means of consumption and as additional constant capital in DI or DII (1974b, 508 [1978, 580]), it seems that this is by no means the case as far as *fixed capital* is concerned, which normally functions in this way, both as *actual* fixed capital (which is consumed productively until such time that it is used up and needs to be replaced in its entirety) and as *potential* fixed capital (which may be accumulated productively until such time that it is needed to replace the fixed capital whose value it represents). But the question we have to consider here is why the capitalists of DI or DII should do this? Why do they, as Marx says in the above letter, 'naturally' accumulate their potential fixed capital *before* such time as it is needed to replace their worn-out fixed capital (i.e. *sooner* than they apparently need to do so on the basis of simple reproduction), and thereby *extend* the scale of the process of production without apparently having any material motive to do so? This is where the concept of 'precipitation' comes into play.

Marx discusses the concept of precipitation in two places in Vol. II and it is possible to distinguish two distinct meanings of this term (although the second of these is so unclear in Marx's discussion that it is hard to be sure that this is in fact what he intended). The first usage of this concept is discussed in the first half of Chapter 21 (1974b, 493–509 [1978, 565–81]) and then again in section 11 of Chapter 20 (1974b, 453–73 [1978, 524–45]) where Marx considers the question of the replacement of fixed capital. Here Marx generally uses the term precipitation in a way that would be immediately understood by a student of chemistry or meteorology, to mean the suspension of the active function of something – in this case capital – as a result of its separation into fine particles (e.g. in the case of meteorology, as water vapour before it falls as rain and, in the case we are considering here, as money before it is converted into capital).[6] Marx makes use of this concept of precipitation to try to argue that one group of capitalists is compelled to accumulate their potential fixed capital while it still exists in its commodity form, at the stage 'C' in the circulation process M–C–M (where 'M' stands for money and 'C' stands for commodities). This he argues is due to the suspension of the function of *another* part of fixed capital while it exists in the form of money and, consequently, to the unwillingness or inability of another group of capitalists to buy the commodity product of the first group as a result of a shortfall that the suspension of the function of fixed capital in the form of money brings about in the money supply generally.

Thus, in both Chapters 20 and 21, Marx divides DI and DII between two groups of capitalists (called variously A, A', A'' and B, B', B'', in Chapter 21, and section 1 and section 2, in Chapter 20). One of these groups is relatively near to the time when the capitalists must replace their fixed capital at its full value (and who consequently have in their hands a large money–supply with which to replace their worn-out fixed capital). The other group is relatively remote from this stage in the process of production, having just renewed their fixed capital (and who consequently do not have a very large money supply to hand). In order then to create a disequilibrium *within* the system of production which does not upset the equilibrium *between* DI and DII, Marx argues that capitalists within the department expanding the scale of the process of production must also provide the means of exchange necessary to circulate this expanded production. He then investigates in detail the question of whether the hoarding of money capital by one group of capitalists (e.g. DI, A, A', A'', or DII, section 1) can in any way be said to compel another group of capitalists within the *same* department as the first group (e.g. DI, B, B', B'', or DII, section 2) to accumulate their potential fixed capital and thereby extend the scale of the process of production in this way. The argument here is that where there is a strict limit to the money supply, as in this case, one group of capitalists will be unable to sell their commodity product if the other group of capitalists are unwilling to buy this (see Ch. 21, section 1, 1974b, 496–500 [1978, 568–71]).

There are a number of problems with an explanation of this kind. Firstly, it is difficult to see how the unwillingness of the capitalists of DI, A, A', A", or DII, section 1, to buy can compel the capitalists of DI, B, B', B", or DII, section 2, to accumulate their commodity product, since, as we have already seen, they might simply *waste* this if they were unable to sell it. Of course, DI, B, B', B", and DII, section 2, need to sell their commodity product in order to reproduce the existing process of production on the same scale. But the fact that the capitalists of DI, B, B', B", and DII, section 2, cannot even reproduce the prevailing process of production on the same scale, is not by itself a sufficient reason to explain why expanded reproduction should take place, or, in fact, why under these circumstances a complete collapse of the entire process of production is not a much more likely result. Secondly, except in a very few cases such as transport (where the product of the process of production is consumed immediately it is produced) or coal mining (where the *product* of this process of production may in certain cases be reused directly to help to mine more coal), it is very unlikely that those capitalists who are unable to sell their commodity product will be able to employ this directly in the process of production which produced it without first exchanging it for the commodity product of some other process of production. Once again, therefore, the result of withdrawing money from circulation, and the subsequent inability of one group of capitalists to exchange their commodity product for something that can be consumed productively, is likely to be a general breakdown in the system of simple reproduction as a whole rather than an expansion in the scale of any particular part of the process of production. Finally, it is difficult to see what possible motive the capitalists of DI, A, A', A", or DII, section 1, could have for withdrawing money from circulation in order to compel *another* group of capitalists to expand the scale of the process of production, when, by definition, it is the group of capitalists who are in possession of a hoard of money and who are near to the time when they must renew their fixed capital, who may shortly be expected to *re-enter* the market. Of course, Marx supposes that the capitalists of DI, A, A', A", and DII, section 1, withdraw money from circulation in order to accumulate a hoard of money capital with which to eventually renew their fixed capital, but since they must indeed renew their fixed capital at some point, hoarding money capital for this reason can at best have only a temporary effect on the capitalists of DI, B, B', B", and DII, section 2.

If then hoarding by one group of capitalists is not enough to explain the transition from simple to extended reproduction, how does Marx's discussion of precipitation help us to explain capitalist accumulation? What we would seem to require here is not an explanation in which the group of capitalists who have just renewed their fixed capital (and who consequently do not have in their possession any very substantial potential fixed capital) are required to accumulate their own commodity product. On the contrary, what is required is an explanation in which the group of capitalists who are near to the point where they must renew their fixed capital (and who consequently have in hand *both* an actively functioning fixed capital *and* a relatively large potential fixed capital in the form of money) are in some as yet unspecified way compelled to accumulate this hoard of money capital *simultaneously* as their actually functioning fixed capital continues to operate at its full value, and therefore *sooner than they otherwise would have done so* on the basis of simple reproduction. In other words then, not an explanation in which DI, B, B', B'', or DII, section 2, accumulate their *commodity product*, but one in which DI, A, A', A'', or DII, section 1, are compelled to accumulate their slack or temporarily surplus money capital.

This brings us to the second, and in point of fact, far more common meaning of the term 'precipitation', which may simply be defined as *causing something to happen sooner than it otherwise would*, or in other words 'precipitously'. In this context, precipitation carries with it the suggestion that capitalists who are in possession of money capital are compelled to accumulate this productively sooner than they otherwise would on the basis of simple reproduction. This definition therefore *exactly* answers the problem that Marx is considering here, even though it is not clear that he is using this concept in this way (and, in fact, it would probably be more accurate to say that he does *not* do so). The problem we have here is that there seems to be no way that capitalists who are in possession of capital in its *money* form can be materially compelled to do *anything* with it, since as Marx says money is a commodity which 'everyone can use for everything' (1974b, 94 [1978, 172]) and which therefore money capitalists can either use unproductively or not use at all. In Chapter 20, section 11 ('Replacement of Fixed Capital'), Marx presents us with a number of unsuccessful attempts to illustrate the process by which capitalists convert their potential fixed capital from its money form to its material form as actually functioning fixed capital. Especially interesting here is the illustration (1974b, 459–60 [1978, 531–2]) in which Marx concentrates on the question of the reproduction of the fixed capital of DII. All Marx succeeds in doing here, however, is reversing one of the main problems of his previous discussion of the transition from simple to extended reproduction. Instead of assuming that it is the capitalists of DII who are always obliging enough to reduce their surplus expenditure on articles of luxury in order to convert part of the surplus product of DI into means of consumption (although DII apparently has no motive of its own for doing this), here it is assumed that the capitalists of DI are the ones who convert part of the commodity product of DII into money simply because DII cannot do this for itself. A similar, albeit more successful, illustration is presented in Chapter 20 (1974b, 465–6 [1978, 536–7]). However, even this seems to be incomplete, since Marx cannot find any materially compelling reason why the capitalists of either DI or DII in possession of potential fixed capital in the form of money should do anything with this other than hoard it until it is needed to replace actually functioning fixed capital on the basis of simple reproduction.

The only satisfactory – i.e. materially compelling – reason Marx has so far presented to explain the transition from simple reproduction to reproduction on an extended scale relates to the necessity of expanding the scale of the process of production for even *simple* reproduction to take place. Paradoxically, however, we now find ourselves in the position of apparently only being able to explain expanded reproduction if the capitalists who are in possession of money capital accumulate their potential fixed capital *sooner* than they apparently need to do so on the basis of simple reproduction. How are we to overcome this problem? There would seem to be only one possible explanation which can account for capitalist accumulation under these circumstances: the capitalists who are in possession of *money* capital must convert it into the *material* form in which it will later on be required to function as fixed capital for the purposes of *simple reproduction* and employ this productively in the process of production in the meantime – alongside their existing fixed capital – in order to secure or *preserve* its value as potential fixed capital.

At the same time that one group of capitalists, DI, A, A', A'', for example, are accumulating a hoard of money capital, another group of capitalists, DI, B, B', B'', or DII, B, B', B'', are accumulating a supply of commodities, part of which must eventually go to renew the fixed capital of DI, A, A', A''. Unless these commodities are employed productively more or less *as soon* as they are produced, they may begin to lose their value, either as a result of neglect, or because they become obsolete. Further, unless the capitalists who produce these commodities sell them more or less as soon as they are produced, there is a possibility that these capitalists will go out of business due to the deterioration in value of what they produce and that these commodities will therefore not be available to the first group of capitalists when they come to replace their worn out fixed capital. Therefore, the capitalists who need to renew their fixed capital on the basis of simple reproduction (i.e. the group who would otherwise form a hoard of money capital on the assumptions of Marx's argument; DI, A, A', A'', in this case) are forced to buy these commodities *as soon as they are produced* and to employ them in the process of production *alongside* the fixed capital they are intended to replace, rather than buy them at a later date when they are actually required to replace worn out fixed capital, *simply* in order to preserve the value of these commodities and ensure their continued existence in their present form which will later be required for the purposes of simple reproduction.

If the capitalists who are in possession of potential fixed capital in its money form employ this capital in its material form in the process of production at the same time as the actually functioning fixed capital which they are intended to replace continues to operate at its full value, then the scale of the process of production will have been expanded, and when this new process of production is set in motion, reproduction on an extended scale will take place. Marx it seems was therefore on the wrong track when he sought to explain the transition from simple to extended reproduction as a result of the *suspension* of the active function of fixed capital in fine particles by its hoarding in the form of money as potential fixed capital (let us call this 'precipitation *i*'), since the formation of a monetary hoard can never by itself lead to an expansion in the scale of the process of production but only to a crisis of simple reproduction. Nevertheless, a form of precipitation does take place here (we will call this 'precipitation *ii*') in which the function of capital that has been suspended in fine particles in its money form is released into circulation sooner than it would otherwise be on the basis of simple reproduction in order to function as fixed capital in the process of production. The group of capitalists who would otherwise have formed a hoard of money capital until such time that it was needed to renew their fixed capital are thereby (a) forced to convert this potential fixed capital from its existing money form into its material form as actually functioning capital sooner than they otherwise would have done so in order to ensure that they have this capital to hand later on, in the material form that they require when they need it for the purposes of simple reproduction, and (b) to employ this fixed capital productively in the process of production precipitately (i.e. as soon as they acquire it and before such time as it is needed on the basis of simple reproduction), alongside the fixed capital it is intended to replace, in order simply to preserve its value in its presently existing material form.

Points for Further Discussion

Those chapters in the second half of *Capital*, Vol. II in which Marx attempted to find a *materially* compelling reason for capitalist accumulation (as opposed to an explanation which relies on the will of the capitalist and/or the effects of capitalist competition) are undoubtedly among the most difficult of all to understand in the three volumes of *Capital*,[7] and I think we have no choice here but to say that they are in fact largely unsuccessful. Marx, I believe, simply could not find a solution to this problem and this, as I have already suggested, might well be the reason why he failed to publish *Capital*, Vols II and III during his own lifetime. There is no problem in explaining the expansion of the capitalist mode of production – either in the form of reproduction on an extended or progressively extending scale – once this process is up and running, capitalist competition will account for this. But unless one is willing to explain the origins of this process in terms of the will of the capitalist – a spirit of entrepreneurialism, a love of innovation, or the lust for greater and greater profits – then it is hard to see how this can be done without abandoning a materialist perspective. Such an explanation is of course perfectly satisfactory – and this is almost certainly the reason why the expansion of capital takes place – but the problem we have here is that any such explanation simply was *not* acceptable to Marx. Marx could not accept that something as fundamental to the CMP as capital accumulation – the defining feature of this particular mode of production in many ways – could, or should, be explained in terms of the will of the capitalist or even the lust for profit. There simply had to be a more fundamental explanation of this phenomenon he thought.

But what if there is *in fact* no materially compelling reason for the accumulation of capital, either on the same scale or on a progressively extending scale? What if capitalists might simply choose to accumulate or *not* to accumulate as the case may be? If this is the case, then the entire character of the capitalist mode of production as Marx understood this is changed. Instead of developing inexorably towards socialism, as Marx expected it would, it might develop in some other way that was not anticipated by Marx. This is therefore the question that we will now go on to consider in detail in Part III of this study, on the subject of the *circulation* of capital and I will argue that where capital exists in its money form – as in fact all capital must do as a *normal* part of its circulation – there is indeed no such material compulsion for capitalists to accumulate and hence no very good reason why the capitalist mode of production should continue to expand on a *progressively* extending scale.

Reading: Essential: *Capital*, Vol. II, Ch. 21, sections 1 and 2 (1974b, 493–510 [1978, 565–81]), Ch. 20, section 11 (1974b, 453–73 [1978, 524–45]). Background: Marx's letter to Engels of 24 August 1867; letter no. 91 (*MESC*, 1953, 232–3); and see also Marx and Engels, *Letters on 'Capital'* (1983, 111–13), for Engels's reply to Marx on this point.

CONCLUSION TO PART II

In the second part of this study we have looked at the nature of the capitalist mode of production itself and, specifically, at the question which is at the heart of Marx's discussion of this point, how the capitalist claims to be the *legitimate* owner of the capitalist enterprise. In doing this we have considered two further questions. Firstly, how is it possible that a single primitively accumulated capital can support the capitalist and/or his or her family, in perpetuity as it sometimes seems, without apparently ever becoming worn-out or needing to be replaced or renewed? And secondly, what is it then that causes the capitalist to accumulate their capital not just on an extending scale but on a progressively extending scale when it appears to reproduce itself on the same unchanging scale without any intervention on their part? As we have seen, Marx's answer to the first of these questions is quite clear: it is that the primitively accumulated capital with which the capitalist enterprise begins is not immortal but is in fact renewed and replaced in a successful capitalist enterprise on a more or less daily basis by all the people who work for the capitalist. As such, the capitalist's claim to be the legitimate owner of the enterprise in question is undermined to the extent that this is the case. However, Marx's answer to the second of these questions is much less clear and, as I have argued, is in fact incomplete. Why should capitalists accumulate their capital *at all*, and still less on an extended or a progressively extending scale, when there appears to be no materially compelling reason for them to do so? Why don't they simply reproduce this on the same *unchanging* scale and what are the consequences for the development of the capitalist mode of production itself if they were to do this? This is the issue we will now go on to consider in detail in Part III of this guide to *Capital* where we will look at the question of the possible underdevelopment of the CMP.

Part III

THE UNDERDEVELOPMENT OF THE CAPITALIST MODE OF PRODUCTION

PREFACE TO PART III

In the first half of this book we looked at the historical development of the capitalist mode of production and what might be said to be the preconditions for this (in Part I) and then at what Marx understood to be the conditions of the capitalist mode of production itself (in Part II). The question I consider in the second half of this study is to what extent the development of the pure capitalist mode of production *itself* might be said to have been undermined – or, as I think we might say in this connection, *underdeveloped* – as a result of trade between the more highly industrialized economies of Europe and North America during the late nineteenth and early twentieth centuries and other as yet non-capitalist modes of production at that time. In short, from now on, we will drop the closed economy model employed by Marx in Part I of this study and examine the effects of trade not just on the development of the non-capitalist world – i.e. through capitalist colonialism or imperialism – but on the development of the CMP itself. Specifically, we will now look at the *circulation* of capital – an issue we have so far almost entirely neglected – and in particular at the differences between the circulation of two very different types of capital, the more highly developed form of merchant's capital and the circuit of industrial capital generally. The main question we will be considering here is whether the development of finance capital and imperialism signified a higher stage in the development of capitalism (as both Rudolf Hilferding and Lenin believed), or whether both of these development would be better regarded as a more highly developed form of *mercantile* capitalism and therefore might be said to signify a step backward in the development of the capitalist mode of production itself.

INTRODUCTION TO PART III

In Part II of this book, we examined just how *difficult* it is to compel capitalists to accumulate their capital on an extended scale, and therefore still less on a *progressively* extending scale, with *simple* reproduction being the normal or preferred state for the capitalist mode of production. Unless simple reproduction takes place there will be no extended or progressively extended production. The question we now have to consider is why it is that such a dramatic extension in the scale of the capitalist mode of production does in fact take place and, perhaps even more interestingly, what happens when *no* such expansion in the scale of the CMP occurs.

I have argued that there is no very good reason why accumulation should take place on anything other than the same unchanging scale except under the most *exceptional* circumstances (viz. (i) that a closed economy actually does obtain, (ii) that at least a part of the surplus product of the capitalist mode of production is produced in a form in which it cannot be consumed unproductively, and (iii) that the owners of surplus value, against their will as it were, are *precipitated* into accumulating part of this surplus value sooner than they would otherwise have done so on the basis of simple reproduction). I have also argued that, on the contrary, outside this set of conditions the owners of capital have every reason *not* to expand the scale of the process of production due to the risk that this entails of undermining what they have already. Of course, it may well be possible to substitute for the above set of conditions an *alternative* set which might also compel capitalist accumulation, and we will look at some of the most frequently mentioned alternative possible conditions in the final chapter of Part III of this study when we turn our attention to what Marx has to say on the subject of competition and the falling rate of profit. However, as I have already pointed out, competition between capitalists can only explain accumulation *once* the process of reproduction on an extended scale is already underway, while, as we will now see, a falling rate of profit also requires the assumption of a closed economy model to explain capitalist accumulation since, as Marx points out, foreign trade has the effect of equalising the rate of profit and therefore undermines what is in effect only a *tendency* that the rate of profit has to fall.

Since a falling rate of profit can only explain reproduction on an extended scale on the assumption of a closed economy model, and since this condition is probably just as unlikely to actually obtain as the set of conditions outlined by Marx in the Department I and Department II model, what seems to be required here is an account of the way that capital is actually accumulated *outside* the conditions of a closed economy model. However, although capital accumulation undoubtedly does take place under these conditions, the type and circulation of capital associated with an international economy is very different indeed from the type that Marx had in mind when he considered the conditions of existence of a purely capitalist mode of production. In fact, I will argue that this type of international trade and investment is closer to the pattern of accumulation found in the case of a highly developed form of *merchant's capital* than it is to the pattern of accumulation characteristic of a fully developed capitalist mode of production. It is because the development of a purely capitalist mode of production in Europe in the nineteenth century was undermined by contact between this still developing mode of production and the rest of the non-capitalist world at this time that the fullest possible development of the capitalist mode of production itself did not take place. In its place we have something else altogether – a hybrid between a capitalist and a non-capitalist mode of production – or, in other words, the more highly developed mercantile system which today is sometimes also known as 'finance capital'.

Let us begin our discussion of this point by looking at the distinction Marx makes between the circuit of merchant's capital and the circuit of industrial capital.

10. MERCANTILISM AND THE CIRCUIT OF INDUSTRIAL CAPITAL IN *CAPITAL* VOL. II, PART I, CH. 1–4

Marx discusses the circulation of merchant's capital in all three volumes of *Capital*, as follows: in Vol. I, Part II, Chapters 4 and 5, the first two chapters of the part, entitled 'The Transformation of Money into Capital' (1974a, 145–63 [1976, 247–69]); in Vol. II, Part I, Chapter 1–4, in the section entitled 'The Metamorphoses of Capital and Their Circuits' (1974b, 25–123 [1978, 109–99]); and in Vol. III, Parts IV and V (1977, 267–613 [1981, 379–748]), but especially Chapter 20, entitled 'Historical Facts about Merchant's Capital' (1977, 323–37 [1981, 440–55]). However, since Marx's Vol. III discussion of merchant's capital is almost entirely descriptive while his Vol. I discussion is entirely concerned with a highly abstract distinction between the simple circulation of commodity capital (C–M–C), merchant's capital (M–C–M), and money-dealing capital, M–M (where 'C' stands for commodity capital, and 'M' stands for money capital), what we will mainly be concerned with here is Marx's detailed discussion of the circulation of what he calls 'the more highly developed forms of merchant's capital', in Vol. II.

Marx devotes one chapter each at the beginning of Vol. II to the circuit of money capital (M–C…P…C'–M'), the circuit of productive capital (P…C'–M'–C…P') and the circuit of commodity capital (C–M'–C…P…C') and then summarizes his argument in the fourth chapter of *Capital*, Vol. II (1974b, 25-123 [1978, 109–99]) where he describes these three circuits of capital as the more highly developed forms of the simple circuit of money capital (M–C–M) and commodity capital (C–M–C). Marx says that these three circuits are more highly developed *precisely* because in each of these circuits the process of production (P) is included to show that a production process is an integral part of the circulation of capital in all three cases. The expressions M', C' and P' are then used to indicate where the value of money, commodity and productive capital have been augmented. In M–C…P…C'–M' the process of production is seen to intervene midway between the two phases of what would otherwise be the normal circulation of money capital, with the value of the commodity capital being augmented by the production process as shown at C' and M'. In the case of P…C'–M'–C…P', the circulation of capital begins and ends with productive capital, where the value of the production process itself is augmented at P' and M'. While even in C'–M'–C…P…C', although a simple circulation of commodity capital (C'–M'–C) has already taken place before the process of production intervenes, the simple reproduction of this circuit of capital requires that the process of production (P) should renew the surplus value withdrawn from this circuit by the owner of money capital at M'–C.

However, apart from noting the all important point that the process of production ('P') is central to each of these three more highly developed circuits of capital (and that this is precisely what distinguishes them from the more simple circuit of these three forms of capital), here we are less concerned with the very important part played by the process of production in the circulation of a more highly developed commercial or mercantile system as we are with the following three extremely important points that Marx also makes in the first three chapters of *Capital*, Vol. II. Firstly that, according to Marx, the circuit of *industrial capital* (defined here as comprising every branch of industry that is run on a capitalist basis)[1] is made up as Marx says of the 'uninterrupted' (1974b, 50 [1978, 133]) and 'fluent and ever renewed' (1974b, 63 [1978, 142]) circuits of money capital, productive capital, and commodity capital as follows:

M–C…P…C'–M', M–C…P…C'–M', M–C…P…C'–M…etc.
(1974b, 63 [1978, 142])

Consequently, where this fluent circulation *is* interrupted at any point it follows that *no* such circuit of *industrial* capital will take place at all. Secondly, the circuit M–C…P…C'–M' viewed by itself, and fixed as Marx says as the 'exclusive form' of capital, constitutes what Marx describes as 'the basis of the *more highly developed mercantile system* in which not only the circulation of commodities but also their production appears as a necessary element' (1974b,62 [1978, 141]; emphasis added). Thirdly, while there may be said to be a material compulsion to resume the circuit of industrial capital in the case of the circulation of productive capital (since in this case capital is once more present at the end of the circuit in a form that can only function anew as productive capital), and even in the case of commodity capital (since Marx argues that C', the end result of the circuit of commodity capital, represents the reappearance of *industrial* capital in its commodity form, and must therefore re-open the process of circulation with the reconversion of this industrial capital into its money form in the circulation phase C'–M'), there cannot possibly be *any* material compulsion whatsoever to resume the circuit of industrial capital at the end of the circuit of money capital M–C…P…C'–M', since *this* circuit of capital begins and ends with money. As we have seen money is a commodity which anyone can use for anything (and which therefore the capitalist might either save or consume unproductively) and as Marx says on this all important point, 'It is a full and complete business cycle that results in money, something everyone can use for everything. A new start is therefore only a *possibility*' (1974b, 9 [1978, 172]; emphasis added).

According to Marx, money capital, commodity capital and productive capital do not represent independent forms of capital which function as separate branches of industrial capital. Rather, they denote distinct forms of industrial capital itself, which assumes all three of these different forms one after the other at different stages of the circulation of industrial capital. And Marx goes even further than this to claim that industrial capital describes its circuit *normally* only so long as these three phases pass into one another without any interruption.

> Capital describes its circuit normally only so long as its various phases pass uninterruptedly into one another. If capital stops short at the first phase M–C, money capital assumes the rigid form of a hoard; if it stops at the phase of production, the means of production lie without functioning on the one side, while labour-power remains unemployed on the other; and if capital is stopped short in its last phase C'–M', piles of unsold commodities accumulate and clog the flow of circulation. (1974b, 50 [1978, 133])

However, as we have seen, since there can be no material compulsion at the money stage to renew the circulation of industrial capital – since the capitalists can simply withdraw their money capital at this stage and hoard this if they choose to do so – it is in fact highly unlikely that industrial capital would ever complete such a fluent or uninterrupted circuit, let alone one that, as Marx says, is 'ever renewed'.

To overcome this problem, Marx tries to argue that we are somehow mistaken or wrong if we regard merchant's capital as either an independent or an exclusive form of the circulation of industrial capital. Thus, for example, in *Capital*, Vol. II, describing the circuit of money capital, he claims that:

> the illusory character of M–C'…P…C'–M' and the correspondingly illusory interpretation exists whenever this form is fixed as occurring once, not as fluent and ever renewed; hence whenever this form is considered not as one of the forms of the circuit but as its exclusive form. (1974b, 63 [1978, 142])

While in Vol. III, in the chapter entitled 'Historical Facts about Merchant's Capital', Marx adds:

> It is self-evident from what has gone before that nothing could be more absurd than to regard merchant's capital, whether in the shape of commercial or money-dealing capital, as a particular variety of industrial capital, such as, say, mining, agriculture, cattle-raising, manufacturing, transport, etc., which are side lines of industrial capital occasioned by the division of social labour, and hence different spheres of investment. The simple observation that in the circulation phase of its reproduction process every industrial capital performs as commodity-capital and as money-capital the very functions which appear as the exclusive functions of the two forms of merchant's capital, should rule out such a crude notion. (1977, 323 [1981, 440])

However, if Marx is really intending to argue that merchant's capital can *never* be regarded as independent of the circuit of industrial capital, simply because the circulation of industrial capital *normally* contains the circuit of merchant's capital as one of its phases, then I think we would have to say that it is Marx who is mistaken on this point since this argument clearly involves an obvious confusion of logical and empirical necessity. It is much more likely that Marx is simply arguing that *when* we are discussing the circulation of industrial capital in its pure form, the circuit of money capital should not be viewed as a separate part of this – that this would be a mistake since all three circuits are integrated here – but when we come to look at the circuit of the highly developed form of money capital by itself no such restrictions apply. Clearly merchant's capital can have an independent existence from the circuit of industrial capital, if not as an exclusive form of the circuit of industrial capital, then as an independent circuit of money capital in its own right, containing if necessary its own independent process of production at the point (P) of the circuit M–C…P…C'–M'. Furthermore, it is not only *logically* possible that just such an independent circuit of money capital might well take place, but it is also more likely than not that this *will* happen since, as we have seen, it is precisely at the money stage that the circuit of industrial capital is most likely to be interrupted. Because the circuit of industrial capital is continually converted into its money form as a *normal* part of its circulation – because, without this, the circulation of industrial capital cannot take place – and because there is no material compulsion to resume the circuit of industrial capital at the stage that ends in the circulation of money capital, it is far more likely that the circuit of industrial capital will be interrupted at the money stage than complete an uninterrupted circuit. This being the case, it is therefore much more likely that the development of capitalism will assume what Marx describes as a highly developed *mercantile* form rather than the form of industrial capital per se.

Points for Further Discussion

Obviously much of what Marx says here is very important indeed if we are to understand the development of capitalism during the late twentieth and early twenty-first century and my own reading of these four chapters at the beginning of *Capital*, Vol. II is no doubt somewhat controversial. These chapters, more than any others in the whole of *Capital*, would therefore seem to demand careful reading. However, if what I say here is correct, then we can speculate that this is one of the major reasons for the relative underdevelopment of industrial production/industrial investment in the former capitalist economies of Europe and North America, and the development in these countries of the phenomenon which is now most commonly known as 'finance capital' or 'post-industrialization'.

Reading: Essential: *Capital*, Vol. II, Ch. 1–4 (1974b, 25–123 [1978, 109–99]; see especially 1974b, 62–3, 94–5 [1978, 141–3, 172–3]). Background: *Capital*, Vol. I, Part II (Ch. 4–5, 1974a, 145–63 [1976, 247–69]); *Capital*, Vol. III, Parts IV and V, 1977 (267–613 [1981, 379–748]; see especially Ch. 20, 323–37 [1981, 440–55]).

11. CREDIT AND THE DISSOLUTION OF THE CMP IN *CAPITAL*, VOL. III, CH. 27

Marx's short chapter 'The Role of Credit in Capitalist Production' (1977, 435–41 [1981, 566–73]) is probably one of the most neglected but also one of the most important things he ever wrote. In it, he not only gives us his views on the role of the credit system in the development and underdevelopment of the capitalist mode of production itself (something which has become even more important since the recent collapse of the credit system); he also outlines his views on the subject of 'joint-stock companies' and the development of shareholding, monopoly capitalism, state interference in the economy, and gives us what is probably the best example in *Capital* of his use of the dialectical method.[2]

Having briefly looked at Marx's discussion of the circulation of merchant's capital in the previous chapter, we are now going on to consider the related issue of what he has to say about the development of the credit system and in particular the claim that the development of the credit system is one of the main factors helping to bring about the destruction of the CMP *from within*. However, as we will see, this superficially attractive claim is in fact incorrect since, as Marx explains, nothing can bring about its own destruction as part of the normal operation of the system without at the same time destroying itself. By itself therefore, the normal operation of the credit system alone *cannot* possibly bring about the end of the CMP.

Marx outlines his general views on this matter in Vol. III, Parts 4 and 5 (1977, 267–613 [1981, 379–748]) and discusses the effects of the credit system on the development of the CMP itself in the first two pages of Vol. III, Chapter 27 (1977, 435–6 [1981, 566–7]), in particular. According to Marx, credit has the effect of reducing the costs of circulation. It does this by doing away with the need for money altogether; by the more rapid circulation of such money that is already in existence; and by enabling paper money to replace precious metals as the usual material substance of money, and thereby doing away, at least in part, with the need to mine precious metals. Secondly, he claims that the availability of credit generally helps to equalize the rate of profit in most processes of production by enabling them all to expand the scale of the process of production irrespective of the particular contribution that each makes to the production of surplus value generally. Thirdly, he points out that credit increases the opportunities for speculation, by extending the time between the act of buying and selling a given commodity. But undoubtedly the most important consequence of the development of the credit system that Marx discusses is that credit brought about an enormous centralization of already existing capitals scattered throughout society and united these in the form of what were known at that time as joint-stock companies (1977, 436 [1981, 567]).

However, along with these generally positive effects on the development of the capitalist mode of production, Marx argues that the development of the credit system has certain destructive effects too. In particular, he notes that while credit accelerates the material development of the productive forces, it also appears as the main lever of over-production and over-speculation in commerce and forces the reproductive system to its extreme. Firstly, Marx claims that this occurs because:

> a large part of the social capital is employed by people who do not own it and who tackle things quite differently than the owner, who anxiously weighs the limitations of his private capital in so far as he handles it himself. (1977, 441 [1981, 572])

Secondly, the development of the credit system, by facilitating the separation of the ownership of capital from its control, encourages the development of the process of production whereby the actually functioning capitalist is transformed into a mere *manager* of other people's capital (1977, 436 [1981, 567]). Thirdly, the development of joint-stock companies and the *socialization of ownership* that this implies, brings about 'the abolition of capital as private property within the framework of capitalist production itself' (1977, 436 [1981, 567]). And, finally, Marx argues that the effects of this socialization of production are so severe that it eventually threatens to bring about the abolition of the capitalist mode of production itself and the development of monopoly capitalism, finance capital, and state interference in its place. However, he stresses that:

> This is the abolition of the capitalist mode of production within the capitalist mode of production itself, and hence a *self-dissolving contradiction*, which *prima facie* represents a mere phase of transition to a new form of production. *It manifests itself as such a contradiction in its effects.* It establishes a monopoly in certain spheres and thereby requires state interference. It reproduces a new financial aristocracy, a new variety of parasites in the shape of promoters, speculators and simply nominal directors; a whole system of swindling and cheating by means of corporation promotion,

stock issuance, and stock speculation. *It is private production without the control of private property*. (1977, 438 [1981, 569]; emphasis added)

So much then for the argument that is sometimes made that Marx did not anticipate the development of finance capital, monopoly capitalism, state interference or even managerialism (although it has to be said that Marx did not develop these observations very much beyond what he says here). But we must be careful not to misunderstand Marx's main argument here, especially what he means when he *appears* to claim that the social ownership of the means of production in the form of joint-stock companies signifies the abolition of the capitalist mode of production within the CMP itself. Marx does *not* mean to suggest that capitalism can bring about its *own* destruction here. On the contrary, he quite clearly states that any such claim must involve 'a self-dissolving contradiction' (i.e. an absolute contradiction). This is therefore an important example of the role that dialectical reasoning played in Marx's thought. Marx is here employing a dialectical argument; namely, one in which the *apparent* claim being made (e.g. the destruction of the CMP) is in fact undermined by the statement of the thesis itself. In such an argument, the contradiction is said to be immanent in the thesis. It is therefore only at first sight that this seems to involve the transition to a new form of production. This is because, in having a *tendency* to bring about its own destruction, capitalism will destroy the very thing which, according to this argument, is supposed to be destroying it; namely *itself*. Diagrammatically such an argument can be expressed as follows:

Figure 16. Self-dissolving contradiction

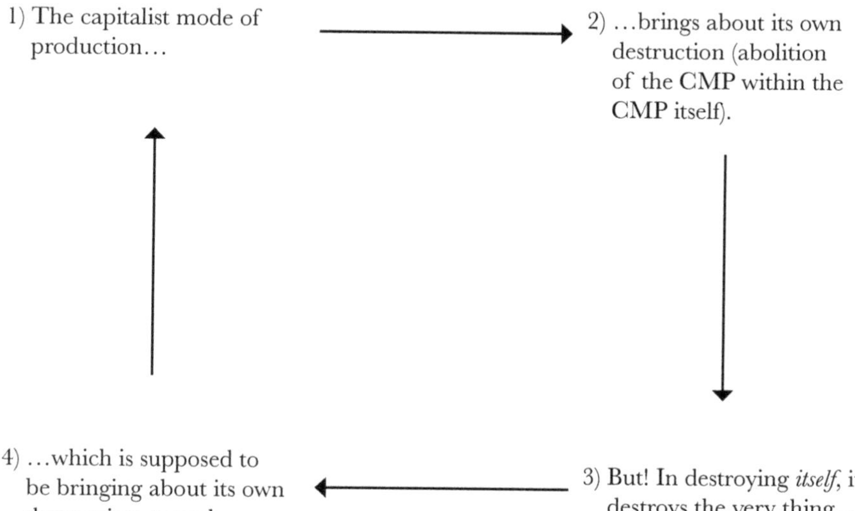

Capitalism does not destroy itself then, but rather destroys the *tendency* it has to bring about this effect. However, this does not means that the development of the pure capitalist mode of production is itself left unscathed. Capitalism cannot undermine the tendency that the CMP has to destroy itself until the process of the socialization of private property has been at least *partially* completed and therefore until that form of the capitalist mode of production based on the ownership of private property *has* been partially destroyed. In place of a capitalist mode of production based on the ownership and control of private property there develops a mode of production characterized by the continuation of individual ownership of private property *at the same time* as there is a significant socialization of the control of private production. There is an increasing socialization of *private* production at the same time as there is an increasing privatization of *social* control and it is to this partial process of destruction alone that Marx refers when he claims that the development of the credit system and the destruction of capital as private property signifies the abolition of the capitalist mode of production from within the capitalist mode of production itself. As Marx says on this point in *Capital*, Vol. I, at the end of the chapter entitled 'Historical Tendency of Capitalist Accumulation':

> The capitalist mode of appropriation, the result of the capitalist mode of production, produces capitalist private property. This is the first negation of individual private property, as founded on the labour of the proprietor. But capitalist production begets, with the inexorability of a law of Nature, its own negation. *It is the negation of negation.* This does not re-establish private property for the producer, but gives him individual property based on the acquisitions of the capitalist era: i.e. on cooperation and the possession in common of the land and of the means of production. (1974a, 715 [1976, 929]; emphasis added)[3]

Since the dialectical contradiction between the tendency that the CMP has to destroy itself has been negated, it simply *cannot* be the case that the phase of transition Marx refers to in his discussion of the role of credit is that between a capitalist and a *socialist* mode of production. This is not his argument at all. On the contrary, what Marx is saying here is that, in place of a capitalist mode of production based on the private ownership *and* control of capital, there will develop a hybrid mode of production between the CMP and a fully developed socialist mode of production. Such a hybrid is characterized by managerialism, monopoly capitalism and finance capital (or finance capitalism as Rudolf Hilferding called this). As Marx says on this point in the chapter on credit in *Capital*, Vol. III:

> In stock companies the function [of management] is divorced from capital ownership, hence also labour is entirely divorced from ownership of means of production and surplus-labour. This result of *the ultimate development of capitalist production* is a necessary transitional phase towards the reconversion of capital into the property of producers, although no longer as the private property of the individual producers, but rather as the property of associated producers, as outright social property. (1977, 437 [1981, 568])

What we have here then, instead of either a purely capitalist mode of production (based on the private ownership and control of industry) or a fully developed socialist mode of production (one in which everyone shares ownership of the means of production of human life in proportion as they produce it), is a hybrid somewhere between these two developments and therefore something which is neither a purely capitalist nor a purely socialist mode of production. As Marx says towards the end of the chapter on the role of credit:

> The capitalist stock companies, as much as the co-operative [*sic*] factories, should be considered as transitional forms from the capitalist mode of production to the associated one [i.e. socialism], with the only distinction that the antagonism is resolved negatively in the one and positively in the other. (1977, 440 [1981, 572])

The development of associated forms of private property, managerialism, finance capital and/or monopoly capitalism must be seen therefore not as the beginning of a transition to a new mode of production but as the *resolution* of the contradictory tendencies that the CMP has to destroy itself. This is not to say that finance capital/monopoly capital cannot become transitional modes of production in their own right, only that for this to be the case they would have to develop their *own* internal contradictions (whatever these might be). However, the really important point here is that the CMP's tendency to socialize the control of capital does not present itself as a contradiction for finance capital or monopoly capitalism; rather it is the very thing on which they are based and this is precisely what distinguishes them from earlier forms of capitalism based on the private ownership *and* control of capital.

Points for Further Discussion

Marx explains that while credit enormously extends the tendency that monopoly capitalism and finance capital have to centralize the control of capital and to expand the capitalist mode of production on a global scale, it also accelerates capitalism's tendency to *over*-extend itself and therefore increases the likelihood that capitalism will suffer periodic crises. As Marx puts it:

> The contradictory nature of capitalist production permits an actual free development *only up to a certain point*, so that in fact it constitutes an immanent fetter and barrier to production, which are continually broken through by the credit system. Hence, the credit system accelerates the material development of the productive forces and the establishment of the world-market. It is the historical mission of the capitalist system of production to raise these material foundations of the new mode of production to a certain degree of perfection. At the same time credit accelerates the violent eruptions of this contradiction – crises – and thereby the elements of disintegration of the old mode of production. (1977, 441 [1981, 572]; emphasis added)

In fact, as we shall see, these two apparently contradictory tendencies of the capitalist mode of production – to both develop on a world scale and to undermine its own development – have much the same effect on the CMP *itself*, since it is not the capitalist mode of production as such that is developed on a world scale by the development of world trade (not the CMP proper, and not even a very highly developed form of industrial capitalism either), but a highly developed form of merchant's capital which takes the form of monopoly capitalism and/or finance capitalism (see Chapter 12). The development of the CMP then is not undermined by its tendency to over-extend itself, but by the fact that the development of a purely capitalist mode of production within a closed economy model had *all along* been undermined/undeveloped by the survival of a highly developed form of merchant's capital in the form of finance capital/monopoly capitalism into the twenty-first century. If this is the case, then this may well mean that it is not the CMP *as such* that has a tendency towards crisis or to over-extending itself, but rather it is this highly developed form of merchant's capital (i.e. the *interrupted* circuit of industrial capital) that has this tendency. We will therefore look at this argument in greater detail in the remaining two sections of Part III of the present study.

Reading: Essential: *Capital*, Vol. III. Ch. 27, 'The Role of Credit in Capitalist Production' (1977, 435–41 [1981, 566–73]). Background: *Capital*, Vol. III, Ch. 36, 'Pre-Capitalist Relationships' (1977, 593–613 [1981, 728–48]), and *Capital*, Vol. I, Ch. 32, 'Historical Tendency of Capitalist Accumulation' (1974a, 713–15 [1976, 927–30]).

12. RUDOLF HILFERDING AND 'FINANCE CAPITAL': *CAPITAL*, VOL. I, CH. 25, SECTION 2

First published in 1910, Rudolf Hilferding's *Das Finanzkapital* (*Finance Capital*) was almost immediately hailed as a fourth volume of Marx's *Capital*.[4] In fact, *Finance Capital* (translated into English in 1981) is less a continuation or an extension of the three volumes of *Capital*, than an updating and restatement of material covered by Marx, with only a very few exceptions to this general rule (e.g. Hilferding's development of the concept of promoter's profit). In addition to this, Hilferding's restatement of Marx's work is badly flawed in certain major respects; in particular, Hilferding's notoriously poor theory of money (which is admittedly derived from Marx's own confusion on this point)[5] and, more seriously, his failure to apply the all important distinction that Marx makes between the concentration and centralization of capital.

However, *Finance Capital* is of interest to us here for two main reasons. Firstly, because the publication of Hilferding's book had a significant influence on the development of the neo-Marxist theory of imperialism at the beginning of the twentieth century (and especially on Lenin's *Imperialism, the Highest Stage of Capitalism*, first published in 1916); but secondly, because it introduced the highly influential but completely mistaken view that 'finance capital' was a stage in the development of the capitalist mode of production rather than something that might be better understood as a stage in the development of a highly developed mercantile system. The reader who is interested in Lenin's concept of imperialism as the *highest* stage of capitalist development (and Hilferding was content to merely describe this as the *latest* phase) will have to study this for themselves. For now, however, if we restrict our attention in this chapter to what Hilferding has to say on the subject of money capital, this will provide us with a useful way of examining what Marx has to say on the subject of 'finance capital' and will allow us to consider in what way, if at all, Hilferding's theory of the role of money capital represents an advance over what Marx had to say on this subject.

In one respect at least, Hilferding may be said to have made a significant advance over Marx's concept of the role of money capital. This is in his explanation of the development of promoter's profit. As we saw in the previous chapter, in so far as Marx can be said to discuss this subject at all, he regarded corporate promotion, stock issuance and stock speculation as 'a whole system of swindling and cheating' (1977, 438 [1981, 569]). However, Hilferding quite rightly points out that corporate promotion is not a swindle in itself (however much it may present opportunities for swindling), but has a real economic basis; namely, making use of money capital lying idle in society. Banks announce a share floatation, and in this way money which otherwise might not have entered into circulation is attracted to the newly formed corporation. However, owing to the fact that these shares are negotiable in their own right, the value of the corporation seems to have doubled overnight with the mere fact of its formation. There are now in existence *two* lots of value: the actual physical value of the assets of the companies that enter into the newly formed corporation, and the values the shares have as negotiable securities rather than as mere titles to the ownership of a certain part of the new corporation. The banks who promoted the formation of the corporation are normally paid for the service they have performed for the corporation, not in the form of a share of the profits of the new company (although they may well become shareholders in the new corporation), but in the form of a fee which is paid according to the size of the difference between the actual stock value of the corporation and its stock value plus its share value. Since the share value of the new corporation seems to have no basis in the corporation's physical value, Marx regards this as fictitious: any profit made on the basis of the corporations share value must, he thought, involve a swindle. However, as Hilferding points out, the share value of a corporation does have a very real basis, not in the form of the stock of the company but in the form of the numerous small investors who deposit their hard-earned savings with the corporation in the form of shareholdings. These small shareholders tend to buy into a corporation when its shares are performing well and when the price of these shares are high, and because they live off the income generated from these shareholdings, they tend to sell their shares when their value starts to fall. Institutional investors, on the other hand, have a quite different pattern of investment. They tend to buy shares when they are performing badly and the price of these shares are low, and to sell their shareholdings to small investors when the value of their shares have increased. In this way, large institutions make a profit at the expense of small shareholders. However, it is only once a corporation has been formed that opportunities for swindling small investors really present themselves: firstly, by speculating in the possible rise and fall in the price of shares; secondly, by making a distinction between ordinary and preferred shares (and by only paying dividends on preferred shares); and thirdly, by artificially inflating the price of shares, often by the mere suggestion that a company may be going to form a new corporation (Hilferding 1981, Part II, Ch. 7; see especially, 112–20).

In other respects, however, Hilferding's analysis of finance capital represents a serious step backwards compared to Marx's analysis. This is particularly so with regard to the *circulation* of money capital. As we saw in Chapter 11 of this study, Marx argues that the circuit of capital that begins and ends with money passing through a productive stage after the initial investment of money has been capitalized and where the value of the initial money capital is withdrawn in the form of profit at the end of the process of production – i.e. the circuit M–C…P…C'–M' – constitutes what he describes as 'the basis of the more highly developed *mercantile* system', rather than the basis of the capitalist mode of production proper (which by contrast is characterized by the fluent and ever renewed circuit of industrial capital). As we saw, this circuit is defined as a *highly* developed form of merchant's capital precisely because it passes through a productive stage. But it just so happens that the circuit that Marx describes as the highly developed form of merchant's capital is *exactly* the form of circulation that Hilferding defines as the normal circuit of 'finance capital'. That is, the 'normal' circuit consists of bank capital in the form of money, which is transformed into productive capital (which Hilferding mistakenly calls 'industrial capital'), but which can always be withdrawn in the form of money (1981, 235). As Hilferding says on this point:

> I call bank capital, that is, capital in money form which is actually transformed in this way into industrial capital [*sic*], finance capital. So far as its owners are concerned, it always retains the money form; it is invested by them in the form of money capital, interest-bearing capital, and can always be withdrawn by them as money capital. (1981, 225)

What Hilferding here calls 'industrial capital' is what Marx calls 'productive capital'; and what Hilferding calls 'finance capital' is what Marx refers to as the highly developed form of merchant's capital. Of course, in conformity with Marx's view, Hilferding treats the circuit of merchant's capital as though it was part of a much larger, fluent and ever-renewed circuit of industrial capital proper (M–C…P…C'–M'–C'…P'…C"–M", etc.). Despite the fact that he discusses Marx's views on the circulation of merchant's capital at length throughout *Finance Capital*, what Hilferding does not appear to understand is the fact that the 'finance capitalist' – the owner of capital in its *money* form – can always withdraw his or her capital from the process of circulation at the money stage, and therefore, as we have seen, that the circulation of industrial capital is likely to be anything but uninterrupted.

Similarly, as we saw in the previous chapter of this study, Marx argues that credit has *both* an integrating and a disarticulating effect on the development of capitalist accumulation. However, despite two really excellent chapters on credit and capitalist crises (Ch. 17–18, 1981, 257–81), Hilferding fails to understand the full implications for the development of capitalist accumulation of writing off enormous amounts of otherwise perfectly good capital as a result of crises brought about by a simple interruption of the normal circulation of money capital. In short, Hilferding simply does not seem to understand the threat posed by the conversion of production capital into money capital to the process of reproduction on an extended scale during the *normal* circulation of industrial capital, whether this transformation takes the form of a reconversion into 'bank capital' or the extension of a new line of credit.

Hilferding's failure to analyse the implications of the development of 'finance capital' for the uninterrupted accumulation of industrial capital can be seen clearly in his analysis of the concentration and centralization of capital. In *Capital*, Vol. I, Chapter 25, section 2 (1974a, 582–9 [1976, 772–81]), Marx is careful to make a clear distinction between the concentration and centralization of capital. According to Marx, the *concentration* of capital in the hands of fewer and fewer individual capitalists is brought about by the accumulation of newly produced surplus value, whether this accumulation takes place within the process of production which actually produced this newly created capital, or within a related enterprise, under the ownership or control of the same group of capitalists as the initial process of production from which the surplus value originated. This type of concentration of capital, Marx argues, 'grows directly out of, or rather is identical with, accumulation' (1974a, 586 [1976, 776]) and it is only as a result of this type of concentration of capital that the total social capital of society can be increased. It must therefore be regarded as essential to the development of the capitalist mode of production. On the other hand, however, Marx defines *centralization*, as distinct from concentration, as the coming together of *already* existing capitals, and therefore as a process which involves no necessary growth in the total social capital of society, even though the size of the new companies formed by this process of centralization and incorporation may be enormously expanded. Centralization is 'the concentration of capitals already formed, destruction of their original independence, expropriation of capitalist by capitalist, transformation of many small into few large capitals' (1974a, 586 [1976, 776]), and this process is often accompanied by a fall in the size of the total social capital, as a result of the liquidation of otherwise perfectly sound capital, the function of which happens to be duplicated in the newly formed company. Astonishingly enough, however, despite the fact that Hilferding himself declared that his purpose in writing *Finance Capital* was to study the process of the *concentration* of capital and the direction of development that this process of concentration implies (1981, 22), and despite the fact that it is impossible to study this question without making an adequate distinction between the concentration and centralization of capital, he simply fails to apply the distinction that Marx makes between these two very different things. Furthermore, he sometimes even refers to a process of 'concentration' which does not involve 'any expansion of production' (a clear reference to a process of centralization), and to cartels and trusts as the culmination of a process of concentration rather than as the result of a process of centralization (1981, 22, 223). As a result of this, Hilferding is unable to analyse whether the growth in size of individual capitalist enterprises represents an expansion in the scale of the capitalist mode of production as a whole or whether it is taking place at the expense of other already existing capitals and he is therefore unable to say what significance the development of finance capital has for the development or underdevelopment of the capitalist mode of production as a whole.

If we set aside for the moment this major failing of Hilferding's work – and it is a failing which left Hilferding totally unable to identify whether the development of finance capital represented a higher stage in the development of the CMP or a new phase in the development of some other mode of production – Hilferding did make at least two significant contributions at a descriptive level to the Marxist theory of the concentration and centralization of capital, and any account of the development of the highly developed form of merchant's capital (or 'finance capital', to use his term) which failed to mention these would be incomplete. Firstly, Hilferding systematically distinguishes between four different combinations of capital – consortia, cartels, mergers and trusts – according to two main factors: the type of control that a corporation has over the market, and the legal status of the type of association between the member companies of a corporation. Thus, according to Hilferding, capital can be associated in the form of a consortia, a cartel, a merger or a trust, depending upon whether the member companies of a corporation are legally or informally incorporated, and whether they have a monopolistic or only a partial control over the market place. A consortia is a corporation which is only informally associated and which has only a partial control over the market place. A cartel is a corporation which is informally associated but which has a monopolistic control over the market place. A merger is a corporation which is formally (i.e. legally) associated, but which has only a *partial* control over the market place. While a trust is a corporation which is both formally associated *and* has a monopolistic control over the market place. Hilferding also distinguishes between the horizontal and vertical integration of previously independent companies, with horizontal integration referring to the incorporation of companies within the same branch of production (e.g. car making), and vertical integration referring to association between companies in successive stages of the same process of production (e.g. car production and car distribution). Further, he differentiates homospheric and hetrospheric associations (within the same sphere of production: agriculture, industry, commerce, or between different spheres) from economic, natural (e.g. geographic), legal (e.g. patents) and distributive monopolies (e.g. control over transport, wholesale, or retailing). Hilferding describes the monopoly of labour – e.g. in the form of trade unions – as 'quota cartels' (1981, 351).

Secondly, Hilferding describes in great detail the process whereby finance capital develops as a result of the centralization of banking and industry. According to Hilferding, finance capital is the synthesis of monopolistic banking and monopolistic or syndicated industry. Syndicated or cartelized industry is the result of the merging of previously independent industrial companies and their synthesis, together with the transport and sales functions of a previously independent commercial sector. Monopolistic banking is similarly the result of a merger between previously independent banks and a previously independent commercial credit sector. Independent industry and independent banks have their origin in handicraft industry and private money-lending ventures. And Hilferding argues that the result of the usurpation of what was previously the function of commercial capital by monopolistic banking and corporate industry is the complete destruction of an independent commercial sector (1981, Ch. 12–14, 204–26). Diagrammatically Hilferding's thesis here can be expressed as follows in Fig. 17.

Figure 17. The development of finance capital

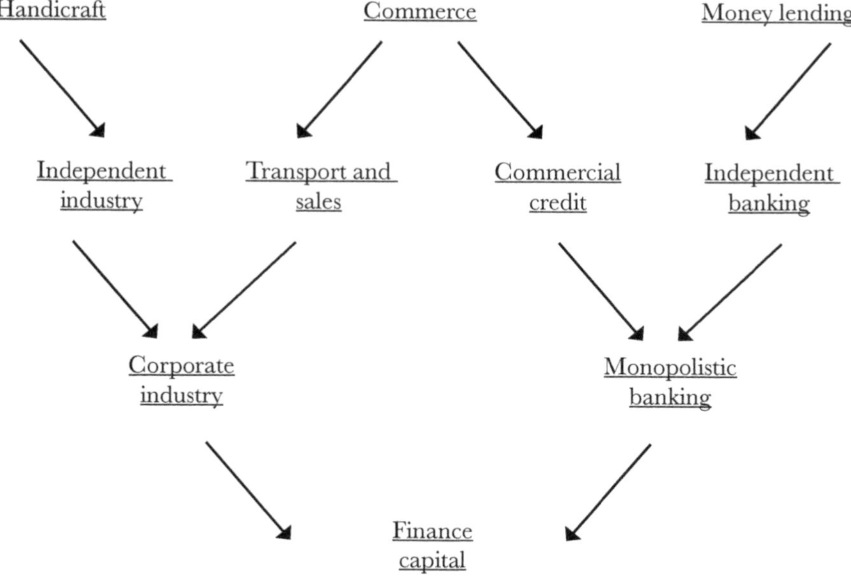

Points for Further Discussion

The reader who is interested in Hilferding's writings on the concentration and centralization of capital might like to follow up this brief introduction to Hilferding's work by reading *Finance Capital* for themselves. It would also be helpful to look at Hilferding's theory of imperialism – the third main aspect of his study and the part of that work which I have entirely neglected here – and at Lenin's work on this same question. Here the key question is obviously whether Lenin was correct to characterize imperialism as the *highest* stage in the development of capitalism, whether Hilferding was right to say that this was merely its *latest* phase, or whether I am right to suggest that colonialism/imperialism – and more generally foreign trade between newly developing capitalist economies and the rest of the as then non-capitalist world – did not represent a stage in the development of capitalism at all but rather a stage in its relative underdevelopment, i.e. a turning away from its pure development within a closed economy model and one from which it has not yet recovered. For the *general* reader of Marx's *Capital*, however, the following reading should be sufficient on this question.

Reading: Essential: *Capital*, Vol. I, Ch. 25, section 2 (1974a, 582–9 [1976, 772–81]), 'Relative Diminution of the Variable Part of Capital Simultaneously with the Progress of Accumulation and the Concentration that Accompanies it'. Background: Rudolf Hilferding, *Finance Capital*, Routledge & Kegan Paul, 1981.

13. MARX ON DEVELOPMENT AND UNDERDEVELOPMENT IN *CAPITAL*, VOL. I, CH. 25, SECTION 5

In the previous chapters of Part III of this book I have suggested that the capitalist mode of production itself is underdeveloped. What I mean by this is that the capitalist mode of production we are all familiar with today has not developed fully in the way that Marx expected that it would, but that the uninterrupted circulation of industrial capital has been undermined in its development by the continuing existence of a highly developed form of mercantile capitalism (characterized by an independent circuit of money capital) and which is erroneously called 'finance capital' by Rudolf Hilferding. If this is the case it seems as well to conclude this discussion by looking at what Marx had to say about the development and underdevelopment of the capitalist mode of production in *Capital*, Vol. I (see especially Ch. 25, section 5, entitled 'Illustrations of the General Law of Capitalist Accumulation', 1974a, 607–66 [1976, 802–70]), as well as what he had to say on this subject elsewhere in his writings, before we go on to look at what he has to say on the question of surplus value and profit at the beginning of *Capital*, Vol. I, in Part IV of this present study.

Until only a few years ago, it was commonplace to argue that Marx thought that capitalism would undermine the development of (or 'underdevelop') the non-capitalist world (Kay 1975; Warren 1980). However, there is in fact surprisingly little in Marx's writings generally to support the argument that this was his view beyond some very general comments on the destructive effects of English colonialism on Irish agriculture in *Capital*, Vol. I, Chapter 25, section 5f (1974a, 652–66 [1976, 854–70]), and a letter by Engels to Marx in which Engels argued that Ireland had been 'stunted' in its development by English colonialism (Marx and Engels 1976, 334). In fact, the genealogy of the neo-Marxist concept of underdevelopment during the second half of the twentieth century would seem to owe more to Paul Baran's 1957 *The Political Economy of Growth*, Paul Baran and Paul Sweezy's highly influential 1965 *Monopoly Capitalism* and especially to (Baran's student) Andre Gunder Frank's 1967 *Capitalism and Underdevelopment in Latin America* than it does to Marx.

On the other hand, however, there *is* quite a lot of evidence to suggest that, in so far as he considered the question of the impact of capitalism on less developed parts of the world at all – and he was *much* more interested in the effects of the non-capitalist world on the development of capitalism than he was in the effects of the development of capitalism on the rest of the world – Marx thought that capitalism would *develop* the rest of the world in its own image rather than undermine its development. Thus, in *The Communist Manifesto*, for example, Marx and Engels argue that:

> The bourgeoisie, by the rapid improvement of all instruments of production, by the immensely facilitated means of communication, draws all, even the most barbarian, nations into civilization. The cheap prices of its commodities are the heavy artillery with which it batters down all Chinese walls, with which it forces the barbarian's intensely obstinate hatred of foreigners to capitulate. *It compels all nations, on pain of extinction, to adopt the bourgeois mode of production*; it compels them to introduce what it calls civilization into their midst, i.e., to become bourgeois themselves. In one word, it creates a world after its own image. (1971, 84; emphasis added)

Similarly, in an essay entitled 'The British Rule in India' (in a collection of Marx and Engel's writings brought together by Progress Press under the title *On Colonialism*) Marx argues that:

> English interference having placed the spinner in Lancashire and the weaver in Bengal, or sweeping away both Hindu spinner and weaver, dissolved these small semi-barbarian, semi-civilized communities, by blowing up their economical basis, and thus produced the greatest, and, to speak the truth, the only *social* revolution ever heard of in Asia. (1976, 40; emphasis added)

While, in *Capital*, Vol. III in the chapter entitled 'Historical Facts about Merchant's Capital' (1977, 333–4 [1981, 451–2]), Marx claims that English commerce exerted a 'revolutionary influence' on Chinese and Indian society and transformed them in the interests of English industry.

However, if Marx did not have an especially significant view of the impact of the development of the capitalist mode of production on the rest of the world, he did have a very significant view indeed of the effects of the underdevelopment of the rest of the world on the development of the capitalist mode of production itself. Thus, in a letter to Engels of 8 October 1858, Marx has this to say:

> The specific task of bourgeois society is the establishment of a world market, at least in outline, and of production based upon this world market. As the world is round, this seems to have been completed by the colonisation of California and Australia and the opening up of China and Japan. The difficult question for us is this: on the Continent the revolution is imminent and will immediately assume a socialist character. Is it not bound to be crushed in this little corner, considering that in a far greater territory the movement of bourgeois society is still in the ascendant? (1953, 134)

Similarly, in 'The British Rule in India', Marx argues that:

> England, it is true, in causing a social revolution in Hindostan [*sic*], was actuated only by the vilest interests, and was stupid in her manner of enforcing them. *But that is not the question.* The question is, can mankind fulfil its destiny without a fundamental revolution in the social state of Asia? If not, *whatever may have been the crimes of England* she was the unconscious tool of history in bringing about that revolution. (1976, 41; emphasis added)

Of course there is no real contradiction between the view that capitalism might develop *and* underdevelop the rest of the world, since it might well do *both* and, in point of fact, Marx tends to argue that capitalism has a short-term destructive impact and a long-term regenerative effect on pre-capitalist social-economic formations. Thus, in another essay on India in *On Colonialism*, entitled 'The Future Results of the British Rule in India', Marx argues that:

> England has to fulfill [*sic*] a double mission in India: one destructive, the other regenerating the annihilation of old Asiatic society, and the laying of the material foundations of Western society in Asia. (1976, 82)

And he further claims that:

> All that the English bourgeoisie may be forced to do will neither emancipate nor materially mend the social condition of the mass of the people, depending not only on the development of the productive powers, but on their appropriation by the people. But what they will not fail to do is to lay down the material premises for both. Has the bourgeoisie ever done more? (1976, 85)

Finally, and in a sense summing up his general view on this question, Marx has this to say:

> I know that the English millocracy intend to endow India with railways with the exclusive view of extracting at diminishing expenses the cotton and other raw materials for their manufactures. But when you have once introduced machinery into the locomotion of a country, which possesses iron and coals, you are unable to withhold it from its fabrication. You cannot maintain a net of railways over an immense country without introducing all those industrial processes necessary to meet the immediate and current wants of railway locomotion, and out of which there must grow the application of machinery to those branches of industry not immediately connected with railways. The railway system will therefore become, in India, truly the forerunner of modern industry. (1976, 84)

What I am suggesting here therefore is that while Marx was interested enough in the question of the effects of the development of capitalism on the non-capitalist world (and especially on Ireland, India and China), he was *much* more concerned with the possible effects that the underdevelopment of the rest of the world would have on the development of the capitalist mode of production itself. I believe that he was right to take this view because the question of the short-term development of the capitalist mode of production was equally important to the long-term development of *both* the capitalist mode of production and the development of the rest of the non-capitalist world. The question that we have to consider here when we are trying to explain the relative underdevelopment of the non-capitalist world is why it has taken the capitalist mode of production quite so *long* to develop the rest of the world in its own image, as Marx clearly expected it would. I have already given my answer to this question in the preceding chapters of Part III of this study; namely, that the capitalist mode of production in Europe *failed* to develop the rest of the world in its own image because it was *itself* both: (a) *un*developed, by virtue of the greater vitality and independence of merchant's capital than was anticipated by Marx and therefore by the survival of this highly developed form of merchant's capital into the twentieth century, and (b) *under*developed, by virtue of its trade with the non-capitalist world in much the same way that the rest of the world is usually thought to have been underdeveloped by virtue of its trade with the CMP. As Marx said in 1858 – with some prescience I think – was not the socialist revolution bound to be crushed in Europe when so much of the rest of the world remained relatively undeveloped?

Points for Further Discussion

1. Despite the fact that the highly developed form of merchant's capital characteristic of modern post-industrial societies has clearly failed to develop the third world in the way that Marx expected it would, many Marxists today still seem to believe that it is the capitalist mode of production *itself* that has undermined the development of the third world during the twentieth century, even when they are aware of the peculiarly mercantile form that the development of capitalism has taken. A good example of this kind of thinking is provided by a now somewhat dated 1975 book by Geoffrey Kay entitled *Development and Underdevelopment: A Marxist Analysis*. According to Kay, 'the history of underdevelopment is the fullest possible expression we have of [the] contradictory tendencies of *merchant's capital* to both stimulate and repress the development of the forces of production and to both open and block the way for the full development of capitalism'(1975, 95; emphasis added). Despite the fact that Kay recognizes that the underdevelopment of the third world is to be explained by the expansion of merchant's capital from Europe, and by the fact that merchant's capital is more interested in developing the means of trade rather than the forces of production, and despite the fact that he further argues that capitalism has underdeveloped the third world not so much by exploiting it as by *failing to exploit it sufficiently*, Kay seems unwilling to draw the obvious conclusion from his own research: that if capitalism failed to develop the third world capitalistically, it must be because it too was underdeveloped itself. Nevertheless, this conclusion is clear enough I think and it makes far more sense of Kay's own findings than the conclusion he draws that the capitalist mode of production itself underdeveloped the third world. After all, if capitalism is less than fully developed, what is the conceptual status of this *not* fully developed CMP?
2. An alternative approach to both the view I am advocating here and to the late twentieth-century neo-Marxist theory of underdevelopment is simply to dispute the fact that capitalism *has failed* to develop the third world in its own image (or, more usually, to dispute that it has failed to develop the third world *yet*). This is the approach adopted by Bill Warren in his deservedly famous essay in *New Left Review* ('Imperialism and Capitalist Industrialisation', *NLR*, Sept/Oct 1973) and in his 1980 follow-up book *Imperialism: Pioneer of Capitalism.* Making very impressive use of a wide range of statistics on annual gross national product, manufacturing labour force as a percentage of total active population, manufacturing output as a percentage of GNP, etc., Warren demonstrates that certain countries which have traditionally been considered to be underdeveloped (writing in the 1980s he mentions Mexico, Iran, Chile, Argentina and Hong Kong, but today this list would

far more likely cite the so-called BRIC countries: Brazil, Russia, India and China) were in fact developing industrially, so much so in fact that he claimed that capitalist imperialism was alive and well. In the case of Hong Kong, for example, Warren points out that in 1971 fully 41.4% of the total working population of Hong Kong were employed in manufacturing, a *higher* percentage than in any other country in the world at that time, and that even if we take a less exceptional example, in the case of Argentina for example, 25.1% of the economically active population of Argentina were employed in manufacturing industry as long ago as 1961 (which compares to only 26.5% of the economically active population employed in manufacturing industry in the USA in the same year). According to this argument then, if the USA is a developed economy then so too must Argentina and Hong Kong be.

The problem with Warren's thesis, however, is that while he irrefutably demonstrates that certain countries which have traditionally been thought of as underdeveloped are in fact more highly *industrialized* than many other countries which have traditionally been thought of as part of the developed world, he does not show that this process of industrialization is the product of a fully developed *capitalist* process of production rather than merely the productive stage of the circuit of a highly developed form of *mercantile* capitalism. In other words, he does not consider that it is precisely a highly developed form of *merchant's capital* – one in which the circuit of capital is interrupted and discontinuous – that is able to export its productive function to the so-called third world, an option that might not have been open to a fully developed (i.e. fluent and ever-renewed) circuit of industrial capitalism. What is more, it seems not to have occurred to Warren that the first-world countries against which he is comparing these highly industrialized third-world countries (i.e. countries in the so-called developed world whose levels of industrialization are in fact *lower* than that of certain countries in the third world) are *themselves* relatively underdeveloped industrially. In short, a similar level of industrialization in first- and third-world countries does not necessarily indicate that it is the third-world countries that are developing industrially. Rather, it might instead suggest that these so-called first-world countries are themselves relatively underdeveloped industrially; the process which today we would describe as one of 'post-industrialization'. Finally, even if the level of industrialization in formerly underdeveloped countries is the same or even better than that of many previously developed economies, it has not been established that such industrialization has been achieved by a fully developed *capitalist* mode of production rather than, as might just as well be the case, as the productive phase of a highly developed mercantile circuit of capital (which has its money stage in the first world and the productive stage in the third). Here a notable oversight in Warren's essay in *New Left Review* is that he simply does not define capitalism at all (a major weakness surely in an essay entitled 'Imperialism and Capitalist Industrialisation'), and this omission is also not corrected in his 1980 book where, in so far as he can be said to define capitalism at all, he does so in terms of *market* relations and what he refers to as the 'self-sustaining momentum, and rapid pace of technological change' (Warren 1980, 12).

Reading: Essential: Marx and Engels, *On Colonialism* (1976), especially the essays on 'The British Rule in India' and 'The Future Results of the British Rule in India'. Secondary: *Capital*, Vol. II (1974b, 113–14 [1978, 190–91]), Vol. III, Ch. 20 (especially 1977, 333–4 [1981, 451–2]). Background: G. Kay, *Development and Underdevelopment: A Marxist Analysis*, and B. Warren, *Imperialism: Pioneer of Capitalism.*

14. THE TENDENCY OF THE RATE OF PROFIT TO FALL IN *CAPITAL*, VOL. III, PARTS I–III, CH. 1–15, BUT ESPECIALLY CH. 14–15

Marx's interest in the question of the tendency of the rate of profit to fall has sometimes been discussed by Marxists in connection with Marx's writings on colonialism and, in particular, with the possibility of establishing a Marxist theory of imperialism. For this reason, it seems appropriate here to look at what Marx has to say on this subject in that part of *Capital*, Vol. III which we have yet to look at in any detail at all: the approximately 250 pages which make up the first three parts of Vol. III (Ch. 1–15; 1977, 25–266 [1981, 117–375]), and especially Chapters 14–15. The reason that this otherwise rather uninteresting discussion is sometimes thought to provide the basis for a Marxist theory of imperialism is because of Marx's observation that there is generally a higher rate of profit to be found in colonial rather than non-colonial trade (Ch. 14, section 5, 'Foreign Trade'; 1977, 237–9 [1981, 344–6]). Once again, however, this is something of a misrepresentation of Marx's actual view of this matter. Marx's interest in the question of a falling rate of profit, like that of the classical political economists before him, had nothing very much to do with establishing a possible theory of colonialism-imperialism, but was *solely* concerned with the implications of the tendency of the rate of profit to fall on the development of the *capitalist mode of production itself*, and in particular, to the question of the *finitude* of the CMP. However, whereas Adam Smith and David Ricardo sought to understand the tendency of a falling rate of profit in order to overcome the threat that it posed to the capitalist mode of production, Marx was interested in the opposite problem; namely, why the fall in the rate of profit was not very much greater and more rapid than it actually was, given that there was any such thing as a falling rate of profit at all, and how this might help to bring about an end to the CMP (1977, 232 [1981, 339]). In order to answer these questions Marx undertook a detailed study of the counterbalancing forces that offset an actual fall in the rate of profit.

But before we go on to look at what these counterbalancing forces were, we must first understand the reasons why Marx accepted that there was indeed a tendency for the rate of profit to fall at all.

Marx expresses the rate of profit in the following formula: r = s/(c + v), in which r equals the rate of profit, s represents the amount of surplus value produced over and above costs, c stands for constant capital costs employed during the process of production – i.e. machinery and raw materials – and v represents variable capital costs, the cost of labour or wages. That the rate of profit (r) must fall if the denominator in this equation (c + v) increases in relation to the numerator (s) is nothing more than a simple mathematical truism. Thus, if for the sake of convenience a factor of 2 is attributed to each of s, c and v, the following equation for the rate of profit emerges:

$$r = \frac{2s}{2c+2v} = \frac{2}{2+2} = \frac{2}{4} = \frac{1}{2} = 50\%$$

If we now increase c to a factor of 4, the rate of profit will obviously fall:

$$r = \frac{2s}{4c+2v} = \frac{2}{4+2} = \frac{2}{6} = \frac{1}{3} = 33\frac{1}{3}\%$$

On the other hand, however, it is equally true to say that the rate of profit would *rise* if either s increased relative to c + v, or if c + v fell relative to s. Thus, if s rose from 2 to 4 we would get the following rate of profit:

$$r = \frac{4s}{2c+2v} = \frac{4}{2+2} = \frac{4}{4} = \frac{1}{1} = 100\%$$

While if c + v each fell to a factor of 1 this would yield much the same result:

$$r = \frac{2s}{1c+1v} = \frac{2}{1+1} = \frac{2}{2} = \frac{1}{1} = 100\%$$

Similarly, even if c rose, the rate of profit would remain unchanged if v fell in proportion to this increase in c:

$$r = \frac{2s}{3c+1v} = \frac{2}{3+1} = \frac{2}{4} = \frac{1}{2} = 50\%$$

The rate of profit will therefore fall where costs (c + v) increase in relation to profits (s). Those factors which might offset a fall in the rate of profit will be those that reduce the combined cost of c + v in relation to s, or, in other words, those factors which can either bring about a fall in variable capital (v) proportionate to any rise in constant capital (c) or which bring about an increase in the mass of surplus value (s) proportionate to any increase in the magnitude of constant and variable capital.

Marx seems to have thought that there would *actually* be a slight falling off in the rate of profit in capitalist societies, as opposed to merely a *tendency* for this to occur, because of the enormous and apparently disproportionate increase in constant capital that accompanied the development of modern industry. He expressed this point in what he terms the 'law of the falling rate of profit' as follows:

> The law of the falling rate of profit, which expresses the same, or even a higher, rate of surplus value states ... that any quantity of average social capital, say, a capital of 100, comprises an ever larger portion of means of labour, and an ever smaller portion of living labour. Therefore, since the aggregate mass of living labour operating the means of production decreases in relation to the value of these means of production, it follows that the unpaid labour and the portion of the value in which it is expressed must decline as compared to the value of the advanced total capital. (1977, 215–16 [1981, 322])

However, the important point to understand here is not that the rate of profit is *actually* likely to fall (due to a progressive relative decrease of the proportion of variable capital to constant capital), but that any actual fall in the rate of profit is likely to be very much less pronounced than an actual increase in the magnitude of constant capital might lead us to expect due to the combined effect of the many other counterbalancing factors outlined above. In other words there is only a *tendency* for the rate of profit to fall, and this tendency might not necessarily manifest itself at all. The 'law' of the falling rate of profit is therefore at best only a conditional one. Marx is merely making a claim of the kind that, other things being equal, the rate of profit will fall if the magnitude of constant to variable capital increases relative to any increase in the magnitude of surplus value produced, but that, for as long as other things are not equal, and in particular where the rate of surplus value (s/v) increases in proportion to any increase in the magnitude of constant capital, the rate of profit will *not* fall. Marx's explanation of the fact that the fall in the rate of profit in the CMP is not anything like as great or as fast as we might otherwise have expected it to be is that this is due to the effect of certain counterbalancing forces.

In Vol. III, Chapter 14, entitled 'Counteracting Influences' (1977, 232–40 [1981, 339–48]), Marx lists a number of counterbalancing factors to the tendency of the rate of profit to fall, as follows:

1. *Increasing the intensity of exploitation of labour and thereby reducing expenditure of variable capital.* In effect this means increasing the speed at which existing machinery is employed, since almost any other way of increasing the intensity of exploitation – e.g. by introducing new machinery – is bound to lead to an increase in constant capital spending as well, and therefore to a probable fall in the rate of profit. Simply speeding up the use of existing machinery, however, allows for greater employment of labour-power without any additional expenditure of either constant or variable capital.
2. *The depression of wages below the value of labour-power and hence a fall in the expenditure of variable capital.* In other words, cheapening the price of labour by not even paying the labourer the cost of reproducing themselves (i.e. what it costs to bring the labourer back to work for another week or another day and therefore the cost of reproducing the labourer's capacity to work). However, this tends to be only a short-term solution to the problem of a falling rate of profit, and it is in any case only possible when labour is abundant, since paying labourers less than what it cost to reproduce themselves very quickly tends to reduce the number of labourers seeking work (either by starvation or simply due to exhaustion), such that the ensuing fall in the number of labourers seeking work will tend to drive up the price of labour once again as a result of competition among capitalists for this now scarce resource.
3. *Cheapening the elements of constant capital.* Although the magnitude of constant capital employed may increase dramatically with the development of modern industry, this increase is not necessarily matched by any increase in the *value* of the constant capital employed. For example, where new sources of supply of raw material are found, the value of constant capital (and hence its price) may fall due to the ease of its reproduction or a glut in its supply.
4. *Unemployment, or what Marx calls 'relative over-population'.* Rather than the supply of labour driving down its price (see point 2), the continued existence of cheap labour tends to make it unnecessary or uneconomical to introduce new machinery until the price of the new machinery has fallen below the price of the labour it replaces, or until foreign competition makes even very cheap commodities more expensive to produce than those produced using new machinery.
5. *Foreign trade.* This tends to raise the rate of profit, firstly by cheapening the elements which go to make up constant capital, and secondly by cheapening the cost of the necessities of life for which variable capital is exchanged.

As we have seen, Marx also argues that the rate of profit is usually higher in foreign, and especially in colonial, trade which would further serve to counterbalance the tendency for the general rate of profit to fall, even if foreign trade did not also have a direct effect on the rate of profit in the home market.

6. *Increasing the level of stock capital.* It is by no means clear how increasing the level of profits taken in the form of dividends is supposed to offset a general fall in the rate of profit (1977, 240 [1981, 347–8]). What Marx *seems* to mean here is that, since investors in stocks and shares are usually prepared to take a lower than average rate of profit, the rate of profit excluding the return on stocks and shares is higher than it would be if stocks and shares were included. However, where the general rate of profit includes the rate of return on stocks and shares (as it should of course) the tendency of the rate of profit to fall would be unaffected by the fact that an increasing proportion of all profits are paid in the form of dividends.

If we then summarize the above argument we can say that the law of the falling rate of profit – i.e. of the *tendency* that the rate of profit has to fall – is nothing more than a mathematical truism which states that if the value of the constant capital employed rises, and if this rise is not offset by a fall in the value of the variable capital employed, or by a rise in the value of the surplus value produced, then the rate of profit will fall, but that where the above is not in fact the case, none of this will actually obtain. The way in which Marx expresses this argument in terms of the above mathematical formulas is interesting enough no doubt but otherwise all of this is of relatively little importance.

Marx's contribution to the long-standing debate in political economy concerning the tendency of the rate of profit to fall was intended to resolve the problem of why capitalists are apparently willing to continually increase their investment in constant capital when the effect of this would seem to be to continually reduce their rate of profit. Marx pointed out that the actual rate of profit probably will not fall even if capitalists do increase their absolute investment in constant capital since any increase in constant capital is likely to be accompanied by a corresponding fall in the amount of variable capital employed, in which case the rate of profit may even rise due to an increase in the intensity of labour or to the introduction of labour-saving machinery. However a *much* more simple and straightforward solution to this problem would have been to point out that the rate of profit is after all a relatively unimportant economic indicator to the type of capitalist who is more interested in the *absolute* magnitude of profits produced by a particular enterprise rather than the *rate* at which these profits are produced. I have already suggested that this type of capitalist is a merchant capitalist rather than an industrial capitalist and that the type of economic process Marx was trying to describe was actually much closer to his concept of a highly developed mercantile process of production than it was to a fully developed capitalist mode of production. A detailed study of monopoly capitalism would show how little those capitalists who are not especially subject to the pressures of competition are able to endure relatively low rates of profit in return for high absolute levels of profits.

Points for Further Discussion

1. It should be clearly understood that there is nothing in the law of a falling *rate* of profit which implies that there will be any *absolute* fall in the *mass* of profits produced by a capitalist mode of production. On the contrary, absolute levels of profits may continue to rise such that greater and greater magnitudes of profit are continually produced by an ever-increasing *mass* of capital, while at the same time the *rate* at which this increasing magnitude of profit is produced continues to fall. Equally, the rate of profit may continue to rise while the absolute mass of the capital employed, and even the absolute mass of the profits produced, falls (1977, 235 [1981, 342]). This would happen, for example, when either the constant or the variable capital employed is reduced, but the intensity of labour is increased. Marx's law of the tendency of the rate of profit to fall, in so far as this can be called a law at all, is not concerned with an absolute fall in the level of profits produced by the capitalist mode of production, but only with a fall in the rate at which these profits might be expected to rise.
2. Since in Marx's concept of the rate of profit foreign trade does not take place under the conditions of an actual fall in the rate of profit, but rather as one of the major counterbalancing conditions which offset this tendency, Marx's concept of the tendency of the rate of profit to fall can only be *directly* employed to explain foreign trade in a situation where the rate of profit does not actually fall, and is only *indirectly* employed (in the form of an ideal-typical construct)[6] to explain foreign trade in a situation in which the rate of profit actually does fall. Paradoxically, therefore, Marx's concept of the *tendency* of the rate of profit to fall – a tendency that does not actually obtain – is better suited to explaining the export of capital in a situation in which the rate of profit is relatively *stable* than it is to an explanation of capitalist crisis: i.e. where the rate of profit actually does fall or there is an absolute fall in the mass of profits produced.
3. This observation highlights a further problem with the conventional interpretation of Marx's concept of the rate of profit; namely, how this

concept of a relatively *stable* rate of profit (a rate of profit which does not actually fall, and which may even increase as a result of the higher profits usually to be found in foreign trade, or due to a fall in the expenditure of variable capital) is supposed to be able to explain capitalist competition? If the *tendency* of the rate of profit to fall is supposed to cause capitalist competition, as Marx seems to suggest, just what is it about a relatively *stable* rate of profit that is supposed to have this effect? On the other hand, if competition between capitalists (and hence investment in constant capital) is supposed to account for the tendency of the rate of profit to fall, as Marx also seems to suggest, what is it that causes this capitalist competition in the first place? (On this point see my earlier discussion of Marx's DI–DII model in Chapter 7–9 of this study for an explanation which suggests that *both* capitalist competition *and* the tendency of the rate of profit to fall are effects of a *third* phenomenon: the material compulsion to accumulate potential fixed capital in a capitalist mode of production.)

Reading: Essential: *Capital*, Vol. III, Part III, 'The Law of the tendency of the rate of Profit to Fall', especially Ch. 13–14 (1977, 211–40 [1981, 317–48]). Background: *Capital*, Vol. III, Parts I and II, Ch. 1–12 (1977, 25–210 [1981, 117–313]), Part III, Ch. 15, (1977, 241–66 [1981, 349–75]). See also Marx's letter to Engels, letter no. 98, 30 April 1868 (*MESC*, 1953, 245–50).

CONCLUSION TO PART III

In Chapter 10 of this study I argued that the circuit of industrial capital M–C…P…C'–M'. M–C…P…C'–M'. M–C…P…C'–M' etc. (or M–C… P…C'–M'–C'…P…C''–M''–C''…P…C'''–M''' etc., as this would be in the case when reproduction on a progressively extending scale took place) is interrupted at the money stage (M'–M, or M minus m), such that (a) the circuit of a highly developed form of merchant's capital, M–C…P…C'–M', becomes an *independent* circuit of money capital (also known as 'finance capital') rather than remaining a continuous and uninterrupted part of the normal circuit of industrial capital, and that (b) as a result of the dominance of merchant's capital, surplus value is withdrawn from the process of production and consumed unproductively by finance capitalists, such that reproduction on a progressively extending scale – and hence capitalist accumulation proper – does not take place. In Chapter 11, I further argued that the capitalist mode of production cannot possibly destroy itself from within – that is to say, *systemically* – since, any attempt to destroy itself will destroy the very thing that is supposed to be bringing about its own destruction: namely, itself. However, I also argued that the CMP is not left unaffected by this development. Rather, within the tendency that it has to destroy itself, the CMP does indeed go some way towards undermining its own conditions of existence (i.e. its fullest possible development in the form of the uninterrupted circulation of industrial capital) before the tendency it has to destroy itself is arrested. It *socializes* the ownership of the means of production in the form of share ownership, while leaving the control of the commanding heights of industry and finance in the hands of *private* interests. To the extent that this occurs the resulting mode of production is neither capitalist nor socialist, but something in between the two that might variously be described as a highly developed form of the mercantile system: finance capitalism, monopoly capitalism or managerialism. In Chapter 12, I looked at Rudolf Hilferding's writings on the circulation of money capital to see how this compared with Marx's views on this question. I argued that what Hilferding calls 'finance capital' (bank capital in its money form which actually takes part in the process of production) is a misinterpretation of what Marx had previously described as a highly developed form of merchant's capital in *Capital*, Vol. II. I further argued that Hilferding was unable to analyse the significance that the development of 'finance capital' had on the question of the direction of development of the CMP itself (i.e. the effect that the development of finance capital had on the underdevelopment of the capitalist mode of production itself) because of his view that finance capitalism represented a progressive development in the history of the capitalist mode of production – its 'latest phase' – rather than, as I suggested, a step backward (i.e. a stage in its underdevelopment). In Chapter 13, we then looked at Marx's views on the development and underdevelopment of the capitalist mode of production and I argued that while Marx did not have a particularly significant view of the effects of the underdevelopment of the capitalist mode of production on the rest of the world, he *did* have a very significant view of the effects of the failure of capitalism to develop the rest of the world on the development of the capitalist mode of production itself; namely, that the development of the capitalist mode of production (and hence the development of capitalism towards socialism) was bound to be crushed in Europe given that, at that time, capitalism had still to develop in the rest of the world. Finally, in Chapter 14 I considered Marx's views on the alleged tendency that the rate of profit has to fall within the capitalist mode of production and the implications of this, if any, for a Marxist theory of imperialism/colonialism.

Interest in the social, political and economic effects of industrialization on what used to be known as 'third-world' countries (i.e. the sociology of development, as this used to be called) has declined recently, due to the incorporation of many of these formerly undeveloped economies into the world market in the late twentieth and early twenty-first centuries, as well as a corresponding decline in interest in Marxist accounts of such underdevelopment. However, as I have indicated here, I think this is a very bad mistake indeed since, in no longer analysing the effects of the development of capitalism on the third world, Marxists have failed to analyse the effects of the underdevelopment of the third world on the development of capitalism. As these formerly underdeveloped economies become increasingly industrialized, and as industry shifts from the first to the third world, we can only wait to see what effects this development will have on the increasing underdevelopment of the capitalist mode of production itself.

In Part IV of this book, we will now go on to look at what the implications of the above arguments are to what Marx has to say in *Capital*, Vol. I on the subject of the rate of surplus value, the circulation of commodities and especially for the question of a so-called labour theory of value.

Part IV

THE VALUE THEORY OF LABOUR

PREFACE TO PART IV

Having looked in some detail at what Marx has to say on the subject of the development of the capitalist mode of production in *Capital*, Vols I and II, and on the underdevelopment of the CMP in Vols II and III, we are now going back to look at what Marx had to ay about the theory of value at the beginning of *Capital*, Vol. I (1974a, 43–222 [1976, 125–339]). In what follows, therefore, I will by-pass Marx's two-hundred page long highly detailed discussion in Part VI of *Capital*, Vol. III (1977, 614–814 [1981, 751–950]) of the question of the transformation of surplus-profit into ground-rent (a short book in its own right and a topic which is of very little interest to us here), as well as his very interesting discussion in the final section of Part VII (1977, 814–86 [1981, 954–1,024]) of what has come to be known as the 'trinity formula' – the three main sources of income (rents, profits and wages). I will however look at Marx's famously incomplete discussion (Ch. 52, 1977, 885–6 [1981, 1,025–6]) of the three major social classes (landlords, capitalists and workers) that are said to correspond to these three main sources of income in the appendix at the end of this study. I say this because although the section on ground-rent and surplus-profit takes up a substantial part of Vol. III, it seems to me that these have more in common with Marx's detailed discussion of surplus value and rent in the three-volume notebook now known as *Theories of Surplus Value* (1975), and that consequently these chapters would have been much better if they had been excluded by Engels from the already overlong *Capital*, Vol. III, while the sections on the trinity formula and social class, when taken together with Marx's other writings on class, require a separate chapter to themselves.

INTRODUCTION TO PART IV

We are now returning to those conceptually difficult sections of *Capital*, Vol. I, Part I (Ch. 1 to 9), which although presented first by Marx in the order which he described as the 'scientific exposition' of his argument, he nevertheless sometimes advises his readers to read last, or at least after they had read the much less demanding second half of Vol. I. Here, therefore, I go back to consider those sections which I have so far deliberately neglected, in which Marx elaborates his views on the rate of surplus value, the degree of exploitation of labour by capital and the labour theory of value (1974a, 43–221 [1976, 125–339]), in the belief that the reader who has come this far, and is now familiar with Marx's way of describing things, will be better able to understand those very difficult chapters at the start of *Capital*, Vol. I than they otherwise would have been.

We have already looked at the difference between Marx's concept of profit and his concept of surplus value earlier in this book (Part II, Ch. 5 and 6). Here we saw Marx argues that the *absolute* surplus value produced by a capitalist process of production is usually very much greater than the apparent surplus, or profit, since unpaid labour not only produces the capitalist's profit but also recreates – and, according to Marx, produces *anew* – the value of the worn-out *constant* capital employed during the process of production. We are now going on to look at what Marx has to say on the parallel question of the difference between the *rate* of profit and the *rate* of surplus value. While Marx argues that profit can at first sight only be *formally* distinguished from surplus value (so much so that this distinction had almost entirely eluded classical political economy before him), he claims that the *rate of profit* can be much more easily distinguished from the *rate of surplus value*, and the magnitude of the free gift that labour makes to capital much more easily demonstrated, than when the difference between profit and surplus value is expressed in absolute terms (*MESW*, 1953, 246).

15. THE RATE OF PROFIT AND THE RATE OF SURPLUS VALUE IN *CAPITAL*, VOL. I, CH. 9, SECTION 3, AND VOL. III, PARTS I AND III

We have already seen that the formula Marx gives for the rate of profit is r=s/(c+v) (in which r equals the rate, s stands for the visible surplus, or profit, c stands for what Marx calls 'constant capital', the cost of reproducing the enterprise, and v stands for what Marx called 'variable capital' or wages). The formula for the rate of surplus value, on the other hand, is simply r=s/v. These two formulae are therefore distinguished *solely* by the fact that, while Marx includes the cost of renewing constant capital (c) in his calculation of the rate of profit, he does *not* include this factor in his calculation of the rate of surplus value. Chapter 5 of this study explains the reason why he does this. It is because, while the cost of renewing worn-out constant capital is undoubtedly a loss to the capitalist when considered from the point of view of the capitalist's profit, and although the cost of reproducing constant capital *is* clearly a loss to the capitalist when viewed from the perspective of the absolute profit capitalists might otherwise take if they were to liquidate their capital entirely, Marx regarded the actual expense of reproducing the worn-out constant capital *not as a cost to the capitalist but as a loss to the labourer*. That is, he saw it as an additional part of the unpaid work that labour provides for capital over and above what they are paid for, and, therefore, as something which should legitimately be regarded as a part of the surplus value of the enterprise. According to Marx then, it is not the capitalists, but the labourers, who pay for the replacement of constant capital in the form of wages they do not receive and who reproduce the substance of worn-out constant capital in the form of their surplus labour. *Capitalists* count the cost of renewing constant capital as a loss to themselves, and this is correct in so far as the profit that the capitalists might otherwise take if they did not replace worn-out constant capital and, in doing so, renew their claim to be the *owners* of the enterprise in question. But the money to pay for the replacement of constant capital has to come from somewhere and it quite clearly does *not* come from the capitalists' profits, since this is calculated only after the renewal of the process of production has taken place. Where then does this *additional* value come from, which is used to replace worn-out constant capital, and which is composed of neither profits nor wages? According to Marx, it can only come from the unpaid labour of all the workers engaged in the process of production. There is a hidden component of surplus value (s), over and above its visible component, profit (p). Surplus value is thus composed of profit (p), *plus* the cost of reproducing worn-out constant capital (c), which is renewed during the process of production (s=p+c), and the *rate* of surplus value is therefore given by the ratio of [s(+c)]/v. The rate of surplus value will therefore always be greater that the rate of profit, s/(c+v), and is usually very much greater than this, except on those rare occasions in which the reproduction of constant capital does not take place at all (i.e. where c = 0) and the enterprise in question is liquidated. Let us look at this argument in more detail.

Marx distinguishes between the rate of profit and the rate of surplus value most clearly in the section of *Capital*, Vol. I entitled 'Senior's Last Hour' (Ch. 9, section 3, 1974a, 215–20 [1976, 333–8]). Writing as a critic of the campaign to reduce the normal working day from 12 to 10 hours, Nassau W. Senior (1790–1864), a well-known economist of the time, claimed that if the normal working day of 12 hours, introduced by the Factory Act of 1833, was to be cut back by only one hour (from 12 hours to 11 on a week day, and from 9 hours to 8 on a Saturday), capitalists would be unable to make any profit at all, since, according to Senior, they derived their entire profit not from the whole of the working day (as might well be supposed) but from only one part of this, the last hour. Furthermore, Senior argued, if the length of the normal working day was cut still further, by two hours, from 12 hours to 10 on a week day and from 9 hours to 7 on a Saturday (as was in fact proposed by agitation for a 10-hour working day, and as was eventually introduced by the Factory Act of 1844), then not only would the capitalists be unable to make any profits at all (in the last hour of a 12-hour working day) but they would be unable even to pay their labourers' wages, since, according to Senior, the last hour but one of a 12-hour working day was spent by the labourers in doing nothing more for the capitalist than reproducing their own wages. For Senior, this extraordinary situation came about because labourers do nothing for the capitalist during most of the working day beyond reproducing the value of the capital which the capitalist already has to hand at the beginning of the working day in the form of machinery and raw materials, etc. It is therefore only the *additional* value (or profit) which the labourers create over and above what the capitalist already had to hand at the beginning of the working day that, according to Senior, we are entitled to take into account when calculating the extent of the labourers' contribution to the capitalist's surplus value (1974a, 215–16 [1976, 333–4]).

Marx easily refutes the first part of this argument, which is dependent upon the claim that labourers perform qualitatively different types of labour during different parts of the working day. If, in an average working day of 11 ½ hours (i.e. 12 hours on weekdays and 9 hours on Saturdays = 69 hours/6 days), the capitalist makes his profit only in the last hour (i.e. in the last 1/11 ½ of the working day), the reduction of the normal working day to 10 hours means that the labourer will, as before, produce the capitalist's profit in the last 1/11 ½ (i.e. the last 53 minutes) of this new 10-hour day. Similarly, if the labourers reproduce their wages in the last hour but one of a working day, the reduction of the normal working day to 10 hours means that they will reproduce their wages in the last 53 minutes but one of this new 10-hour day. The point here, as Marx says, is that the cost of reproducing wages and replacing worn-out means of production is reduced in proportion to the reduction in the length of the working day and the capitalists therefore gains as much in the reduction in the length of the working day as they lose in the form of profit gained by over-working labour (1974a, 216–18 [1976, 334–6]).

The second part of Senior's argument, however, is much more difficult to refute than the first. This concerns the question of what exactly it is that the labourers do for the capitalist during the greater part of the working day (9 ½ hours in the above example) when they are producing neither the capitalist's profit nor reproducing their own wages. As we have seen, according to Marx, the labourers not only produce the capitalist's profit, but maintain the substance and reproduce the value of the capitalist's constant capital during the *whole* of the working day, and not just during a specific part of the day. Marx further argues that it is due to the fact that the capitalist does not pay the labourers for this service that the capitalist appears to be in possession of a peculiar commodity (capital) which seems to be able to renew itself in perpetuity, without ever wearing out, and therefore without ever needing to be renewed by the capitalist. Senior's position is quite different from Marx's, however, and entails two apparently contradictory claims. On the one hand, he argues that the labourers do *nothing* for the capitalist during the greater part of the working day. On the other hand, however, he seems to admit that the labourers do at least appear to do something for the capitalist when they renew and maintain the substance of the capitalist's worn-out constant capital, but he seems to think that this service does not amount to very much. The apparent contradiction between these two claims is resolved by the argument that, while the labourers clearly do *something* for the capitalist when they renew the substance of their worn-out constant capital, this does not amount to very much from the point of view of the *total value produced* since the capitalist *already* had the value of this capital to hand (i.e. already owned it) at the beginning of the working day.

At first, Marx appears to go along with Senior's claim that the labourer does nothing for the capitalist during the whole of the working day except produce the capitalist's profit and reproduce their own wages (1974a, 217 [1976, 335]). If, however, as Marx points out, the labourers produce equal amounts of profit and wages during the working day, and if the labourers do nothing all day for the capitalist beyond producing profit and reproducing their wages, then the labourers must spend not one hour each day, as Senior maintains, producing profits and wages but 5¾ hours (one half) of this 11½-hour working day producing profits and a further 5¾ hours producing wages. Now, clearly, this is not what Senior meant to argue at all. When he claimed that the labourers do *nothing* for the capitalists during most of the working day, he did not mean that they do nothing at all; but simply that they do not *add* anything of value to the process of production that the capitalists already had to hand at the beginning of the working day. However, contrary to what Senior claimed, Marx insists that the labourer *does* add something to the value of the capitalist's original capital, over and above the capitalist's profits and in addition to the cost of reproducing the labourer's own wages. This something is the value of that part of the capitalist's constant capital which is worn-out and renewed during the process of production itself and Marx insists that, in so far as this part of the process of production is concerned, no part of the labourer's work represents a reproduction of any part of the capitalist's *original* capital (which, he argues, is worn out and used up during the process of production itself) but this is all simply new value created by labour.[1]

This whole problem then rests on the question of the renewal of the capitalist's original capital. This capital, which the capitalist brings to the process of production at the beginning of the working day, is not indestructible. If it is employed productively it will wear out through use. On the other hand, if it is not employed productively it will, firstly, not produce any profit for the capitalist and, secondly, lose what value it has by virtue of being neglected, either because, in the case of raw materials, it will decay, or because it is not maintained in its proper working condition, in the case of means of production. When it is employed in the process of production it transfers its value to the new product of this process, part of which is realized by the capitalist in the form of profit. However, at the end of the working day, the capitalist has to replace this worn-out constant capital. Both Marx and Senior are agreed that the money to pay for this constant capital does not come from the capitalist's profit. Where then does it come from? According to Senior, it comes from the unpaid labour of the working class who reproduce the substance of worn-out constant capital, but whose labour is of little or no value to the capitalist since this labour does not *add* anything to the value of the capital that the capitalist already had at the beginning of the working day. According to Marx, however, it comes from *new* value created by the unpaid labour of the working class. One hour's labour, Marx insists, is just like any other, nothing more and nothing less (1974a, 217 [1976, 335]). The amount of value produced in the first hour of the working day will be exactly the same as that produced in the last hour, in the last hour but one, and in any other hour of the working day for that matter. If, in an 11½-hour working day, the labourers produce the capitalist's profit and reproduce their own wages in the last two hours of the day, as Senior maintains, then, according to Marx, in the remaining 9½ hours of the working day they will produce nothing other than 9½ hours worth of *new* value, which the capitalists keep to replace their worn-out constant capital. The capitalist's constant capital transfers its value during the process of production to the product of this process, but, as it does so, it ceases to exist from the point of view of the process of production itself. Whatever else the labourers do during the process of production, Marx argues, it is clear enough that they do not *reproduce* any part of the capitalist's original worn-out constant capital which has been used up during the process of production and no longer exists. The happy circumstance (from the point of view of the capitalist) that the new value created by the labourers during the working day to replace the worn out constant capital is exactly equal to the value of the worn out capital is no accident of course. The magnitude of this value is determined by the magnitude of the worn-out value it is required to replace. Only once this is done can the capitalist calculate his profit. However, this coincidence of values is the means by which the capitalists are able to claim that value newly created during the working day is simply their old capital reproduced in a new form and returned to them unchanged. In fact though the labourer does not perform qualitatively different types of labour during the working day, but simply creates 11½ hours worth of new value through out the *whole* of the working day, one part of which goes towards their wages, another part of which goes towards the capitalist's profit and a third part of which goes to renew worn-out constant capital.[2]

Looked at in this way, the capitalist's rate of surplus value is very nearly always greater than his or her rate of profit and is usually very much greater than this. Senior assumes that the magnitude of profits and wages is proportionate one to the other, and their value is equivalent to the value of one hour's labour. Where this is the case the rate of profit will be equal to a seemingly reasonable 9.5% return on the capital invested (where $r+[s/(c+v)]=1s/[9\frac{1}{2}+1v]=1/10\frac{1}{2}]=9.5\%$). However, where the rate of surplus value ($r=s/v$) is understood to be made up not just of profits (p), but of profits plus the replacement value of worn-out constant capital (c') the rate of surplus value will be very much greater than this. The formula for the rate of surplus value is $r=(p+c')/v$ which, in this case, yields a rate of surplus value of $r=[1p+9\frac{1}{2}c]/1v=[1+9\frac{1}{2}]/1=10\frac{1}{2}/1$ or, in other words, a quite astonishing rate of surplus value of 1,050%. On the other hand, however, where the labourers do *not* reproduce their wages in one hour and the capitalist's profits in another hour, but instead take half the working day to reproduce their wages and spend the remaining half of the working day producing the capitalist's profit and renewing the substance of worn out constant capital, then the rate of surplus value would not be 1,050%, as in the above case, but only a mere 100% (where, $s=p+c'$ and $r=(s/v)=[5\frac{3}{4}]/[5\frac{3}{4}]=1/1=100\%$), as in the example given by Marx towards the end of his critique of Senior (1974a, 218–19 [1976, 335–6]). Ironically then, in attempting to minimize the contribution of labour to the rate of profit, by reducing the length of time the labourers spend producing profit and reproducing their wages, Senior makes the probable rate of surplus value seem even greater than it actually is.

Points for Further Discussion

1. We must be careful not to confuse the *historical* rate of surplus value of a capitalist enterprise, which includes the total cost of the *entire* constant capital of a given process of production (something which may take several years to wear out and renew), with the *daily* rate of surplus value produced, which includes only the replacement of that part of the total constant capital worn out on a day-to-day basis. If we wish to calculate the *daily* rate of surplus value of a particular process of production we must therefore be careful to count as surplus value only that part of the total constant capital that is worn out and renewed on a day-to-day basis ('c'), and not the total constant capital of the entire enterprise itself (let us call this 'C'). Similarly, if we wish to calculate the historical rate of surplus value of a particular enterprise we must not only take into account in the numerator of this fraction the total profit produced by the enterprise during its entire lifetime (P) and the total constant capital renewed during the process of production as a whole (C), but we must also be careful to include in the denominator of this fraction the *total* amount of variable capital paid out in the form of wages during the same period (V). Just as the degree of exploitation of a particular living labourer is not given by the rate of exploitation of 'dead' labour (see Ch. 16 of this study for more on this), so the daily rate of surplus value must not be confused with its historical rate.
2. We must be equally careful here not to misrepresent the rate of profit as in any sense a 'false' concept which fails to measure the true rate of surplus value. The concept of the rate of profit is simply an exact measure for another concept altogether apart from the rate of surplus value; it is in fact the true extent of the capitalist's *disposable* surplus value after the replacement of worn-out constant capital has taken place on the basis of simple reproduction.
3. This point about the correctness or otherwise of a rate of profit analysis as a measure of *value* brings us to another much less important, but no

less interesting, point concerning Marx's critique of Senior's concept of the rate of profit. If, as we have seen, Senior only claims to be giving an account of the rate of *profit*, is Marx being entirely fair when he criticizes him for failing to present an analysis of the rate of surplus value? Although Senior was incorrect to argue that different kinds of labour are performed during different parts of the working day, and although he was clearly wrong to argue that no profit at all would be produced if the length of a 12 hour working day was shortened in any way, what he has to say about the magnitude of the rate of *profit* that is produced in an 11½ hour working day is in fact correct in so far as the remaining 9½ hours labour are indeed spent in reproducing worn-out constant capital. It is an important part of Marx argument that he does not disagree with this part of Senior's analysis or with his calculation of the rate of profit in this case. Since Senior therefore does not pretend to be presenting an analysis of the rate of surplus value produced in this case (a subject on which he quite clearly had no comprehension at all), but only to be analysing the rate of profit, it is hard to escape the conclusion that Marx is presenting little more than a straw-man critique of Senior's views when he criticizes Senior for failing to understand that the rate of surplus value will almost certainly be very many times greater than the rate of profit.

4. Finally, one very puzzling question still remains to be considered here and this concerns the vexed matter of why Marx apparently never considered including the reproduction of variable capital (v) alongside the reproduction of constant capital and of the production of the capitalist's profit, in his formula for the rate of surplus value, given that, except in very exceptional cases (i.e. in the case of primitive accumulation, when the capitalist really does 'advance' money to the labour before the process of production actually takes place), the labourers reproduce their wages in the form of variable capital in exactly the same way that they reproduce constant capital. If the renewal of constant capital by labour is to count as part of the production of surplus value for the capitalist even though this part of the surplus does not form part of the capitalist's profit, why then does not the reproduction of variable capital by labour figure as part of the production of surplus value for the capitalist even though this variable capital is eventually paid to the labourers in the form of wages? We will look at this matter in more detail in the next chapter where we will consider Marx's claim that 'the rate of surplus value is … an exact expression of the degree of exploitation of labour-power by capital' (1974a, 209 [1976, 326]). However, at this point, we may say that there seems to be some confusion on this point between a concept of *expropriation* (in which the reproduction of variable capital cannot be included since this is eventually returned to

the labourer in the form of wages) and the concept of *exploitation*, since an adequate conceptualization of the rate of surplus value would seem to require that we take into account the production of all new value by labour, and therefore the reproduction of variable capital by labour, whether or not this is eventually returned to the labourers. As he conceives it, Marx's concept of the rate of surplus value is an exact expression of the concept of the degree of exploitation of labour. The question we will consider in the next chapter is therefore whether Marx's concept of the rate of surplus value is really such a good measure of the degree of exploitation, or whether, alternatively, this concept should be amended in some way to include a measure of the reproduction of an apparently inexhaustible supply of *variable* capital produced by labour for the benefit of capital.

Reading: Essential: *Capital*, Vol. I, Part III, Ch. 9, section 3, 'Senior's Last Hour' (1974a, 215–20 [1976, 333–8]). Background: *Capital*, Vol. III, Part I, Ch. 2–3, (1977, 41–69 [1981, 132–62]), and Part III, Ch. 13–15 (1977, 211–66 [1981, 317–75]). See also Marx's letter to Engels, 30 April 1868 (*MESC*, 1953, 245–50).

16. THE DEGREE OF EXPLOITATION OF LABOUR BY CAPITAL IN *CAPITAL*, VOL. I, CH. 9, SECTION 1; CH. 6–7

In the previous chapter, we saw that when worn-out constant capital is replaced, or as Marx insists produced anew, during the process of production, the rate of surplus value will always be greater, and usually very much greater, than the rate of profit. If we accept that the rate of surplus value is an exact measure of the degree of exploitation of labour, it would seem to follow that Marx is claiming that the degree of exploitation of labour is likely to be very much greater than its apparent measure; the rate of profit. It therefore comes as something of a shock to discover that while Marx equates the rate of surplus value with the degree of exploitation of labour, and does in fact expect the degree of exploitation to be greater than its apparent level, he also claims that the labourer is paid the *full* value of his or her labour-power when he or she is paid the bare *minimum*, or subsistence, cost of reproducing him- or herself. How then is this paradox to be resolved?

The apparent contradiction between these two claims has to do with the very important distinction Marx makes between two quite separate concepts: *labour* (the amount of work that one may perform in a given time, e.g. during one day), and *labour-power* (one's capacity or ability to work). Since there is no necessary correlation between the amount of time it takes to reproduce one's labour-power (one's capacity to work) and the amount of time one may be asked to work *over and above this* (the amount of *labour* one may be asked to perform), there is also no necessary connection between paying a labourer the full value of the cost of reproducing him- or herself *as a labourer* for a given period of time (the value of his or her labour-power) and paying the same labourer the full value of the amount of labour that he or she may perform during a given period of time (the value of his or her labour). When labour and labour-power are exchanged they become commodities – use values that are exchanged – and it is owing to the confusion between these two quite separate commodities that the capitalist is able to pay the labourer the full value of his or her labour-*power* while still paying them less than the full value of the *labour* they might actually perform during the working day.

Since this is such a crucial argument, let us look at this very important distinction between labour and labour-power more closely:

(i) According to Marx, the value of *all* commodities, irrespective of what they might be, is determined by the cost of their reproduction (1974a, 167 [1976, 274]).
(ii) When it is exchanged for wages, labour-power becomes a commodity like any other.
(iii) Therefore the value of labour-power, like the value of any other commodity, must be determined by the cost of its reproduction (which in effect means reproducing the labourer in which this labour-power is embodied).
(iv) In a capitalist society, the time it takes to reproduce the labourer (i.e. in order to ensure his or her own reproduction and renewal) has no necessary relation to the time the labourer may be required to work over and above this for the benefit of the capitalist.
(v) And when the labourer is required to work for longer than it takes to reproduce him- or herself, he or she may well be exploited.
(vi) Exploitation occurs when, instead of keeping the product of one's own labour, someone other than the labourer – for example, a capitalist – keeps at least part of the surplus labour performed (i.e. surplus from the point of view of the labourer).
(vii) To distinguish the value of labour as a commodity (i.e. what it takes to bring the labourer back to work for another day) from the value of the commodities a labourer can produce, for example during one working day, Marx calls the former the value of labour-power (the cost of reproducing the labourer's capacity to work) and the latter the value of labour (the amount of value a labourer can produce, on average, in a given day). And he calls that labour which the labourer expends in order to reproduce him- or herself *necessary labour* (NL), and that labour which the labourer performs over and above what is necessary to reproduce him- or herself *surplus labour* (SL).
(viii) When the capitalist pays the worker ostensibly for the value of a day's *labour*, neither the labourer nor the capitalist are aware of the fact that the capitalist usually only pays the labourer the cost of reproducing him- or herself as a labourer. The labourer only agrees to sell, and the capitalist is therefore only entitled to buy, labour-power (the cost of reproducing the labourer). However, because this commodity is in fact physically inseparable from the person of the labourer in which it is embodied, and

therefore this quantity of labour cannot go to work without the labourer who sold it, the labourer is forced to accompany his or her own labour-power – the very thing which in fact they have sold – to *its* place of work and to work alongside it until long past the point has been reached at which the labourer has satisfied his or her own reproduction. In this way, the labourer is not only forced to accompany the commodity which he or she has already sold to its place of work, but is forced to go along with the will of the capitalist in determining the length of the working day. Having bought the amount of labour from the labourer that is required to reproduce the labourer's person, the capitalist is then able to extract more labour than has actually been paid for and therefore more than they are actually entitled to.

(ix) The trick that the capitalist plays on the labourer – and both the labourer and the capitalist are in fact equally deceived by this – is to get the labourer to work for longer than it takes to reproduce him or her self, so that the labourer continues to work solely for the benefit of the capitalist. In feudal society, the fact that the labourer worked part of the time for the lord of the manor and part of the time for him- or herself was made clear by the arrangement whereby the labourer worked three days of every week on his or her own fields and three days on the lord's fields (with the seventh day off for rest). It was owing to the clarity of this arrangement that the nobility sometimes had to force the peasantry to work for them. However, no such difficulty exists in capitalist society. The labourer is paid a wage for a day's work that both the labourer and the capitalist believe represents the value of a day's labour (the amount of value that a labourer can produce in one day). While the labourer in a capitalist process of production may reproduce his or her capacity to labour for one day (i.e. reproduce his or her wages) during a relatively short part of the working day, there is nothing to stop the capitalist from making the labourer work for the rest of the day for the capitalist's benefit. Indeed, both the capitalist and the labourer expect this to happen, since this was precisely the reason why the capitalist hired the labourer in the first place.

(x) This argument does not involve any claim to the effect that labourers are entitled to the *full* value of the product of the process of production in which they participate. This product includes the value of raw materials and means of production which entered into the process of production before the labourers acted upon them, the value of which is due to the labour of other groups of workers who may or may not have been exploited in their turn. There are then, in effect, *three* distinct categories of value embodied in the finished product of a capitalist process of production: (a) the value the labourer produces in order to reproduce him- or herself, (b) the value the labourer produces over and above this for the benefit of the capitalist, and (c) the value produced by 'dead labour' that already exists in the means of production, and which Marx claims 'living' labour-power merely helps to revivify, or renew the value of, by acting upon it. The labourer we are considering here is only paid the value of the first part of the product of the process of production, although he or she is entitled to be paid the value of the first and second parts of this product, and is not entitled to any part of the value of the third part of this product (which belongs to the capitalist or other exploited labour). It should also be noted here that not every act of labour involves a corresponding act of exploitation. Where, for example, an exceptionally skilled (or for some other reason, temporarily scarce) labourer *is* paid the full value of his labour (as opposed to the full value of his or her labour-power), or where the producer of surplus value works for him- or herself and is not separated from the product of his or her own labour, then no exploitation occurs even though the labourer may work for very much longer than it takes to reproduce him- or herself.

(xi) In conclusion then, it would be wrong to say that the labourer is exploited when he or she is alienated, or separated from, the product of his or her own labour, since the labourer does not *personify* either labour or labour-power. Nor is it true to say that the performance of surplus labour is always an *impersonal* or alienating act for the labourer. On the contrary, the labourer is *intimately* involved in the creation of surplus value – cannot get away from this in fact – and may even be allowed to keep the product of his or her own labour in certain cases. Rather, the labourer's problem is precisely due to the fact that he or she *cannot* alienate themselves from the thing that they have to sell: either from their labour-power or from the performance of this labour-power in the form of labour.

(xii) Exploitation occurs in the capitalist mode of production then *not* when the labourer is alienated from the product of his or her labour, but when the labourer, having agreed to exchange only a certain amount of labour time in order to reproduce him- or herself, is forced to work for longer than it takes to do this. The labourer, then, goes along to the work place *in place* of what they have agreed to sell – in effect they *impersonate* their own labour- power – and exploitation takes place when this occurs (1974a, 180, 196 [1976, 291–2]). Exploitation in the capitalist mode of production is therefore a *tale of two commodities* in which one commodity (labour) goes along to the work place in place of another commodity (labour-power) and impersonates it, and as we have already seen in the previous chapter, it is usually a far, far greater thing that the labourer does for the capitalist than either of them are aware of.

Points for Further Discussion

1. Marx argues that the value of labour-power, like the value of any other commodity, is determined by the cost of *its* reproduction: this is his key argument and the basis of everything else that he says in *Capital*. Somewhat paradoxically, this means that Marx is forced to argue that the labourer is paid the full value of his or her labour-*power* when he or she is paid a subsistence wage, and that, in effect, the value of labour-power is equal to the bare minimum level at which the labourer can reproduce him- or herself. According to Marx,

   > the minimum limit of the value of labour-power is determined by the value of the commodities, without the daily supply of which the labourer cannot renew his vital energy, consequently by the value of those means of subsistence which are physically indispensable … It is a very cheap sort of sentimentality which declares this method of determining the value of labour-power, a method prescribed by the very nature of the case, to be a brutal method. (1974a, 169 [1976, 277])

   However, things are not quite as straightforward here as they may at first seem since Marx includes in his calculation of the *minimum* cost of labour-power all sorts of apparently extraneous social, historical and even moral factors – the normal standard of living in a given country at a particular time – among the most important of which is the biological, or sexual, reproduction of labour-power in the form of the labourer's children:

   > The owner of labour-power is mortal. If then his appearance in the market is to be continuous, and the continuous conversion of money into capital assumes this, the seller of labour-power must perpetuate himself 'in the way that every living individual perpetuates himself, by procreation'. The labour-power withdrawn from the market by wear and tear and death, must be continually replaced by, at the very least, an equal amount of fresh labour-power. Hence the sum of the means of subsistence necessary for the production of labour-power must include the means necessary for the labourer's substitutes, i.e. his children, in order that this race of peculiar commodity-owners may perpetuate its appearance in the market. (1974a, 168 [1976, 275])

The inclusion of the reproduction of the labourer's family – 'so as to live, labour, and [re]generate' as William Petty expressed this point (quoted in *Capital*, Vol. I, 1974a, 297 [1976, 430]) – among the necessary costs of the reproduction of labour-power seems reasonable enough to begin with until we consider that, as John Urry has pointed out, where there is an adequate supply of unemployed labourers, the replacement of worn-out labour can take place on the basis of the simple destruction of living labour-power (Urry 1981, 124). However, some of the other factors Marx includes in the cost of reproducing labour-power are more controversial. For example, he claims that

> the number and extent of … so-called necessary wants, as also the modes of satisfying them, are themselves the product of historical development, and depend therefore to a great extent on the degree of civilization of a country, more particularly on the conditions under which, and consequently on the habits and degree of comfort in which, the class of free labourers has been formed. (1974a, 168 [1976, 275])

And he therefore argues that '*in contradistinction … to the case of other commodities*, there enters into the determination of the value of labour-power a historical and moral element' (1974a, 168 [1976, 275]; emphasis added).

But it simply *cannot* be the case that the habit and degree of comfort, the normal standard of living, of the working class is a *determinant* of the value of labour-power, or that a moral element can be said to enter into the calculation of the value of this commodity, without making it impossible to distinguish the value of labour-power (the cost of reproducing the labourer's capacity to labour) from the value of that labour which the labourer may have a share in due, for example, to the exceptional scarcity of a particular type of labour-power. Marx is correct to say that there is a historical element which enters into the determination of the value of labour-power, but it has nothing to do with the 'degree of civilization' which a particular country has reached, or with any moral assessment of an acceptable standard of living for the working class. Rather, as Marx himself points out, this would seem to have much more to do with things like the level of education which is required in technologically advanced societies to train a skilled workforce (1974a, 168–9 [1976, 276]). This highly educated labour-power must always be of a greater than normal value due to the higher than average cost of its reproduction, and this factor by itself is therefore more than enough to account for the greater than subsistence value of labour-power in technologically advanced societies without any need to resort to explanations in terms of moral considerations. The degree of comfort of the working class in industrialized countries and the moral perception of what this *should* be are thus effects of the high value of specially qualified labour-power and not determinants of its value, while the greater than subsistence value of the labour performed cannot be considered as a determinant of the value of labour-power without undermining the principle that it is the cost of reproducing a particular commodity that determines its value. Contrary to what Marx says therefore, labour-power *cannot* be an exception to this rule.

2. However, if we cannot determine the value of labour-power with any precision – in other words, if it is not fixed at the level of subsistence – then it follows that we cannot determine the degree of exploitation of labour with any precision either. As we have seen, calculating the degree of exploitation is a relatively straightforward matter. Variable capital is expressed as a fraction of surplus value, in which the amount of surplus value produced is equated to the amount of surplus labour performed (with both surplus labour and necessary labour, and therefore also surplus value, being defined in terms of what is necessary for the reproduction of labour-power). Thus, Marx says:

> Since, on the one hand, the values of variable capital and of the labour-power purchased by that capital are equal, and the value of this labour-power determines the necessary portion of the working-day [*sic*]; and since, on the other hand, the surplus value is determined by the surplus portion of the working-day [*sic*], it follows that surplus value bears the same ratio to variable capital, that surplus-labour does to necessary labour, or in other words, the rate of surplus value s/v=surplus labour/necessary labour. Both ratios, s/v and surplus labour/necessary, express the same thing in different ways. (1974a, 209 [1976, 326])

I have already suggested that Marx's conceptualization of the rate of surplus value might be deficient in some way since he does not include variable capital in his calculation of the rate at which labour produces *new* value for the benefit of capital. Although Marx frequently describes the process by which worn-out constant and variable capital is renewed as a process of *reproduction*, this process does not involve the reproduction of any worn-out capital, the value of which is in fact entirely used up and transformed into that of the finished product of the process of production, but simply involves the production of entirely new value which functions in place of both the worn-out constant and variable capital. This is why Marx includes the 'reproduction' of constant capital by labour in his calculation of the creation of new surplus value by labour for the benefit of capital and, as we have seen, this is why the rate of surplus value is normally so much greater than the rate of profit. But if the replacement of worn-out constant capital must be included in the calculation of the rate of surplus value r=(s+c)/v, in order take into account the reproduction of this capital by labour for the benefit of capital, why not include the reproduction of variable capital by labour in the calculation of the rate of surplus value in just the same way, r=(s+c+v)/1, since, except in the case of primitive accumulation (where the master-capitalist really does 'advance' wages to labour prior to the process of production), labour reproduces its own wages during the process of production in just the same way that it reproduces the capitalist's worn-out constant capital? The obvious objection to this argument is that the production of variable capital, although the creation of new value, is necessary for the reproduction of labour-power and therefore cannot be counted as part of the capitalist's surplus value since this is paid directly to labour in the form of wages. But this objection applies equally well to constant capital since the labourer too requires that this should be recreated in order to reproduce the means of production and therefore the objection simply begs the question why surplus value is defined in terms of what is surplus to the requirements of reproducing labour-power, rather than in some other way (e.g. in terms of what is surplus to reproducing the mode of production as a whole).

Although it obviously makes sense to define surplus value in terms of the requirements of reproducing labour-power when calculating the degree of *expropriation* of labour from the ownership of capital (the amount that the capitalist claims to own), it is not at all clear that defining surplus value in this way makes sense when calculating the rate of surplus value or the degree of *exploitation* of labour. Clearly, the capitalist benefits from the reproduction of variable capital – and hence of the labourer's capacity to labour – in just the same way that he or she does from the reproduction of constant capital and hence from the reproduction of the mode of production. On the other hand, it seems irrefutable that labourers are exploited when they are overworked *whether or not any surplus value is actually produced by their labour.* Further, where the capitalist has an interest in the continuous reproduction of constant capital, labour too would seem to have a similar interest in the continuous reproduction of the means of production and, therefore, of variable capital (i.e. wages). Unless therefore it is claimed that labourers' interest in the reproduction of constant capital is entirely taken into account in the form of the variable capital that is paid to the labourers by the capitalist (and this is indeed what Marx seems to have thought) then it must be the case that the labourers too share in the benefit to be derived from the continuous reproduction of constant capital, even though they do not share in the ownership of the means of production as such. If this is the case, then the degree of exploitation of labour must be significantly less than the rate of surplus value where (a) the degree of exploitation includes a measure of the labourers' interest in the reproduction of constant capital [$r=(s+c)/(v+c')$], and where (b) the rate of surplus value includes some recognition of the capitalist's interest in the continuous reproduction of variable capital [$r=(s+c+v)/1$].

On the one hand then, while the rate of surplus value must be much greater than the degree of exploitation where it is accepted that the capitalist has an interest in the continuous reproduction of variable capital, it seems clear that the degree of exploitation must be much less than the rate of surplus value where labour has an interest in the continuous reproduction of constant capital. While, on the other hand, it seems that there is no very good reason to identify the degree of exploitation with the production of surplus value in the first place, where what is 'surplus' to the requirements of reproducing labour-power does not seem to be an especially good way of defining what one means by surplus value.

Reading: Essential: *Capital*, Vol. I, Ch. 6 (1974a, 164–72 [1976, 270–80); Ch. 7 (1974a, 173–92 [1976, 283–306]), Ch. 9, section 1 (1974a; 204–12 [1976, 320–29]). Background: István Mészáros, *Marx's Theory of Alienation*, especially Part II, Ch. 4.

17. THE LABOUR THEORY OF VALUE AND THE VALUE THEORY OF LABOUR IN *CAPITAL*, VOL. I, CH. 1, SECTIONS 1–3

It is commonplace today, even among people who have never read Marx's *Capital*, to believe that Marx shared a broadly similar theory of value to that developed by classical political economists; namely, that which has come to be known as 'the labour theory of value'. However, I wish to suggest that this is *not* the case and that any such interpretation which presents Marx's view as a labour theory of value (or even as a more sophisticated version of this) is a very bad misreading of what Marx has to say in the first few chapters of *Capital*, Vol I. In making this claim I am basing my argument on the reading I have just presented in the previous chapter of this study. In trying to explain the difference between labour and labour-power Marx is forced to discuss the value of labour itself. This then gives the impression that his is a sophisticated labour theory of value when in actual fact he was a critic of this theory. The argument that labour is the source of all value (i.e. a crude labour theory of value of the kind presented by Adam Smith and David Ricardo) depends on an equally crude antithesis between nature and labour. In fact however, as Marx points out in the *Critique of the Gotha Programme* (*MESW*, 1968, 315), labour is not separate from nature, but is itself a *manifestation* of this: labour in the form of human labour-power is a force of nature too. Once this antithesis is resolved – in other words, once we realize that labour is natural too – we can see the actual basis of Marx's theory of value and in what way it differs from a crude labour theory.

In making the apparently startling claim that Marx's theory of value is not a labour theory I am not saying anything that has not been said before. Geoffrey Pilling, for example, has argued that 'this notion – of a "labour theory of value" in Marx – is at best confusing and at worst quite wrong' (Pilling 1980, 41); while, in place of a crude theory of value in which labour is not only said to be the *measure* of all value, but also its *creator*, Diane Elson has argued that what we require is not a labour theory of value of any kind, but rather what she calls a 'value theory of labour' (a theory of what it means to say that labour has, or can create, value). Furthermore, in order to be able to measure the value of labour itself, both Pilling and Elson have, in slightly different ways, attempted to identify the substance of value itself – and therefore the basis of such a theory of the value of labour – with much the same thing: *social* or *abstract* human labour, or labour *in general*, rather than the labour of any particular individual (Pilling 1980, 45; Elson 1979, 159–60).

In what follows I will support the argument that Marx's theory of value represents a radical departure from the views of Adam Smith or David Ricardo, but I will go further than either Pilling or Elson in claiming that Marx's theory of value is *not* based on labour at all (whether 'abstract', 'social', 'general' or otherwise), but rather involves some idea of what it means to say that something has value *in or of itself* (and therefore without needing to reduce our understanding of what *this* something is to something else, the nature of which would then have to be explained in its turn). In short, I disagree with Pilling and Elson's claim that abstract labour is the *substance* of value. Abstract labour is not the substance of value I think, but is merely the sum of that *part of value* which is added to things by labour, the *substance* of which is already to be found in *nature* in the form of raw materials which human labour acts upon and in which such value is then embodied. Unless that value which already exists in nature *independently* of human labour (the value of a tree, for example, before it is turned into wood, or of grassland before this is cultivated) is said to be valueless, then labour – abstract, general or otherwise – cannot be the substance of *all* value, or even the substance of that part of value which is created by labour. On the contrary, value created by labour must be embodied in something and that thing must already have some form before it is acted upon by labour. The substance of all values is use values – nothing is valuable which is not useful – and the substance of value added by labour is the use values that already exist in nature and of which human labour is a part. As Marx says at the very beginning of *Capital*, Vol. I, 'Human labour-power in motion, or human labour, creates value, *but is not itself value*. It becomes value only in its congealed state, when embodied in the form of some object' (1974a, 57 [1976, 142]; emphasis added). Labour cannot possibly be the basis of a Marxist theory of value therefore, not only because labour is not the substance of value, but also because the value of labour, like the value of anything else, cannot meaningfully be expressed in terms of itself. If labour was the basis of all value then the one thing that could *not* be expressed in terms of a labour theory of value would be the value of labour *itself* – which was of course the very thing that Marx was most keen to understand.

In order to develop a sophisticated concept of the value of labour then, Marx's theory of value – properly understood – cannot be reduced in any way to an understanding of the value of something other than the concept of value itself (i.e. of what it means to say that something has value), and this concept certainly cannot be expressed in terms of the value of labour itself. What is required therefore is not a concept of labour as a measure of value, or even a theory of the value of labour, but a concept of the nature of value which is not reducible to something else. As Marx says on this point: 'The problem of an "invariable measure of value" was simply a spurious name for the quest for the concept, the nature, of *value* itself, the definition of which could not be another value' (Marx 1972, 134; emphasis original).[3] Fortunately, the basis of *just* such a sophisticated theory of value is to be found in the first nine chapters of Vol. I. Here, as we have already seen, Marx argues that it is not labour or labour-power that determines the value of every other commodity, but rather *the cost of reproducing something* (commodities and non-commodities alike) that determines the value of labour-power itself. It is therefore the cost of reproducing something – what it would cost to make something anew – that is the basis of the Marxist theory of value and this applies equally to the value of labour or labour-power as it does to anything else. When therefore Marx discusses the value of labour, it is natural that he does so in terms of what appear to be a labour theory of value, just as when he is discussing the value of commodities he does this in terms of their exchange value rather than their use value. But this does not mean that Marx is presenting us with a labour theory of value here, any more than it means that all use values are commodities when he is discussing the value of commodities.

It is only too easy to argue that there is no such thing as a universal or absolute standard of value 'in the real world', or that, at best, the concept of value is nothing more than a 'scholastic invention of economists'.[4] However, this assertion seems to contradict the intuitive notion we have that some things *do* indeed have more value than others. The real problem then is not how to do away with the concept of value, but how to explain what it is we mean when we say that one thing has value while something else has little or none. According to Marx, in order to establish the basis of a theory of value it is necessary first of all to identify a common denominator, so that the value of unlike *qualities* can be made commensurable and compared *quantitatively*. Thus, in the first chapter of Vol. I, section 3, he gives the example of the value of 20 yards of linen compared to that of one coat. In themselves, the value of any number of yards of linen cannot be directly compared with the value of any number of coats. There is nothing about coats or linen by which we can meaningfully compare the magnitude of their values, in the way that for example we might compare the value of 10 yards of linen to that of 20 yards of linen of the same quality and arrive at the conclusion that 20 yards of the linen are worth twice as much as 10 yards. In order to be able to say that one coat is worth 20 yards of linen, Marx argues that the value of one of these commodities must be expressed relatively in terms of the other such that the other commodity becomes an equivalent expression of the first. If, for example, we say that the value of one coat is worth 20 yards of linen, the 20 yards of linen become the equivalent expression of the relative value of the coat. On the other hand, if we say that the value of 20 yards of linen is one coat, then the value of the linen is expressed relatively in terms of the value of the coat which then becomes the equivalent expression. In this case, it does not matter very much which commodity acts as the equivalent form of value or which commodity's value is expressed relatively. Coats and linen, however, are not especially suitable commodities to act as the equivalent expression of the value of all other commodities generally, both because the quality of coats and linen may vary from one case to another, and because the value of both these commodities is not especially durable. Eventually therefore certain commodities, such as salt and ivory, or gold and silver, which either have a more durable material form and a relative value that can be more easily measured, come to stand as the equivalent expression of the values of all other commodities generally, until such time that one of them comes to assume the form of the universal expression of the relative values of all other commodities; that is to say, *money*. We can then measure the relative value of all other commodities, one against another, in terms of their equivalent expression as so many units of money. However, as the universal equivalent of the value of all other commodities, Marx argues that, in itself, money comes to be seen as having no value in its pure form, i.e. as money as such (1974a, 54–75 [1976, 138–63]).

This argument about the relative nature of the value of commodities raises a number of problems for Marx's theory of value. If the value of all commodities is only relative, one to another, then it might well be the case not only that all values are relative but that there are different standards of value – moral, aesthetic and personal for example – such that diamonds or gold are worth one thing to one person while one's family or peace and quiet are worth something else altogether to another? Of course, it may be objected here that Marx's theory of value is not intended to encompass aesthetic or moral values; it is merely an economic concept of the value of commodities, and especially of labour as a commodity. But any such argument would have to ignore what Marx has to say about the moral value of labour-power in highly industrialized societies and would seem to accept the argument that different standards of value cannot be compared. Further, while Marx's concept of value may not have been intended to account for the value one attaches to one's children, Marx clearly *did* expect his theory to be able to account for the high value that is generally attributed to something like diamonds (1974a, 44, 47–8 [1976, 126, 130–31]). If then one can explain the value of diamonds in terms of Marx's theory, can one also account for the value of a great work of art, which after all is only intrinsically made up of paper, stone or paint? And if one can account for the value of a work of art, then why not the value of one's parents or one's children?

If it were possible to establish a universal concept of value this would clearly be an advance over a theory which asserts that different standards of value are incommensurable. What then is the common denominator in terms of which we can establish, if not an invariable measure of value, then at the very least a meaningful idea of the nature of value itself? It is not money. Money, in whatever material form it takes, gives us an accurate measure of the different magnitudes of the value of these commodities. However, it does not by itself tell us anything about their value, since when we attribute different monetary values (i.e. prices) to commodities we are taking for granted the very thing we are trying to establish here; namely, that we *already know* the equivalent value of the commodities in question. What then of labour or labour-power? Might these provide us with a suitable basis with which to understand the concept of value? As we have already seen, a crude labour theory of value measures the value of different commodities in terms of the amounts of labour embodied in them. This measure of value will certainly tell us why one commodity is worth more than another, and is therefore perfectly acceptable, when what we are comparing is the different amounts of value *added* to commodities by 'living' labour (e.g. in the case of the working up of raw materials into new products, or putting these products together in the form of components of something else, or in the distribution and exchange of the finished product itself). But, as I have already indicated, this measure of value is not particularly useful to us where what we want to measure is the value of labour itself or even the value added to something by living labour compared to the value of raw materials and the contribution made to the value of raw materials by 'dead' (or past) labour. However, even if we put the question of the value embodied in raw materials to one side, labour time still does not seem to be an especially useful way to measure the value of certain rare or precious commodities. If I find an uncut diamond lying on the ground at my feet, the value of that diamond is obviously not a reflection of the amount of labour embodied in it when I bend down to pick it up, or even the additional labour time spent in cutting and polishing it or in taking it to market in order to sell it. Similarly, labour time does not seem to be an especially good measure of the value of a painting by Leonardo da Vinci compared to the time it would take someone else to produce the same painting. Of course, in the case of the painting by Leonardo da Vinci, it may be said that we are comparing labour-power of different values when we compare the skill of a Leonardo to that of any other painter. But can the cost of *reproducing* Leonardo da Vinci's labour power really account for the difference in value of the product of his work and that of another painter, since any such reproduction, however well done, would always be regarded as having much less value than the original? Similarly in the case of diamonds, it is the diamond produced by a sophisticated mining process that is the product of the more highly skilled labour (and which therefore should be more valuable according to a labour theory of value), rather than the much larger diamond I find at my feet by chance. Rather it is the fact that diamonds are relatively rare, and hence hard to come by, or that Leonardo da Vinci's paintings are *literally* irreplaceable, that seems to make them so valuable.

What then of a more sophisticated labour theory of value in which it is claimed that the value of any particular commodity is determined by the *average* amount of socially necessary labour required to produce it? Might not the average amount of labour time spent on discovering, mining, processing, polishing and distributing diamonds generally account for their very high value, as Marx seems to suggest in the first chapter of Vol. I (1974a, 47 [1976, 129–30])? After all, the diamond I find by chance is of no greater or lesser value than a diamond of equal weight and purity which is the product of a highly sophisticated labour process. But to argue that the value of a diamond which is not the product of a sophisticated labour process is determined by the high cost of producing diamonds generally is to imply that the value of diamonds would fall to little or nothing if the production of diamonds produced by mining was to come to an end, since the cost of producing diamonds by mining would no longer be taken into account when calculating the average cost of their production. In fact, the opposite would seem to be that case. It is more likely that the value of those diamonds still in circulation would rise due to their relative scarcity. Further, even if a more sophisticated labour theory of value could account for the price of diamonds in terms of their average cost of production, it seems clear enough that such a theory still could not account for the value of certain rare or precious commodities. Even if we were to take into account the history of Western art up to the time of the Italian Renaissance, and were to try to argue that Leonardo da Vinci's talent was merely the highest expression of this development, we still would not be able to claim that the value of a painting by Leonardo is a reflection of the average cost of producing works of art of this kind.

Of course, it may still be argued that the high cost of a diamond or a work of art is not a reflection of its value at all, but merely of its market *price* (i.e. what people are willing to pay for it) and that a Marxist theory of value is not intended to account for the transformation of value into prices. This may well be the case; however, before accepting this proposition, there is one other possibility that should be considered here which has the advantage of being able to consider sympathetically both a Marxist theory of the value of labour and a rival theory which claims that it is the relative scarcity or rarity of a commodity that determines its value. This is if we modify Marx's argument slightly here and argue that it is not labour time or the scarcity of a particular commodity, or even the cost of reproducing something, that determines its value, but rather that it is the *degree of ease or difficulty with which something can be reproduced* that determines its value.

According to Marx, 'the value of labour-power is determined, as in the case of every other commodity, by the labour-time [*sic*] necessary for the production, and consequently also the reproduction, of this special article' (1974a, 167 [1976, 274]).[5] However, as we have already seen, Marx also argues that no commodity can stand in relation to itself as the equivalent expression of its own value (1974a, 62 [1976, 148]). Therefore neither labour, nor labour time, can stand as the equivalent expression of its own value, any more than diamonds can meaningfully express the value of diamonds or linen can meaningfully express the value of linen (1974a, 55 [1976, 140]). It is not labour time, then, that determines the value of all other commodities, but rather the cost of reproducing these commodities *measured* in terms of labour time that determines their value, and this is especially the case when something *cannot* be reproduced (recreated) and therefore is literally priceless. Diamonds are valuable, not because of the amount of labour embodied in them generally, or even because they are scarce, but because they cannot *easily* be reproduced and the larger the stone the more this is the case. Similarly, apart from its intrinsic value (by which I mean that it must be first thought of as a work of art and as something which we like to look at), a painting by Leonardo do Vinci is especially valuable precisely because it cannot be reproduced *at all*. Marx is correct to say that if we could succeed in converting carbon into diamonds, the value of diamonds might well fall below that of bricks (1974a, 48 [1976, 130–31]), but this would have nothing especially to do with any reduction in the amount of labour embodied in the production of diamonds, as Marx seemed to think, but would be solely influenced by the ease or difficulty with which the transmutation of carbon into diamonds could be effected (i.e. by the availability of carbon, by the cost of installing and maintaining the means of production, and by the running costs of the process of production itself, including the cost of labour involved in this process). Similarly, a great deal of labour goes into the production of motor cars, but cars are still relatively cheap, not because of the relatively small amount of labour embodied in them, but because commodities which are mass produced are more or less identical and because one car is therefore as easy to (re)produce as the next.

On the other hand, a vintage car or a painting by Leonard da Vinci is very valuable, not because they are scarce or because of the amount of labour embodied in their production, but because they simply cannot be reproduced at all. My children are highly valuable to me, not because of the amount of labour time embodied in their production but because I could not reproduce them at all, *not even if I started another family*. However, my children are of no particular value to anyone else, not because they are not unique or because they did not cost very much to produce (and children are very expensive to produce as every parent knows), but because, for most people and for most purposes, one child is much the same as any other. Finally, a painting by Leonardo da Vinci is more valuable than a painting by me, not because the Mona Lisa is more scarce or more rare than my painting – all paintings are equally unique, just as are all children – but because almost anyone could produce a painting of the same quality as mine while no one, *not even Leonard da Vinci*, can reproduce the Mona Lisa.

Points for Further Discussion

1. The idea of a labour theory of value did not originate with Marx, or even with David Ricardo or Adam Smith. During the period before the French Revolution a number of writers developed a crude form of this theory in opposition to the writings of Francois Quesnay and a school of French economists known as the Physiocrats, who claimed that since the inherent natural order governing society was based on land, the natural products of land were the only true source of all wealth. Thus, according to Michel Beaud, Rousseau argues that 'it is impossible to conceive of the idea of property arising from anything except manual labour, because one cannot see what man can add, other than his own labour, in order to appropriate things he has not made'. Linguet, a publicist and lawyer, argues that 'it is not wealth that is the source of life for the "hired man"; it is the life of the "hired man" that creates the opulence of the rich'. While Turgot, although greatly influenced by the Physiocrats, sought to discover the truth underlying their most basic claim. 'What', he asks, 'gives value to the lands, if not the number of their inhabitants?' (Beaud 1984, 56–9). Similarly, Adam Smith, who knew Quesnay personally, argued that 'labour [is] the real measure of the exchangeable value of all commodities' (Smith 1986, 133) but is not the basis of value itself (the all important point for Smith in determining the value of a commodity being the amount of labour that a commodity could be *exchanged* for, rather than the amount of labour that had gone into its production). While David Ricardo criticized Smith's view that labour was not only the *measure* of value but also its basis. As Ricardo

says on this point on the very first page of his major work, *Principles of Political Economy and Taxation*:

> The value of a commodity, or the quantity of any other commodity for which it will exchange, depends on the relative quantity of labour which is necessary for its production, and not on the greater or less compensation which is paid for that labour. (Ricardo 1971, 55)

As we have seen, Marx's writings on value are generally seen as a continuation and an extension of the Ricardian school of thought, in which Marx replaces Ricardo's rather crude labour theory of value with a more sophisticated version in terms of abstract human labour or socially necessary labour time. Thus, in *Capital*, Vol. I, for example, Marx argues that:

> We see then that that which determines the magnitude of the value of any article is the amount of labour *socially* necessary, or the labour time socially necessary for its production. Each individual commodity, in this connection, is to be considered as an average sample of its class. (1974a, 47 [1976, 129–30]; emphasis added)

Elsewhere, Marx puts this same argument a slightly different way:

> [W]e [must] bear in mind that the value of commodities has a purely social reality, and that they acquire this reality only in so far as they are expressions or embodiments of one identical social substance, viz., human labour. (1974a, 54 [1976, 138–9])

However, things are not quite as straightforward as they may seem here and this is because it is necessary to make a distinction between those occasions when Marx talks about labour as a *measure* of the value of any article, and when he talks about labour as the *basis* of all values. We must also be careful to distinguish between Marx's discussion of the value of *commodities* – use values which are exchanged for something else – and when he talks about those use values which are not exchanged. The value of all *commodities* may well have a purely social reality – the exchange of commodities is after all an unavoidably social activity – but this is not to say that all things which have *value* are commodities or have a purely social existence, any more than it would be correct to say that labour is the basis of all value simply because a given amount of labour time of a certain quality can act as a measure of the comparative value of all things. But what of the example quoted above, and others like it, where Marx seems to be saying that the amount of socially necessary labour is not only a measure of the magnitude of value, but actually *determines* this, and where he is not only talking about the magnitude of the value of commodities but of all other things. Surely he is presenting a sophisticated labour theory of value here? I think a good case can be made out here for saying that Marx is merely claiming that labour is a measure of the value of all things – that it is something which can be used to determine the magnitude of the value of any article – but not that he is claiming that socially necessary labour is the *determinant* of the value of all things. It is significant here, I think, that Marx does not make any distinction between the value of commodities and non-commodities, something he is normally very careful to do (see below). On the other hand, it must be said that this is one of the very few occasions when Marx's object is not to try to establish the value of labour and labour-power, but where he does clearly say that it is the amount of socially necessary labour time that determines the magnitude of the value of every commodity other than labour. But, however things are with Marx, I think we can say that there is the basis of a more comprehensive, and therefore a better, theory of value to be found in his writings on the concept of value than that which is usually presented in his name; namely, one that claims that something is more or less valuable according to the degree of ease or difficulty with which it can be reproduced and that it is therefore unnecessary for contemporary Marxists to restrict themselves to a labour theory of value however sophisticated this might be, when we might instead characterize Marx's theory of value as a value theory of labour.

2. As I suggested in the introduction to this chapter, the crucial point in attempting to evaluate the claims of a labour theory of value (and really therefore the whole basis of the difference between a sophisticated labour theory of value and a fully developed value theory of labour) is the question of whether or not any such thing as value exists *in nature* independent of or prior to the activity of human labour. *If* value does exist in nature in this way, human labour (whether individually, socially, or in the form of socially necessary labour, abstract labour, or labour in general) simply cannot be the basis of *all* value, albeit we would still want to argue that labour is the basis of all value *added* to nature and therefore the basis of all *surplus* value. Marx devoted a considerable amount of his attention to this question, most famously in a short pamphlet now known as the *Critique of the Gotha Programme* in which he argues that

> Labour is *not the source* of all wealth. *Nature* is just as much the source of use value (and it is surely of such that material wealth consists!) as labour, which itself is only the manifestation of a force of nature,

> human labour power. (*MESW*, 1969, 3:13; also Pilling 1980, 45; emphasis original)

Similarly, in *Capital*, Vol. I, section 2, Marx argues that:

> The use values, coat, linen, &c. [*sic*], i.e. the bodies of commodities, are combinations of two elements – matter and labour. If we take away the useful labour expended upon them, a material substratum is always left, which is furnished by Nature without the help of man. The latter can work only as Nature does, that is by changing the form of matter. Nay more, in this work of changing the form he is constantly helped by natural forces. We see, then, that *labour is not the only source of material wealth*, of use values produced by labour. As William Petty puts it, labour is its father and the earth its mother. (1974a, 50 [1976, 133–4]; emphasis added)

However, just two pages before the above quotation, Marx writes:

> A thing can be a use value *without having value.* This is the case whenever its utility to man is not due to labour. Such are air, virgin soil, natural meadows, etc. (1974a, 48 [1976, 131]; emphasis added)

What then are we to make of the apparent contradiction between this quotation and the two above? How can something be described as a use *value* which is said not to have any value itself? Surely what Marx means to say here is that such things have no exchange value, for how can nature be a source of material wealth and of the use values which he says are the substance of this wealth, without having any value in itself? Presumably what Marx means here is that it is only because they are acted upon by labour that the products of nature have value and come to be seen as 'material wealth'. But it is difficult to see how Marx could sustain this argument when he says in the *Critique of the Gotha Programme* that the usual antithesis between nature and labour (and, incidentally, also the usual dichotomy between nature and society) is misleading (*MESW*, 1968: 315); labour too is natural and therefore every bit as much a 'force of nature' as land and water, or for that matter air and diamonds.

There is however another possibility open to us here and this is simply to say that Marx is wrong when he says that something can be a use value and yet not have any value in itself. In addressing the question of the value of utilities that are not the product of human labour, Marx considers a problem that had already been identified by Smith in a celebrated passage from *The Wealth of Nations*:

> The word value, it is to be observed, *has two different meanings*, and sometimes expresses the utility of some particular object, and sometimes the power of purchasing other goods which the possession of that object conveys. The one may be called 'value in use'; the other, 'value in exchange'. The things which have the greatest value in use have frequently little or no value in exchange; and, on the contrary, those which have the greatest value in exchange have frequently little or no value in use. Nothing is more useful than water: but it will purchase scarce anything; scarce anything can be had in exchange for it. A diamond, on the contrary, has scarce any value in use; but a very great quantity of other goods may frequently be had in exchange for it. (Smith 1986, 132; emphasis added)

Ricardo, who quotes this passage at the beginning of his *Principles of Political Economy and Taxation*, agrees with Smith that it is not the utility of a particular object that determines its value and, like Marx, mainly confines himself to discussing the value of commodities which he attributes to labour. However, unlike Marx, Ricardo argues that there are some commodities whose value is determined by their scarcity alone (Ricardo 1971, 56), while Marx, as we have seen, argues that the value of even very rare commodities like diamonds is determined exclusively by the average amount of socially necessary labour required for their production. However, the fact that Ricardo agrees with Marx that it is labour that determines the *additional* value of commodities over and above their value as utilities does not mean that some things cannot have value already before that value which is then added by labour, while some other things might still be said to have use value (i.e. value in nature) without having any exchange value. Where Ricardo is mistaken however is in identifying the scarcity of these commodities, rather than their *reproducibility*, as the factor which determines their value. Commodities, or use values of any kind, are not valuable because they are scarce but are scarce because they are difficult to reproduce. The value of virgin land, for example, does not increase in proportion to the amount of labour embodied in it over time, this value being taken out of the soil each year in the form of the product of this labour. Land which is used *loses* value over time if a certain amount of labour is not spent on replacing (i.e. reproducing) the nutrients removed from the soil. Nor is the value of this land determined by the value of the labour that is socially necessary for its exploitation, although the value of this labour does determine the value of the product of this labour, and therefore the value of the product of the land. Similarly, it cannot be said that the value of land is determined by its increasing scarcity or even by its relative scarcity, although there is obviously a direct relationship between the density of population (the ratio of land to labour) and the *price* of land, with the price of land increasing in direct proportion to the increasing density of population. Rather, it is the fact that there is only so much land to go round that makes land first something of value, and secondly, a commodity. Where land can be had for no more labour than it takes to clear a piece of ground and plant crops on it, it is worth nothing more than the value of this labour (which in this case, therefore, does indeed determine the value of the land), but where it is plentiful such land cannot be exchanged as a commodity. But as soon as no more land is to be found in this way, what land there is acquires a value, not because of its scarcity (it is no more scarce than it ever was, not even relatively speaking, and in fact land may be in plentiful supply and more than adequate to meet the needs of feeding the entire population, but still have a high value) but because the supply of land is finite and simply cannot be reproduced at all. Similarly, where they are plentiful, water and the air we breath are of little or no value at the moment, despite the fact that they are both vital for the reproduction of human life, not because they are plentiful or because they require little or no labour to reproduce but because they virtually reproduce themselves. However, as soon as air or water became in short supply (due to pollution, for example, or climate change), then they would increase in value according to the degree of ease or difficulty with which they could be *reproduced* and of course, where they could not be reproduced at all, they would be literally invaluable.

3. Finally, before we leave the question of why those things which have the greatest value in use frequently have little or no value in exchange, we might briefly look at the other side of this question; namely, why those things which frequently have little or no value in use have the greatest value in exchange. Marx argues that the value of diamonds is determined in the same way as any other commodity, by the amount of socially necessary labour embodied in the production of diamonds generally. As he says on this point, 'Diamonds are of very rare occurrence on the earth's surface, and hence their discovery costs, on an average, a great deal of labour time' (1974a, 47 [1976, 130]). However, as we have already seen, Marx also claims that if we could produce diamonds artificially their value might fall dramatically: 'If we could succeed at a small expenditure of labour, in converting carbon into diamonds, their value might fall below that of bricks' (1974a, 48 [1976, 130–31]).

Interestingly enough – and if he were still alive today Marx himself would have been *very* interested in this indeed – it *is* now possible to convert carbon into diamonds at a fraction of the cost of the real thing, but this has not led to the fall in the value of diamonds that Marx anticipated. This is because, although cubic zirconia, or CZ 1.7 as it is known, is several thousand times cheaper to produce than genuine diamonds and is indistinguishable from diamond in appearance, it is much heavier than diamond (1.7 times in fact; and hence its name) and therefore cannot be passed off as the real thing. If CZ 1.7 and diamonds were identical in appearance, weight and in the uses to which they could be put, then it is indisputable that the price of diamonds would fall to that of cubic zirconia. But the question remains whether this fall in the price of diamonds would be a reflection of their fall in value, given that they cost just as much to produce as before, or some other factor, e.g. a glut in the market for diamonds. Marx implies that it is the fall in the absolute mass of labour employed (rather than a fall in the value of labour itself) that would lead to the dramatic fall in the value of diamonds in this case, and it is no doubt true that, other things being equal, as one of the most important factors in the cost of production of diamonds a fall in the magnitude of labour employed would lead to a fall in the value of the product of that labour. But I would still claim that it is not the fall in the mass of the labour employed in this case that would lead to a fall in the value of diamonds, but rather a fall in the difficulty of reproducing diamonds that would lead to a fall in the mass of labour employed. It is not the value of the labour employed in the production of diamonds that determines their value therefore, but rather the ease or difficulty of producing diamonds that determines the mass of labour employed in producing them, and hence determines the value of the diamonds themselves.

Reading: Essential: *Capital*, Vol. I, Ch. 1–3 (1974a, 43–144 [1976, 125–244]). Background: *Theories of Surplus. Value*, Vol. III, Ch. 20 (1969, 133–9); A. Schmidt, *The Concept of Nature in Marx*.

18. THE REIFICATION OF COMMODITY FETISHISM IN *CAPITAL*, VOL. I, CH. 1, SECTION 4, AND VOL. III, CH. 24

We cannot leave our discussion of the first nine chapters of *Capital*, Vol. I without looking at what is perhaps the most difficult to understand and really enigmatic section of any chapter in the whole of *Capital*; even more difficult than the first few chapters of *Capital* on the subject of value. I am referring to section 4 of Chapter 1, Vol. I, entitled 'The Fetishism of Commodities and the Secret Thereof' (1974a, 76–87 [1976, 163–77]). Following Georg Lukács deservedly famous essay entitled 'Reification and the Consciousness of the Proletariat' (*History and Class Consciousness*, 1971, 83–222), most discussion of commodity fetishism has been in terms of Lukács' concept of reification, and has focused on the question of 'false' consciousness (i.e. the alleged failure of the working class to develop a revolutionary class consciousness) and/or the question of realism: the level of reality that is said to underlie the appearance of things. In what follows I will adopt a very different approach to this question partly because I will be concerned to present a close textual analysis of Marx's discussion of commodity fetishism in *Capital*, Vol. I (especially the first four pages, 1974a, 76–9 [1976, 163–8]), but mainly because I will argue that Marx's concept of commodity fetishism has nothing at all to do with the question of the false consciousness of the working class or with Lukács' concept of reification. When one reifies something one treats something which is abstract, social or ideal as though it was merely thing-like, concrete or non-social. However, when one fetishizes something one attributes to something which really is a thing (e.g. high-heeled shoes or a totem pole) the quality of being more than just a thing and, specifically, of being social, sexual or spiritual. When we fetishize commodities therefore, we do not *falsely* attribute a social relationship between people at work to a relationship between things, as Lukács claims, but, on the contrary, we attribute to something which really is a thing (in this case a commodity) the property of having a spiritual reality or a social or sexual existence over and above its thing-like appearance. It is important to note here that this is not to suggest that the concept of reification is itself in any way 'false' or mistaken – this would be to reify the concept itself – but it is simply to say that Lukács was mistaken in believing that this was the concept that Marx was trying to describe in *Capital*.

In what follows therefore, I will argue:

(i) That commodities are things that really do have a social existence over and above their merely thing-like form and that what Marx means us to understand by the term 'the fetishism of commodities' is therefore the attribution to commodities of a social level of reality beyond their every day existence as things.
(ii) That, according to Marx, the whole secret of commodity fetishism is precisely that, contrary to what Lukács claimed and however 'fantastic' this idea might seem to be, commodities really do have a social existence in the process of circulation and in the part they play in exchange; it is *in fact* commodities that interact with each other on the world stage and not the people who produce these commodities.
(iii) That people at work do not in fact have a very significant *social* relationship with one another beyond those relationships which are mediated by the exchange of commodities (including the reproduction of themselves *as* commodities and the exchange of their own labour-power with their employer).
(iv) And that, in so far as the fetishism of commodities has any bearing at all on the question of the consciousness of the working class, people do not form social classes, and do not develop a revolutionary class consciousness, not because they *falsely* attribute a fantastic social existence to things – as Lukács apparently believed – but because they *correctly* perceive the limited nature of their social situation at work and the limited opportunity for class association that this provides them with.

In short, I will argue that, for Marx, commodities *really do* have a social existence in the process of circulation, while people at work do *not* have any very great social relations with each other, other than those which are mediated by commodities, and that paradoxically, it is therefore Lukács who *fetishizes* the relations of people at work when he attributes to them a social reality which they do not in fact possess and who *reifies* the concept of commodity fetishism when he denies that commodities have a social existence and treats them as mere 'things'.

According to Lukács,

> the essence of commodity-structure has often been pointed out. Its basis is that a relation, between people takes on the character of a thing and thus acquires a 'phantom objectivity', an autonomy that seems so strictly

> rational and all-embracing as to conceal every trace of its fundamental nature: the relation between people. (1971, 83)

And Lukács quotes the following passage from Marx's description of commodity fetishism in *Capital*, Vol. I to support this concept of reification:

> A commodity is therefore a mysterious thing, simply because in it the social character of men's labour appears to them as an objective character stamped upon the product of that labour; because the relation of the producers to the sum total of their own labour is presented to them as a social relation, existing not between themselves, but between the products of their labour. This is the reason why the products of labour become commodities, *social things* whose qualities are at the same time perceptible and imperceptible by the senses … It is [only] a definite social relation between men that assumes, in their eyes, the fantastic form of a relation between things. (Marx 1974a, 77 [1976, 164–5], cited in Lukacs 1971, 86; emphasis added)[6]

Lukács claims that Marx describes 'the basic phenomenon of reification' in this passage, which involves attributing thing-like qualities to abstract, social or ideal/spiritual phenomena. Thus, according to Lukács, what Marx is saying here is that the product of labour (and therefore of the social existence of people at work) takes on the appearance of a phantom objectivity in its commodity form such that what they produce seems to be entirely independent of their control by virtue of its autonomy from them (i.e. by virtue of its objectification). But, in fact, this is *not* what Marx says here and, elsewhere in the section on commodity fetishism, Marx makes it quite clear that he is not describing the phenomenon of reification at all, but something else altogether. According to Marx, commodities do not merely take on the *appearance* of having a social existence (fetishism) or of being thing-like (reification), but they really are thing-like and they really do have a social existence. They really are, as he says, '*social things*', some of whose qualities are perceptible by the senses (such as that of being things), while some of these qualities are not (such as that of being the embodiment of the social character of labour). And since, according to Marx commodities *really do* have a social existence, it cannot possibly be the case when he says there is 'a definite social relation between men, that assumes, in their eyes, the fantastic form of a relation between things' that he means that commodities have a fantastic (i.e. phantasmagorical) appearance *and* that this appearance is *false* (as Lukács believed). Marx can only mean one of two things: either (a) commodities really *do* have a fantastic existence in the part they play in the process of circulation, and that therefore the *appearance* that commodities have of seeming to have a social existence, though fantastic, is nevertheless *correct*, or (b) although it seems fantastic to the producers of commodities ('in their eyes', as he says) that the product of their labour should have a social existence separate from the producers of these commodities, this is nevertheless the way things are as far as commodity production is concerned. The important point to understand here is that it is no part of Marx's thesis to argue that capitalist relations of production are in any way rational or straightforward. On the contrary, Marx claims that the relations of production within a *capitalist* mode of production are grotesque in the extreme and that they therefore assume a correspondingly grotesque or fantastic appearance in reality. In other words, we cannot simply 'read-off' reality from the appearances of things in the CMP, but neither should we assume that the appearances of things are simply false. In fact it is only by interpreting the appearances of things that we can gain any understanding of the nature of reality underlying appearances.

Although this interpretation of Marx's concept of commodity fetishism is controversial, it is supported by a careful reading of the rest of the section on the fetishism of commodities in *Capital*, Vol. I. Here, it can be seen that much of what Marx has to say, which seems to be ironic in the light of Lukács' reading of fetishism-as-reification, can in fact be read quite literally in terms of the above interpretation. In particular, in the following passage (1974a, 78 [1976, 165–6]) Marx quite clearly argues that relations between individuals at work appear '*as what they really are: material relations between persons* and *social relations between things*'. Furthermore, Marx not only confirms that commodities really do have a social existence, but also that, for the most part, people at work really do *not* have a social relationship with each other except in so far as these relationships are mediated via the exchange of commodities: this is of course precisely why capitalist relations of production are quite so alienating. As Marx says on this point:

> The labour of the individual asserts itself as part of the labour of society, *only* by means of the relations which the act of exchange establishes directly between the products, and indirectly, through them, between the producers. To the latter, therefore, the relations connecting the labour of one individual with that of the rest appear, not as direct social relations between individuals at work, *but as what they really are*, material relations between persons and social relations between things. (1974a, 78 [1976, 165–6]; emphasis added)

In the capitalist mode of production commodities then really do have social relations with each other, and, in this way, act as the expression of the social character of the labour of the producers of commodities. However, these producers do not themselves have a social existence at work only 'material relations' with each other, by which Marx appears to mean relations mediated by the exchange of material things (e.g. labour-power as a commodity for the products of labour in the form of wages). Furthermore, the producers of commodities do *not* mistake their social situation, but understand things as they really are. How then are we supposed to reconcile the apparent contradictions between what Marx says here with Lukács' interpretation of the passage quoted above? Unless we say that the passage in question is a complete aberration on Marx's part, and that he said something here that he did not really intend, there is only one conclusion we can possibly draw from this statement: Marx did not mean by the fetishism of commodities what Lukács says he did.

But what of mystification? 'A commodity is … a mysterious thing,' Marx says, 'simply because in it the social character of men's labour appears to them as an objective character stamped upon the product of that labour' (1974a, 77 [1976, 164–5]). But, if the producers of commodities do not mistake their social situation, why then does Marx say that a commodity is such a mysterious thing? It is the *objectification* of the social labour of the producers that brings about mystification. However, this mystification does not arise from any false appearances of the commodity *form*, but rather from the much more serious fact that commodities not only *seem* to us to have a social existence but actually do so in the capitalist mode of production. Lukács is correct to say that the veil of mystification which surrounds the commodity form is due to the objectification of the social character of labour and to the alienation between labourers and the product of their own labour that results from this (Lukács 1971, 87), but he is incorrect to say that this mystification results from any false appearance of things. Rather, it is only through its objectification in the form of commodity production that the *social* character of the producers' labour gains any expression at all in the capitalist mode of production. The full extent of the labourer's alienation in this mode of production can only be grasped from the realization that this is the case; i.e. that the labourer *really is* separated from the product of his or her labour when this is exchanged as a commodity. In the capitalist mode of production then, commodities have a fetishized, and even a *transcendental* existence (1974a, 76 [1976, 163]), and the mystification of the commodity form arises from this fact rather than from any misunderstanding of the nature of the appearance of these peculiar things. Marx makes this point quite clearly in his introduction to the section on commodity fetishism, in a passage which is normally interpreted as being ironic in the light of Lukács reading of fetishism as reification:

> A commodity appears, at first sight, a very trivial thing, and easily understood. Its analysis shows that it is, in reality, a very queer thing,

> abounding in metaphysical subtleties and theological niceties. So far as it is a value in use, there is nothing mysterious about it, whether we consider it from the point of view that by its properties it is capable of satisfying human wants, or from the point that these properties are the product of human labour. It is as clear as noon-day that man, by his industry, changes the forms of the material furnished by Nature, in such a way as to make them useful to him. The form of wood, for instance, is altered by making a table out of it. Yet, for all that, the table continues to be that common, every-day thing, wood. But, so soon as it steps forth as a commodity, it is changed into something *transcendent*. It not only stands with its feet on the ground, but, in relation to all other commodities, it stands on its head, and evolves out of its wooden brain grotesque ideas, far more wonderful than 'table-turning' ever was. (1974a, 76 [1976, 163]; emphasis added)[7]

Commodities then really do have a transcendental existence, that is to say, an existence beyond the apparent limitations of their material form and of our conscious understanding of them, and they really do 'stand on their heads' in relation to all other commodities, as the equivalent expression of the value of all these other commodities and as the expression of the value of a given quantity of human labour. Commodities are then *both* mere things *and* the expression of something very much more than this.

But if a degree of mystification is involved in the fetishized-form that commodities normally assume, who is mystified by their appearance? I have suggested that the producers of commodities do not mistake their own social situation – that they are not 'falsely conscious' – but correctly understand that their social existence is limited by the exchange of commodities in the capitalist mode of production. Rather it is intellectuals like Lukács who have a reified understanding of the social situation of the working class when they argue that commodities do not have a social existence of their own and claim that labourers therefore have a false conscious of their own class situation. Nevertheless, Marx does say that *something* is obscured by the fetishized existence of commodities, albeit not the class situation of the producers. According to Marx, it is not the class situation of the labourer that is obscured from him or her, but a specific aspect of the labourer's social situation; namely, 'the *two-fold* social character of the labour of the individual' which, Marx argues, appears to the labourer only under those forms which are impressed upon it in the every day practice of exchange (1974a, 78 [1976, 166]). What this means is that the characteristic that the individual producer's labour has of being qualitatively equal in its commodity form to all other kinds of human labour (i.e. of being different quantities of homogeneous human labour) assumes the form that physically different use values have only one common property: that of being values in their own right irrespective of the labour that produced them. For Marx then it is not the social character of human labour *per se*, but the fact that commodities are the equivalent expression of the value of all different kinds of human labour that is obscured by the form that commodities appear to have of having value in their own right. As Marx says on this point;

> When we bring the products of our labour into relation with each other as values, it is not because we see in these articles the material receptacles of homogeneous human labour. Quite the contrary: whenever, by an exchange, we equate as values our different products, by that very act, we also equate, as human labour, the different kinds of human labour expended upon them. *We are not aware of this*, nevertheless we do it. Value, therefore, does not stalk about with a label describing what it is. It is value, rather, that converts every product into a social hieroglyphic. (1974a, 78–9 [1976, 166–7]; emphasis added)

It is not the class situation of the producers then that is obscured by the fetishized existence of commodities, but a specific exchange relationship within the capitalist mode of production, the *full implications of which* are not clear to us when we equate the value of one commodity with that of another and when we attribute value to commodities in their own right. Of course, commodities really do have value in their own right as objects of exchange, but they are also 'material receptacles of homogeneous human labour', and while we are well aware of the former point, we are not always aware of the latter. When we fetishize a commodity, therefore, we do not attribute a transcendental or a social existence to something that does not in fact have these qualities (*pace* Lukács), but we recognize the existence of certain transcendental qualities which commodities do in fact possess and act accordingly towards them, without always being aware of the full implications of what it is that we are doing. Commodities then really do have a fetishized existence in the capitalist mode of production.

Points for Further Discussion

1. One of the most serious problems with Lukács' concept of reification concerns what I think we will have to call the assumption of a theoretically privileged position that is inherent in this concept. Put simply, what this means is that in order to be able to claim that someone else, or some other group of people in society, have a *reified* consciousness, we must be able to say that we are ourselves free from this reified perspective. As Lukács says,

we must be able to assume 'a vantage point other than that of a reified consciousness' (1971, 104). The obvious problem with this perspective, however, is how we can be sure that we are not presenting a reified analysis ourselves if the tendency to reify things in the capitalist mode of production really is as all pervasive as Lukács says it is. Lukács does not have anything to say about this point, but presumably, if we follow the logic of his analysis that it is class location that determines class consciousness, he would have to say that he is able to develop a non-reified perspective by virtue of the fact that, as an intellectual, he does not share the same class position as that of the producers of commodities. However, any such argument might just as easily be used against the concept of reification as in support of it, since we might reasonably argue that it is only intellectuals like Lukács who have the time to develop the *truly* fantastic idea that relations between people at work appear to them as relations between things, or the even more grotesque idea that the whole of the working class is falsely conscious of the limitations of their own class situation, while the 'true' picture is revealed to only a very few intellectuals who are not directly engaged in the process of production at all ('an idea far more wonderful than "table turning" ever was', as Marx says). In fact however, as we have seen, the true situation is that the producers of commodities do not reify their social situation at all, but only fetishize it, while it is Lukács who presents us with a reified analysis of fetishism when he denies that commodities have a social existence and insists instead on treating them as mere things.

2. If we are to develop a truly sophisticated understanding of the concepts of appearance and reality what is required here is a suitably complex concept of the nature of reality. This must include: some idea of mankind's relation to nature (corporeality); some idea of the embodiment of human labour in its material form (incorporation); some idea of the incorporation of abstract ideas in human form (incarnation); and some notion of the idea that there are certain things that are insubstantial and which are not embodied either in human form or in the form of the product of nature (the transcendental or metaphysical). In other words, it simply will not do to criticize something as possessing only 'phantom objectivity' without having first established the 'truth' of the counter-theory, or real situation, against which what is being criticized is said to be 'false'. This is not to say that we must disprove the existence of any metaphysical reality before we can reasonably claim to believe in the existence of the physical world. It is simply to say that we must have some way of conceptualizing the existence of a metaphysical reality before we can adequately discuss the objectivity of mankind's relationship to the natural world. As Mihailo Markovic has pointed out in an essay criticizing Lukacs' concept of reification, where

Figure 18. The nature of appearance and reality

	Appearance		Reality	
	Realize:	Correctly take to be a thing that which has the appearance of a thing.	Nature:	*The Natural*; nature unacted upon by mankind: matter.
Perception	Mistake:	Falsely take to be a thing like that which has the appearance of a thing	Corporeality:	*The Corporeal*; mankind's relations with nature.
	Deify:	*Deification*; falsely take to be a spirit that which has the appearance of being human or thinglike.	Substantiality:	*The Material*; mankind's relations with man and nature.
Explanation / Conception	Fetishize:	*Fetishism*; correctly take to be social or spiritual that which has the appearance of a thing.		
	Objectify:	*Objectification*; correctly make seem thinglike that which has the appearance of being social or spiritual.	Incarnation	*The Metaphysical*; knowledge of the unobservable. Mankind's relations with mankind.
	Reify:	*Reification*; falsely make seem thinglike that which appears to be spiritual.		
Preconception	Mystify:	*Mystification*; falsely make seem spiritual that which appears to be spiritual.	Insubstantiality:	*The Transcendental*; beyond knowledge and the material world.
	Spiritualize:	Correctly make seem spiritual that which appears to be spiritual.	Spiritualism:	*The Mystical*; undefinable; inexpressibly divine.

reification is taken to mean treating something as a thing, all social science must be understood as having a tendency to reify to whatever extent it generalizes (i.e. to the extent that it abstracts from reality) (Markovic, 1974). In addition to a concept of reification-fetishism, what is therefore required is some conception of the possibility of non-false abstraction (i.e. of objectivity), as well as some idea of the fact that there are certain things which are insubstantial, and the reality of which can therefore only be expressed metaphysically. My suggestion for a preliminary taxonomy of this kind, based on Marx's writings in *Capital*, can be seen in Fig. 18.

3. Finally, no discussion of Marx's concept of commodity fetishism in *Capital*, Vol. I would be complete which did not also look at his other extensive discussion of the concept of fetishism in the form of interest-bearing capital in the section entitled 'Externalisation of the Relations of Capital in the Form of Interest-Bearing Capital' in *Capital*, Vol. III, Chapter 24 (1977, 390–99 [1981, 515–24]). Here Marx not only presents us with a discussion of what he claims is the most extreme, the most externalized, and, as he says, the most fetish-like form that capital assumes in the capitalist mode of production (i.e. capital in the form of interest-bearing capital), but he also makes a clear distinction between reification and fetishism and, at the same time, gives us what is probably the most concise account in the whole of *Capital* of his view of the nature of appearance and reality (see above Fig. 18).

According to Marx, the relations of capital assume their most externalized and hence most fetish-like appearance in the form of interest-bearing capital (1977, 391 [1981, 515]). This is characterized by the circuit of money capital M–M', in which money (M) not only appears to have expanded its own value (M') but seems to have done so without the help of any actual process of production (the cycle C…P'…C', of the circuit M–C…P…C'–M') and, apparently, without having even been exchanged for commodities (M–C–M'). In other words what we have here is the appearance of money capital in the form of a *self-expanding value.* In the circuit M–C–M' (i.e. the simple form of merchant's capital), Marx argues that the general form of the capitalist process is at least made apparent. Money has at least been exchanged for commodities, and has expanded its value, even though it is not clear in this case how this has happened and whether this is due to the exchange of commodities or to some process of production in which the value of these commodities has been enhanced. Nevertheless according to Marx, profit made as a result of this transaction 'is at least seen to be the product of a social *relation,* not the product of a mere *thing*' (1977, 391 [1981, 515]; emphasis in original). However, this is not the case with interest-bearing capital, in which money appears to possess the fantastic ability to create more value than it has itself, simply by placing money into circulation, and without recourse to any process of production in which this surplus value is in fact created. It is here, however, in the fantastic form of interest-bearing capital, that the distinction between reification and fetishism is externalized and made clear. On the one hand, Marx argues capital (money, commodities, value, etc.) is now seen as a mere thing (reification). On the other hand, 'the result of the entire process of production [now] appears as *a property inherent in the thing itself*' (1977, 392 [1981, 516]); i.e. fetishistically. Money capital therefore appears both as a thing, and *as something very much more than this*: as a thing possessed of the fantastic property of being able to enhance its own value merely by entering into the market place, and without any process of production or social relations of any other kind taking place. As Marx says:

> In interest-bearing capital, therefore, this automatic fetish, self-expanding value, money generating money, are [*sic*] brought out in their pure state and in this form it no longer bears the birthmarks of its origins. The social relation is consummated in the relation of a thing, of money, to itself. Instead of the actual transformation of money into capital, *we see here only form without content.* (1977, 392 [1981, 516]; emphasis added)

Both reification and fetishism therefore involve the same phenomenon: the appearance of *form without content.* However, in the case of fetishism, the appearance of this 'form without content' is very different from the appearance of form without content in the case of reification. In both cases, the 'content' which is concealed from us is exactly the same: the relations of production underlying the creation of new value and the reproduction of existing values. But in the case of fetishism, the form taken by this process of concealment is different from the form it assumes in reification. In the case of fetishism, money, commodities and interest-bearing capital take on a fantastic, even magical, appearance, seemingly able to apparently create value out of nothing. Capital generally, but interest-bearing capital in particular, comes to be seen as something like wine stored in a cellar which improves its use value with age (1977, 393 [1981, 517]) or, in a yet more extreme form, as something like the fabled goose that laid the golden egg; a source of value *which never needs replenishing.* But things are quite different in the case of reification. Here, instead of taking on a magical or fantastic appearance, the relations of production underlying the creation of surplus value are concealed by the *dull* appearance of a common every day thing. Where reification occurs, the apparently magical properties of capital and labour, that of being able to create a value greater than they have themselves (1977, 392 [1981, 516]), take on the appearance of not having this capacity;

that is, the appearance of being a mere thing possessed of no special abilities. Reification and fetishism then are quite different, though clearly related things; the difference between them being due to the different *form* which the relations of production assume in each case. In the case of fetishism, the form which the relations of production assume is fantastic; in the case of reification the form which the relations of production assume is mundane. In both cases, however, the underlying relations of production are obscured.

In the case of interest-bearing money capital, the obscurity (i.e. distortion) brought about by the particular form which capital assumes takes on the appearance that interest (which is usually only a small part of the capitalist's profit and an even smaller fraction of the total surplus value produced by the capitalist mode of production) comes to be seen as the main product, and indeed as the main aim and sole purpose of investing money in the form of capital. Profits, on the other hand, seem to be a mere sideline – a by-product of the capitalistic (mercantile) process of production – and something which is literally of little or no *interest* at all to the investor of money capital (1977, 392 [1981, 516]). Does the investor of money capital care if the capitalist does not make a profit, so long as their interest is paid? *Mystification* occurs here when the appearance that capital has in this case (i.e. as interest-bearing money capital able to create value by itself) is presented to us as a full and complete explanation of what is in fact taking place; for example, when 'vulgar political economy … seeks to represent [interest-bearing] capital as an independent source of value, [as a source] of value creation' separate from the actual process of production (1977, 392–3 [1981, 517]). Finally, *objectification* takes place when the creation of surplus value is presented to us in its most perverse and meaningless form, because the *appearance* that capital has in this case of being able to create something out of nothing *reveals* to us that something else altogether *must* in fact be taking place. It is therefore only in its most extreme (i.e. its most externalized) form that the reality of the fetishism of interest-bearing money capital is made most clear to us (1977, 392 [1981, 516]).

Reading: Essential: *Capital*, Vol. I, Ch. 1, section 4 (1974a, 76–87, see especially 76–80 [1976, 163–77, especially 163–8]). Background: *Capital*, Vol. III, Ch. 24 (1977, 391–9, especially 391–4 [1981, 515–24, especially 515–19]). Non-essential: Georg Lukács, *History and Class Consciousness*, Ch. 4, 'Reification and the Consciousness of the Proletariat' (1971, 83–222, especially section 1, 'The Phenomenon of Reification', 83–109).

CONCLUSION TO PART IV

In Part IV of this book I have distinguished Marx's concept of the rate of profit from his concept of the rate of surplus value and hence brought out even more dramatically than before the distinction between profit and surplus value. We have also seen how Marx distinguishes between the concepts of labour-power and labour, and surplus and necessary labour. In doing this I have shown how this method of distinguishing between two things that are usually thought of as being one and the same thing is characteristic of Marx's method generally and therefore of his usual way of proceeding in these matters. I have also gone to some lengths to outline what I have called a general theory of the value of labour – one in terms of the degree of ease or difficulty of *reproducing* something – in order to distinguish this from what Diane Elson calls a value theory of labour. In this way I have tried to apply Marx's theory of value to a wider range of things than mere exchange values, or commodities, and in doing have tried to account for the value we attach to those things which are not usually exchanged or exchangeable. As Adam Smith suggested more than two hundred years ago now, those things which have value are of two kinds: those which can be reproduced, which are therefore exchangeable as commodities, and which hence have a value that can easily be measured, and those things which cannot be reproduced at all, which are more often than not use values rather than exchange values, and hence the value of which cannot easily be measured. This second category of things is literally priceless to us, however, just because the value of a thing cannot easily be measured is not to say it does not have any value at all. As Marx says, nature – in which the value of labour-power is itself embodied – is the source of all use values, some of which can be exchanged and some of which cannot, and labour merely *adds* value to that which already exists in nature. Labour is not the source of all value therefore, but only of all *surplus* value (i.e. the additional value which labour creates and which it adds to that which already exists in nature). Finally, I have outlined a very different theory of Marx's concept of fetishism (in terms of the fetishism of commodities as well as that of interest-bearing capital) to that which is usually presented in terms of the concept of reification. I have argued that Georg Lukács' concept of fetishism as reification is simply wrong – a mistaken interpretation of what Marx meant – but in saying this I hope I have made it clear that I do not mean to suggest that the concept of reification *itself* is in any way 'wrong' or 'mistaken'. Reification is a very interesting concept, which might usefully be applied to all sorts of social situations but it is just that it should not be applied to what Marx understood by the concept of commodity fetishism (and still less to what he meant by the fetishism of interest-bearing capital). To this end I have therefore suggested a more complex model of the nature of appearance and reality which incorporates *both* reification and fetishism, objectification and mystification (see Fig.18).

CONCLUSION

The reader who is new to *Capital* might well wonder why Marx chose to begin his study of the capitalist mode of production with a detailed account of *commodity* production – of the lowly commodity of all things? In a book entitled *Capital*, why not start with a definition of the concept of capital itself – something which in fact we do not get until nearly *five hundred* pages later (*Capital*, Vol. I, Part VII, Ch. 24) – or at the very least start with the concept of capital in its money form as Marx does in the *Grundrisse*, the notebook he wrote in 1857–8 in preparation for writing *Capital* itself? What have commodities got to do with anything, we might ask, and why apparently are they *quite* so important to this question? In fact, the reason Marx begins *Capital* with a discussion of commodities is fairly clear: he wished to take seriously one of the most fundamental claims of vulgar and classical political economy; namely, the belief that, even when they are paid only a minimum or subsistence wage, labourers are in fact paid the *full* value of their labour-power when they exchange this as a commodity. Marx was forced to accept this claim because he wanted to be able to argue in his turn that capitalists too are paid the *full* value of their labour-power (as it were) when they have received back from their enterprise a sum equivalent in value to what they put into it, and *nothing* more than this. If it was fair to say that the labourer is paid the full value of their work when they are paid only a subsistence wage – the bare minimum required to live and reproduce themselves as labourers – then it must *also* be fair to say that the capitalist is only entitled to get back from the capitalist enterprise nothing more and nothing less than they have themselves put into this. In order to make this point, Marx was forced to accept (a) that labour-power was a commodity and (b) that, as such, it therefore must exchange at its full value.

In order to be able to claim that the capitalists are entitled to get back *exactly* what they put into enterprises they founded and nothing more than this, Marx was forced to take seriously what might otherwise have seemed to be an absurd claim, that commodities exchange at their full value and therefore that labour-power as a commodity must also be exchanged at its full value. In order to do this, before he said anything about money, capital or surplus value, he therefore needed to explain exactly what a commodity was. This provides us with a very good example of the Marxist method of 'immanent criticism' (Desai 2002, 6, 55, 75). What this means is that Marx adopted the Hegelian method of criticizing something from within the rules and assumptions of that thing itself and – having mastered completely the theory to be criticized and accepted its logic as it were – trying to show how such beliefs were flawed *in their own terms* (Smith 2004, 204). If vulgar or classical political economy really wanted to insist that the labourer, *however badly paid they might seem to be*, was nevertheless still paid a fair wage (i.e. the full value of their labour even though they only received a subsistence wage), then Marx wanted to show what other consequences followed from such a theory. If the value of something, even a human being, was always the same as the minimum cost of its *own* reproduction, then it must *also* be the case that the value which the capitalist who set up a new process of production was entitled to get back was the same as the value of the original sum invested, and *nothing more than this*.

Writing to Ferdinand Lassalle in 1858, nearly ten years *before* the eventual publication of *Capital*, Vol. I, Marx worried that revolution in Europe might occur before he finished his book on political economy.

> I have a presentiment that now, when after fifteen years of study I have got so far as to be able to get down to the thing [i.e. actually writing the book], turbulent movements without will most likely interfere. But never mind. If I finish too late to find the world still interested in that sort of thing, the fault will obviously be mine. (*MESC*, 1953, 125)

This raises the question why the superbly clever Marx (and Engels too) thought that the death of capitalism was imminent – due at any moment as they seem to have thought – when this mode of production had only just got started in much of the greater part of the rest of the world. As we have seen, Marx dated the beginning of manufacture by machines rather than manufacture by hand from sometime around 1775. When he wrote to Lassalle in 1858 industrial capitalism had therefore only been underway in England for just over 75 years and in Europe and North America for an even shorter period of time. Marx and Engels were well aware that both feudalism, the mode of production based on conquest and serfdom, which immediately preceded the development of capitalism, and the mode of production of ancient Greece and Rome, which had been based on slavery, had both lasted for several *hundred* years or more. Why then should capitalism in Europe – and still less the development of capitalism in the rest of the world – wither away after only 75 years or so? Of course there is no very good reason – no natural law, as it were – why different modes of production should, or somehow *ought*, to last roughly the same length of time; feudalism might well last for several hundred years and capitalism for less than a century. But, as we have seen, Marx himself had already observed that until the capitalist revolution was completed in every corner of the world – in India, in China, in Russia and North and South America, all of which he studied very carefully (and this to say nothing of Africa) – there was a very real danger that the nascent development of the capitalist mode of production in Europe and/or North America would be undermined by the existence of non-capitalist modes of production in the rest of the world. And this, as we have seen, is just exactly what did happen.

In this book, I have argued that it is mercantilism (put crudely, buying cheap in order to sell dear) rather than accumulation (investment in industrial enterprises) that characterizes the mode of production we are all so familiar with today. Accumulation is no longer (if it *ever* was) the driving force of the capitalist mode of production in its present highly developed mercantile phase [M–C…P…C'–M']; but speculation is. Mercantile capitalists are *not* materially compelled to accumulate their capital in productive enterprises, but seem to prefer to leave this for someone else to do. They buy commodities cheaply which have been manufactured in low-wage economies in one part of the world and sell these same things dearly in high-wage economies in another part of the world. If they pay to have these commodities transported, then this is as near as they get to an actual process of production. It is no longer General Motors or the Ford Motor Company but Calvin Klein or Matalan that are characteristic of the mode of production we find today. Not being compelled to invest their money capital at all, such companies are still less compelled to *reinvest* their capital, but can always withdraw this from the process of circulation when their investments go wrong and reinvest it as and when they chose to do so in other speculative enterprises at a later date or else not reinvest this at all (with disastrous consequences for the rest of us). Marx's model of uninterrupted, or as he described this 'fluent and ever renewed', *industrial* capitalism – the model of the CMP characterized by reproduction on a progressively extending scale: M–C…P…C'–M'–C'…P'…C''–M''–C'''…P…C'''–M'''… – simply never came to pass, and the reasons why this was the case are quite clear. It was due firstly to the existence of a non-capitalist 'third world' – and particularly the existence of cheap labour – *outside* the confines of the closed economy model characteristic of the pure model of the CMP, the existence of which allowed European capitalism to *export* its problems to the third world. And secondly, it was due to certain fundamental problems in the nature of the capitalist mode of production itself, especially the survival into the twenty-first century of a highly developed form of mercantile-capital (mistakenly called 'finance capital' by Rudolf Hilferding).

It must be an enduring question for Marxist scholarship why Marx, having published *Capital*, Vol. I in 1867, did not complete the publication of Vols II and III during his own lifetime. We have already seen from his famous letter to Engels of August 1867, in which he announced the publication of *Capital*, Vol. I, that Marx claimed he was *already* well underway with the work required to complete Vols II and III. – originally intended to be published as a single volume presumably of about the same length as the existing Vol. I (see *MESC*, Marx to Meyer, 30 April 1867, 225, 2n) to be published together with a 'third' volume of *Capital* on the history of classical economy based on material that has since been published as *Theories of Surplus Value*. Marx died in March 1883 and although he was often very ill during the last few years of his life, he nevertheless had nearly thirteen years from the publication of Vol. I in August 1867 until sometime around 1880 to complete the rest of his life's work. Why then didn't he do this? The answer to this question, as I have suggested, is that Marx quite simply became stuck sometime during the early 1870s on the question that he set out to answer in what we now know as *Capital*, Vol. II (but which was in fact the *last* of the three volumes of *Capital* to be written) and which he therefore left unresolved. This was the question of what *materially* compelling reason there could be for capitalists, who might otherwise simply chose not to do so, to reproduce their capital on an extended scale (and still less on a *progressively extending* scale), with all the risk that this involved of over-extending their capital in this way? Why not, once it was up and running, simply reproduce a successful capitalist enterprise on the same *unchanging* scale? What was there, apart from capitalist competition and the desire of the individual capitalist for ever greater profits, that *apparently* compelled capitalists to accumulate on a progressively extending scale and thereby gave modern capitalism its unique identity?

Living in England during the middle of the nineteenth century Marx was profoundly influenced by the very high degree of capital accumulation that he saw all around him, which must have seemed at that time to be the defining feature of the capitalist mode of production, and he could not be satisfied with an explanation of this phenomenon simply in terms of the will of the individual capitalist (i.e. lust for profits) or capitalist competition (i.e. the unavoidable need to invest in new machinery in order to compete on level terms with other newer capital). Although he knew that it was competition between capitalists that caused accumulation to take place once this process got underway, he still wanted to understand what it was that caused capitalist competition in the first place. Marx thought that there must be some *materially* compelling reason that caused this apparently fundamental aspect of the capitalist mode of production, and he thought that this must have something to do with the nature of fixed capital and the way in which it was 'precipitated' during the normal circulation of industrial capital. In the end, however, he simply could not discover what this missing 'something' was. By extending Marx's discussion of the concept of precipitation (the suspension of the active function of capital in fine particles in its money form; or what I call 'precipitation i') to another more common definition of this term, namely, doing something *sooner* than one otherwise would (which I have called 'precipitation ii'), I claim to have solved Marx's discussion of this problem. The solution to this problem was there in front of him all along, I think. It is in his writing in *Capital*, Vols II and III, but due to his own dissatisfaction with this solution, for reasons which remain unclear, Marx felt he could not publish *Capital*, Vol. III until he had solved this problem in Vol. II, and of course he never did this. However, this is not the issue here. The real problem is less the question of whether Marx did or did not complete his own project, or the reasons why this was the case, and more the implications of this question for the development of the capitalist mode of production itself. If there really is no materially compelling reason why capitalists should accumulate their capital – if in the end it comes down to nothing more than the will of the individual capitalist and the lust for greater and greater profits – then there is no *materially* compelling reason why capitalism should develop in the way that Marx thought that it would. What we have in place of Marx's model of the pure CMP is a highly developed mercantile circuit of capital which instead of developing towards socialism might well develop in some other direction, or fail to develop altogether, with all the consequences which we see before us today.

These observations about Marx's failure to publish *Capital*, Vols II and III during his own lifetime raise questions about the way in which these two volumes were eventually edited by Engels (see for example Engels letter to Adler, 16 March 1895, in which Engels advises Adler how to read Vols II and III in an order different to that in which it was published; *MESC*, 1953, 566–8). The present ordering of Vols II and III – both considered individually and taken together – is in my opinion just plain wrong and this is one of the main reasons why I have not considered these two volumes of *Capital* in their published order in this book. The first and second 'halves' of Vol. II – as edited by Engels – are in fact the wrong way round I think, or, to put this another way, Vol. II, Parts I and II would come better after Part III. Vol. III might well have been published before Vol. II, but even if these two volumes are read in their present order, I would have first included Part III, then Part II before Part I (on the circuit of the three main forms of capital) since Part I of Vol. II (as Engels has it) goes much better with Vol. III, and in fact might even be thought to serve as an introduction to this. From this perspective, there is a *very* strong case for a new edition of *Capital*, Vols II and III.

Finally, in case Marx's basic thesis in *Capital* – that which distinguishes Marx's philosophy (and therefore Marxism as such) from all other writings on this subject – is still unclear let me see if I can explain this one more time in terms of the well-known story about the caretaker and his favourite broom. The caretaker insists that he has had this same broom for the past twenty years; in fact it's the best broom he's ever had, he says. He has only had to change the head three times and the handle twice! In reality, of course, the broom in question is now somewhere between its second and third manifestation. The caretaker *thinks* that it is the same broom that it ever was because it looks the same to him as it always did and he has looked after it carefully and kept it safely locked up in a cupboard each night while others caretakers repeatedly lost theirs, but in point of fact this is an entirely *new* broom several times over. Things are just the same with the capitalist and his original investment. Because it occupies much the same site as it ever did, and looks much the same as it ever was, the capitalist thinks he is in possession of the same factory and much the same machinery (he is less sure about the raw materials used up during the process of production) that he purchased originally thanks to his own hard work and effort. In fact however, after a period of years perhaps (the reproduction period of the original sum of money invested, as Marx calls it), this is no longer the case. Everything in nature, including ourselves, wears out, either through being used too much or by not being used enough and the capitalist's original investment is no exception to this rule.

After a relatively short period of time, the value of the original investment is entirely used up and in place of this value are new commodities produced by the process of production in which the capitalist has invested. The capitalist sells these and realizes their value in the form of his profit. But, in addition to this, on the *same* site and occupying much the *same* space as before, there is now an entirely *new* process of production which looks very much like the old one it has replaced. The factory, the machinery and the raw materials that it uses have all been reproduced and renewed by the unpaid labour of others – all the people, including even the capitalist himself if he performs the labour of supervision, who have ever worked in the factory during its lifetime – and *together* with the profit of the enterprise, this unpaid labour of reproduction and renewal – the replacement of the worn-out fabric of the capitalist enterprise itself – is called by Marx *surplus* value. Like the caretaker with his broom, the capitalist continues to claim to be the owner of this entirely new enterprise and no one can persuade him or her otherwise. The legitimacy of the capitalist's claim to be the owner of the factory depends on the hard work that he or she performed in order to set up the *original* enterprise, but, by the same token, it is the hard work and unpaid effort of all the people who ever worked in the enterprise who are, in proportion to their labour, the legitimate owners of the enterprise in question.

Further Reading

Apart from Chapter 52 on classes (see the Apppendix below for more on this) the reader should not leave the study of *Capital* without reading the remainder of Vol. III, Part VII, in which the chapter on classes occurs. This is especially the case with Chapter 48, which focuses on the so-called 'Trinity Formula', without which it is difficult to make sense of what Marx has to say on the subject of the three different sources of income of the three main classes in capitalist society at the beginning of Chapter 52. Vol. III, Chapter 50, 'Illusions Created by Competition', is also not without interest and might usefully be read in conjunction with what Marx has to say on the subject of competition in Vol. I (see especially 1974a, 257, 302, 555 [1976, 381, 436, 739]). Vol. III, Chapter 51, 'Distribution Relations and Production Relations', is also interesting from the point of view of the different forms that distribution has taken historically; while Vol. III, Part VI, Chapter 47, 'Genesis of Capitalist Ground Rent', which forms the last section of Part VI of Vol. III, is of great interest to anyone seeking more information on the subject of Marx's writings on pre-capitalist modes of production, and can be usefully read in conjunction with Chapter 36, of Vol. III, 'Pre-Capitalist Relationships', and with the concluding chapters of Vol. I, Chapters 31 and 33, on 'Colonialism, and on the Genesis of Industrial Capitalism'.

There is one other section of *Capital* which I have neglected to consider; namely, the whole of Vol. III, Part VI, 'Transformation of Surplus-Profit into Ground-Rent'. Although this section forms 200 pages of Vol. III, I do not propose to give a detailed analysis of it here for the reasons I gave earlier on in this study. With the conspicuous exception of Chapter 47, 'Genesis of Ground Rent', this section reads much more like a part of Marx's *Theories of Surplus Value* than it does a section of *Capital*, as it is concerned mainly with a critique of Ricardo's and Smith's writings on ground rent, and would therefore, in my opinion, have been better excluded from *Capital* altogether by Engels when he edited the final two volumes for publication. The reader who *is* interested in this subject might usefully read this section of *Capital* before going on to look at the first part of *Theories of Surplus Value*, Part II, Chapters 8–14, but as far as the general reader is concerned I would recommend ignoring this section altogether.

Finally, I also do *not* recommend the general reader to go on to read *Theories of Surplus Value* (*TSV*), published posthumously, and sometimes referred to – incorrectly in my view – as the 'fourth volume' of *Capital*. My reason for saying this is that *TSV* is really very difficult to understand indeed. This is not because it is badly written – it is not in fact especially difficult to read – but because it is very difficult to understand what is Marx's own view, what is simply a view that he is outlining in his notes, and what he meant to go on to criticize. *TSV* is comprised of a collection of notes Marx was making on the history of classical political economy which were intended by him to become the third volume of *Capital.* What was subsequently published as *Capital*, Vol. III was originally intended to be incorporated into a slimmed down *Capital*, Vol. II. However, because of this, it is often very difficult indeed to separate what Marx is saying here as the expression of his own view on a particular question from when he is giving an account of what someone else has said. At times it is quite clear that Marx is criticizing Adam Smith or David Ricardo's formulation of a particular point, but at other times it is not at all clear that this is the case. Therefore, rather than read *TSV*, it is probably better for the general reader of *Capital* to leave this book well alone.

APPENDIX: ON SOCIAL CLASSES

I – Marx on Social Class in *Capital*, Vol. III (Part VI, Ch. 52 and elsewhere)

Apart from some additional 'supplementary remarks' added by Engels, Marx's short discussion of the concept of social class is the final chapter of *Capital*, Vol. III (Part VI, Ch. 52) and is in fact incomplete. The three volumes of *Capital* famously end with the words, 'Here the manuscript breaks off', added by Engels, perhaps to give the impression that Marx was working on the manuscript of *Capital* to the very end and died, with pen in his hand as it were, after a lifetime of intellectual labour. The fact that this chapter was never finished is sometimes presented as a tragedy comparable to the loss of Aristotle's *Comedy*: if *only* Marx had completed this section – and surely Engels could have put some pressure on him to do so – we would know *exactly* what Marx's views on social class were and there would be no need to debate the matter any further. But any such argument is absurd, firstly because it represents the Marxist concept of social class as an a-historical category – as something which is fixed for all time and unchanging from one social situation to another – and this could hardly be further from Marx and Engels's actual views on this question. And secondly because it ignores the fact that there are numerous *other* explanations of Marx and Engel's views on the subject of social class elsewhere (especially *The Communist Manifesto,* but also *The Eighteenth Brumaire of Louis Napoleon*, *The Class Struggle in France* and *The Civil War in France*), which give us a very good idea indeed of what their views on this very important concept were.

Because Chapter 52 of *Capital*, Vol. III is so short – it is in fact a mere 355 words long, apart from a footnote to the end of this chapter which is unimportant and which I will therefore leave out here – it is possible to quote this chapter in its entirety, as follows:

> The owners merely of labour-power, owners of capital, and land-owners, whose respective sources of income are wages, profit and ground-rent, in other words, wage-labours, capitalists and land-owners, constitute the

> three big classes of modern society based upon the capitalist mode of production.
>
> In England, modern society is indisputably most highly and classically developed in structure. Nevertheless, even here the stratification of classes does not appear in its pure form. Middle and intermediate strata even here obliterate lines of demarcation everywhere (although incomparably less in rural districts than in the cities). However, this is immaterial for our analysis. We have seen that the continual tendency and law of development of the capitalist mode of production is more and more to divorce the means of production from labour, and more and more to concentrate the scattered means of production into large groups, thereby transforming labour into wage-labour and the means of production into capital. And to this tendency, on the other hand, corresponds the independent separation of landed property from capital and labour, or the transformation of all landed property into the form of landed property corresponding to the capitalist mode of production.
>
> The first question to be answered is this: what constitutes a class? – and the reply to this follows naturally from the reply to another question, namely: what makes wage-labourers, capitalists and landlords constitute the three great social classes?
>
> At first glance – the identity of revenues and sources of revenue. There are three great social groups whose members, the individuals forming them, live on wages, profits and ground-rent respectively, on the realisation of their labour-power, their capital, and their landed property.
>
> However, from this standpoint, physicians and officials, e.g., would also constitute two classes, for they belong to two distinct social groups, the members of each of these groups receiving their revenue from one and the same source. The same would also be true of the infinite fragmentation of interest and rank into which the division of social labour splits labourers as well as capitalists and landlords – the latter, e.g., into owners of vine-yards, farm owners, owners of forests, mine owners and owners of fisheries. [Here the manuscript breaks off.] (1977, 885–6 [1981, 1,025–6])

Apart from the fact that it is incomplete, what else can we say about this very famous chapter? The first thing we can say – and this is very clear indeed – is that this is not Marx's final formulation of his thoughts on the question of social class in a highly developed capitalist mode of production, but simply the beginning. If nothing else, his use of the expression 'At first glance…' would serve to make this point clear, as does his comment that even in England – the country with the most highly developed capitalist mode of production in the world at the time that Marx was writing – the stratification of classes does not appear in its pure form as yet, but all sorts of middle and intermediary classes intervene. What Marx says here therefore is quite clearly an *opening* statement of his views on this question – something which is in fact typical of his method – and as we can see he immediately goes on to retract the point that wage-labourers, capitalists and land-owners are the three big classes of modern society based on the capitalist mode of production. The *alleged* identity of classes with the sources of their revenues – which at first glance seems to be so compelling – *cannot* be the basis on which the three big social classes are demarcated in capitalist society, Marx thinks, since if this really were the case this would mean that we would also have to identify numerous other social classes on the basis of *their* income too – classes within classes as it were and even within the labouring class(es) as well – and clearly this is not what Marx intends us to do.

In fact, as is well known, the idea that there are just three main classes in modern society was advocated by Ricardo in the preface to his *On the Principles of Political Economy and Taxation* (1817) and Ricardo himself borrowed this idea from the French economist François Quesnay, as Marx explains to a correspondent of his, one Maxim Kovalevsky, in a letter dated April 1879:

> If Mr Karayev had recalled the main idea of Ricardo's Preface to his famous creation, in which he examines three classes of the state (land-owners, capitalists and workers; the latter tilling the soil by their labour), he would have seen that the first invention of the three classes in the economic sphere and their mutual relations could find a place *only* in the system of agriculture, where Quesnay put it. In addition, a writer should distinguish between what an author really gives and what he gives only in his own imagination. This is true even of philosophical systems; thus, what Spinoza considered the cornerstone of his system and what actually constitutes the cornerstone are two entirely different things. It is not surprising, therefore, that some of Quesnay's adherents … saw the essence of the whole system in its paraphernalia while the English Physiocrats, writing in 1798, were the first to demonstrate – on the basis of Quesnay's concepts and contrary to Adam Smith's – the need to abolish private ownership of land. (*MECW*, 1991, 45:452)

The sources of revenue alone then, although necessary, are *not* sufficient by themselves to identify the three great social classes of capitalist society. Beyond this, however, we cannot say what *other* factors Marx thought might be necessary to distinguish these social classes from one another or what difference there was, if any, between the dominant class(es) of capitalist society and all those other classes that were subordinate to them. Based on this fragment alone then, we can only guess what Marx might have gone on to say.

II – Marx on Social Class in *The Communist Manifesto* and in *Capital*, Vol. I

Fortunately for us however, as I say, we do not need to guess what Marx might have meant to say because we have other sources at our disposal, and even other references to social class in *Capital* itself. It is therefore possible to fill in the 'gaps' in Marx's writing here and, in effect, to say what he *might* have gone on to say had he completed this chapter. Before we do this however the first thing that we need to say about Marx's *general* concept of social class is that this is very complex indeed. It simply will not do therefore to try to say in a straightforward way what this concept means given that the concept itself is neither simple or straightforward. Marx variously claimed that there were two, three, five and seven classes (but not as far as I am aware four or six classes) and therefore what we have to do is to come up with a Marxist concept of social class that can accommodate *all* of these different claims. The usual explanation of this apparent anomaly in Marx's writing (and it is really surprising how often this is said) is that Marx is 'contradicting' himself. But this is very unlikely indeed since Marx was far too clever for this to be the case. One of the greatest intellectuals of his time, and surely of the second half of the nineteenth century, it is extremely unlikely that Marx could *not* see through this 'contradiction' in his own work as easily as his critics could. On the contrary, it is quite clear that what Marx was doing here was describing a number of very different social situations each with their own very different class structures. When Marx describes a highly industrialized society like Britain in the 1840s – his exemplar case of the capitalist mode of production – he talks about there being two or perhaps three main classes, depending on the stage of development that the CMP is supposed to have reached. But when he describes pre-industrial societies – his exemplar case here being France in the period from 1850–70 – he claims that there are five or even seven classes. At other times again, where he discusses certain transitional cases mid-way between the agricultural/feudal model exemplified by France and the industrial/capitalist model exemplified by Britain, he identifies three or more classes. That there is no 'contradiction' between these different views should go without saying. All that Marx is doing here is discussing different social situations at different stages in their development.

In the most extreme cases – those in which he says there are only two major classes – Marx is usually only referring to highly industrialized societies in which classes stand in hostile, irreconcilable opposition to one other. In capitalist societies, these circumstances can be further identified with those which Marx characterizes in terms of the increasing 'immiseration' of the working class (i.e. the 'increasing misery' or abject poverty of the working class). In these circumstances, the capitalist class is said to be progressively compelled to cut costs by the pressures of competition from other capitalists until eventually the only costs left to cut are the wages of the working class. Eventually (the onward progress of capitalist competition being relentless in the closed economy model of the CMP) the capitalists, having reduced all other costs as far as they are able to do so, are not only forced to cut the workers wages to a *subsistence* level (at which point the workers can still reproduce themselves and their families, albeit at a very poor standard of living), but to cut wages *below* the level of subsistence, a situation in which the working class cannot reproduce themselves *at all*. At this point, the working class (and large sectors of the middle class(es) too who are wholly or even partly dependent on wages for their living) are forced to rebel against a system of production which can not only no longer support them, but which in point in fact cannot even sustain itself, since no system of production can exist without workers of some kind. As Marx and Engels say on this point in *The Communist Manifesto*:

> The various interests and conditions of life within the ranks of the proletariat are more and more equalized, in proportion as machinery obliterates all distinctions of labour, and nearly everywhere reduces wages to the same low level. The growing competition among the bourgeois, and the resulting commercial crises, makes the wages of the workers ever more fluctuating. The unceasing improvement of machinery, ever more rapidly developing, makes their livelihood more and more precarious. (1971, 89)

And they continue:

> But in order to oppress a class, certain conditions must be assured to it under which it can, at least, continue its slavish existence. The serf, in the period of serfdom, raised himself to membership in the commune, just as the petty bourgeois, under the yoke of feudal absolutism, managed to develop into a bourgeois. The modern labourer, on the contrary, instead of rising with the progress of industry, sinks deeper and deeper below the conditions of existence of his own class. He becomes a pauper, and pauperism develops more rapidly than population and wealth. And here it becomes evident, that the bourgeoisie is unfit any longer to be the ruling class in society, and to impose its conditions of

> existence upon society as an overriding law. It is unfit to rule because it is incompetent to assure an existence to its slave within his slavery, because it cannot help letting him sink into such a state, that it has to feed him instead of being fed by him. Society can no longer live under this bourgeoisie, in other words, its existence is no longer compatible with society. (1971, 93)

An important point to note here is that the working class acts *as a class* in opposition to the capitalist class – the hostile and irreconcilable contradiction to which Marx and Engels refer – *not* because the working class are politically committed to the philosophy of communism or socialism, or to any other form of anti-capitalist ideology for that matter, but *simply* because they cannot live under these conditions any more. Having no other option they have to rebel against a mode of production which can no longer sustain them or else they will starve. This is not a question then of the *consciousness* of the working class of their position as a class, but rather of the sheer necessity to live. Society becomes polarized into two hostile and irreconcilable camps: on the one hand, there is the capitalist class (and all those on the periphery of this class), who, however temporarily, still have access to the means of production of life; on the other hand, the working class (and those of the middle classes who are increasingly driven into the ranks of the working class), who have nothing to sell but themselves, and now find that they cannot even sell this. Marx and Engels make a number of references in *The Communist Manifesto* to the fact that the working class must organize itself into a political movement if it is going to get anywhere in its struggle against the capitalist class. They insist that 'every class struggle is a political struggle', and argue that the 'organisation of the proletarians into a class, and consequently into a political party, is continually being upset again by the competition between the workers themselves. But it ever rises up again, stronger, firmer, mightier' (1971, 90). But when it comes to the class struggle proper (i.e. when it comes to the socialist revolution), Marx and Engels always talk of this in terms of compulsion: the compulsion of the material circumstances in which the working class, and indeed the capitalist class, finds themselves. Thus, as Marx and Engels say on this point in a famous reference at the end of Part II of *The Communist Manifesto*:

> If the proletariat during its contest with the bourgeoisie is compelled, *by the force of circumstances*, to organize itself as a ruling class, if, by means of revolution, it makes itself the ruling class, and, as such, sweeps away by force the old conditions of production, then it will, along with these conditions, have swept away the conditions for the existence of class

> antagonisms and of classes generally, and will thereby have abolished its own supremacy as a class. (1971, 105)

Support for the view of Marx's concept of social class *as* class struggle (and therefore for the idea that classes only *really* exist at all during what Marx calls those 'historical' periods of transition from one mode of production to another) is not only to be found in *The Communist Manifesto*, but also in *Capital* itself. For example, Marx comments in *Capital*, Vol. I:

> Along with the constantly diminishing number of magnates of capital, who usurp and monopolise all advantages of this process of transformation, grows the mass of misery, oppression, slavery, degradation, exploitation; but with this too grows the revolt of the working class, a class always increasing in numbers, and disciplined, united, organized by the very mechanism of the process of capitalist production itself. (Marx 1974a, 715 [1976, 929])

This reference from Vol. I, and several other similar references throughout the three volumes of *Capital* (see Hall 1977, 29–30), give the lie to the suggestion that is sometimes still made (Desai 2002, 81) that Marx's concept of class polarity is only to be found in his earlier or 'immature' works.

III – Marx on Social Class in France

But what of Marx's many other writings on social class apart from *Capital* and *The Communist Manifesto*; what does Marx say here? Elsewhere, but especially in his writings on the political situation in France in the nineteenth century – *The Eighteenth Brumaire of Louis Bonaparte*, *The Civil War in France* and *The Class Struggle in France* (incidentally the only one of Marx's many books which actually has the word 'class' in its title) – Marx seems to present us with a very different concept of class in terms of a model of society composed of (i) a lumpenproletariat (i.e. a kind of underclass), (ii) the industrial working class, (iii) peasantry, (iv) the petty bourgeoisie (i.e. small business concerns), (v) the bourgeoisie proper (the capitalists), (vi) the financial aristocracy (i.e. financiers) and (vii) the aristocracy proper (i.e. the landed classes).

Thus, in *The Eighteenth Brumaire*, Marx identifies 'the aristocracy of finance, the industrial bourgeoisie, the middle class, the petty bourgeois, the army, the lumpenproletariat…, the intellectual lights, the clergy and the rural population' (1968, 102), while in *The Class Struggle in France*, he refers to the financial aristocracy as 'one faction' of the French bourgeoisie, as well as the 'industrial bourgeoisie proper', the 'petty bourgeoisie', 'the peasantry' and 'the ideological spokesmen of all the above classes' (1969a, 206). Even in the famously incomplete Chapter 52 of *Capital*, Vol. III, as we have seen, Marx refers not only to the three big classes of modern society – the wage-labourers, capitalists and landowners – but also to certain 'middle and intermediate strata' and other classes within classes (1977, 885), while in *The Communist Manifesto* Marx and Engels refer to the middle class as 'the small trades people, shopkeepers, and retired tradesmen generally, the handicraftsmen and peasants'(1971, 88, 91), and to the aristocracy, and even a '"dangerous class", the social scum, that passively rotting mass thrown off by the lowest layers of old society' (1971, 92) – i.e. the lumpenproletariat – all the while however making it clear that they expected these 'intermediate classes' to be absorbed into either the working class or the capitalist class (1971, 91).

What implications then does all of this have for the nature of class in late industrial society? Some Marxists have claimed that the three, five or seven class models are Marx's more sophisticated, subtle, or complex view of social class, and that the two class polarization model represents Marx's earlier immature view on this question. I have already criticized this argument on the grounds that Marx seems to reiterate the two-class model in his most mature work, *Capital*, Vol. I, even though he also presents us with a three-class model in Chapter 52 of Vol. III. The solution to this apparent problem is not to be found in Marx's maturity or otherwise but in a closer look at the *circumstances* Marx describes when he employs a three, five or seven class model. In all of these cases, with the possible exception of the three-class model in Vol. III, he is referring to the class struggle in France in the middle of the nineteenth century, *a very different situation altogether* from the class struggle in England, Germany or even America at this time. And where Marx refers to three classes in the English context (e.g. in *The Communist Manifesto*), he seems to expect the third class to wither away in the face of the development of modern industry. The question we then have to ask ourselves is what were the conditions that existed in France in the middle of the nineteenth century which caused Marx to refer here to a multiplicity of classes when elsewhere he refers to only two, or at most three, social classes? Here the answer is quite clear. For Marx, the bourgeois republic in France which preceded the dictatorship of Louis Bonaparte signified 'the unlimited *despotism of one class over the other classes*' (Marx 1968, 103, 119, 170; emphasis original), while the apparent autonomy of the Bonapartist dictatorship itself was due to the fact that it represented the interests of a class which he says had *no historical role*: the small-holding peasantry. Unless those Marxists who prefer a multiple-class model to the model of two classes are prepared to say that modern post-industrialized societies too are characterized by the *despotism* of one class over all the others and moreover that this class and this period in our history has no historic role (and I might be prepared to agree with them if they did say this), then I think they must be prepared to say that the two- or three-class model was Marx's preferred model for historically progressive societies, while the five- to seven-class model applies to more socially stationary periods in history.

IV – Marx on the Concept of A-historical Development

Very much influenced by Hegel's philosophy of history – very much influenced by Hegel's philosophy in general in fact – Marx had a significant concept of 'non-' or 'a-historical' development. Hegel defines 'despotism' (see above) as 'the repetition of majestic ruin' (1956, 105–6). In Marxist terms, this concept might easily be expressed as the reproduction of the same highly developed mode of production over and over again, but without any historical progress from one mode of production to the next; and hence the absence of class struggle. The concept of 'history' for Marx (as also for Hegel) did not refer straightforwardly to 'all past events' or even 'all known past events' in the way that we understand this term today, but Marx and Hegel both describe as 'a-historical' periods in the past when they claim no historically *progressive* development took place. Paraphrasing Hegel, Marx claimed that 'Indian society has no history at all, at least no known history ... What we call its history is but the history of successive intruders who founded their empires on the passive basis of that unresisting and *unchanging* society' (Marx and Engels 1976, 81). Similarly, *The Communist Manifesto* begins with the famous claim that '[t]he history of all hitherto existing society is the history of class struggles' (1971, 79), but this is not to say that Marx and Engels think that all societies *are* characterized by class struggle or that they have always been historically progressive. Rather, certain societies, like India in Marx's view, have no *history* at all. This is because these societies are characterized by the absence of class struggle and this is precisely why Marx says that French society at the time he was writing was a-historical or despotic: because it was dominated by a *multiplicity* of classes, none of which could make any headway against each other. At the same time that England was becoming more and more polarized between the interests of two hostile and irreconcilable classes, as Marx supposed, French society was dominated by the survival of the peasantry into the modern era, and – characterized by a multiplicity of other classes – historically speaking, was going nowhere.

Although *The Communist Manifesto* begins with the statement: 'The history of all hitherto existing society is the history of class struggles' (Marx and

Engels 1971), the idea that this means (a) that *all* historical periods are characterized by 'class struggles' and therefore (b) that classes must *always and everywhere exist* is one of the most widespread but, in my view, mistaken beliefs about Marx's concept of class today. Because Marx and Hegel both had a significant concept of a-historical development (i.e. of relatively stationary periods throughout history in which particular societies were not progressing historically from one mode of production to another), this opens up the possibility that, for Marx at least, *not* all societies or all past events *are* characterized by classes or by class struggle. In my view, the Marxist concept of class is therefore not to be identified with *every* possible 'gradation of social rank' (Marx and Engels 1971, 80), but *only* with certain very specific – or, better still, *fundamental* – social situations; basically those in which access to and separation from ownership of the means of production, and hence the reproduction of human life, is at a critical stage in its development. Defined in this way, 'social classes' in the Marxist sense of this term may be said to exist only under certain very *exceptional* and therefore quite rare, transitory and fleeting conditions, conditions found only during historically progressive (or in other words, revolutionary) periods in history. For most of the time however most societies are not to be characterized by this type of class conflict (i.e. class struggle) and this is precisely *why they are not* developing historically.

Marx's clearest definition of social class is one in which he makes it quite clear that not everyone always and everywhere *has* a class location. This occurs in his discussion of the French peasantry in the middle of the nineteenth century. France at this time was despotic, by which, as we have seen, Marx means us to understand that it was not developing historically precisely because the French peasantry did not constitute a meaningful social class. In *The Eighteenth Brumaire of Louis Bonaparte*, Marx comments:

> In this way the great mass of the French nation is formed by simple additions of homologous magnitudes, much as potatoes in a sack form a sack of potatoes. In so far as millions of families live under economic conditions of existence that separate their mode of life, their interests and their culture from those of the other classes, and put them into hostile opposition to the latter, they form a class. In so far as there is merely a local connection among these smallholding peasants, and the identity of their interests begets no community, no national bond and no political organisation among them, they do not form a class. (Marx 1968, 170–71)

Based on this quotation we can say that a social class is a class for Marx *only* when the following conditions apply but not otherwise:

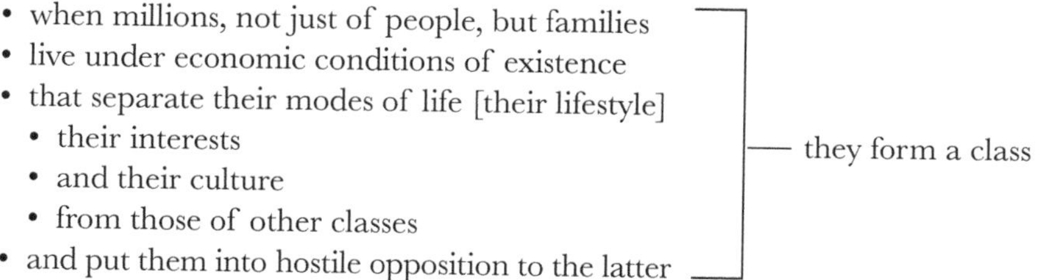

But that, in so far as:

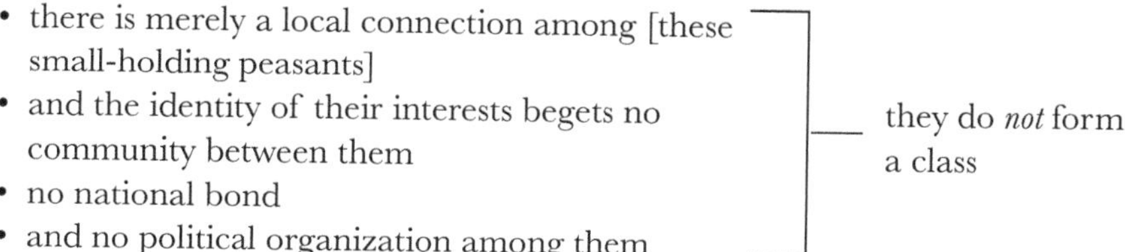

Conclusion

We are now in a position to answer the question which of the above concepts – the two-class polarized model or the three/five/seven multiple-class model – is Marx's concept of social class and of course the answer to this question (as we might well have expected all along) is that *both* and/or *all* three of these two/three class models are Marx's 'true' view of class. Where Marx is describing a historically stagnant, or relatively stationary, period in the history of a country's development he employs a *multiple*-class model and the less historical the development of a particular society is at that time the more classes he says it has. However, the more this situation conforms to a period of historical development the more he employs a *two*-class model. In between these two extremes he uses a more or less finely gradated model of class to describe historically progressive periods in history. In other words, Marx is *not* employing two or three different concepts of class here at all, but simply *one complex concept of class* in which he employs two or three different models to analyse completely different class situations. This concept of class can be expressed in Fig. 19.

Figure 19. Marx's concept of social class

	Number of classes/strata	*Source*
Historically progressive	One class/no classes (achievement of socialism/ communism)	*Communist Manifesto*
	Two-class model: class polarity 'class struggle'; 'class warfare' bourgeoisie and proletariat	*Capital*, Vol. I, 1974a, 715 *Communist Manifesto*
	Three-class model: 'three big classes of modern society': 'wage-labourers, capitalists and landowners'	*Capital*, Vol. III, Ch. 52
Transitional	Three-class model: aristocracy, bourgeois (lower and, by implication, higher middle class) and proletarians or working class	*Communist Manifesto*
A-historical or 'despotic'	Five-class model: big landowners bourgeoisie (including a financial aristocracy, industrial bourgeoisie), various middle 'strata' (peasants petty bourgeoisie), 'working class' and the lumpenproletariat	*The Class Struggle in France*, 1969a, 206, 219, 223–7
	Seven-class model: aristocracy of finance, industrial bourgeoisie, middle class, petty bourgeoisie, lumpenproletariat, intellectuals, and the proletariat	*The Eighteenth Brumaire of Louis Bonaparte*, 1968a, 102–3, 121, 168, 170

Finally, what is the situation as far as social class is concerned in post-industrial societies today? Are we living in a historically progressive period of history, characterized as we have seen by a two-class model of society, or in a period of relative social stationariness and the absence of any real historical progress, characterized by a multiple-class/absence-of-class model? Clearly the a-historical model fits the situation we find ourselves in today much better than one characterized by class polarity. The growth, rather than the expected withering away, of the so-called 'middle classes' in post-industrial society, the continued survival of the aristocracy – and especially of the British royal family – into the twenty-first century, and of all sorts of other intermediate fractions and strata, including all sorts of ethnic divisions in society, indicates the absence of any historically progressive period in the development of the capitalist mode of production and hence, at the moment, the absence of anything that might reasonably be called *class* struggle.

NOTES

Introduction

1 I am grateful to Chris Arthur, formerly lecturer in philosophy at the University of Sussex, for this information.

2 I am grateful to the late Professor Tom Bottomore, formerly Professor of Sociology at Sussex University, for this information.

3 The exact quotation is as follows: 'Should you wish to leaf through some of *Capital*, it would be best to *start* with the *last* section, 314. In the scientific exposition the order is prescribed for the author, although some other arrangements might often be more convenient and more appropriate for the reader' (*Marx and Engels Collected Works* 1991, 45:212).

4 That is, we start with *Capital*, Vol. I, Part III, Ch. 10 and 12, 'The Working Day and the Concept of Relative Surplus Value' (missing out altogether the technical and rather uninteresting Ch. 11, 'The Rate and Mass of Surplus Value'). We then go on to look at Ch. 13–15, 'Co-operation', 'The Division of Labour and Manufacture' and 'Machinery and Modern Industry', and conclude this introductory section by looking at Vol. I, Part VIII, on 'primitive', or pre-capitalist, accumulation. Having started with these more descriptive chapters of Vol. I, we then come back to Part VII, Ch. 23 and 24, 'Simple and Extended Reproduction', with a detailed discussion of the qualitative difference between the capitalist mode of production (the CMP), and pre-capitalist types of accumulation.

5 I know of one other guide to *Capital* that, at least in intention, has the ambition to cover all three volumes of *Capital* that by Ben Fine, *Marx's Capital* (1975) and recently reissued in its fourth edition in 2004 together with Alfredo Saad-Filho. Another book – the so-called *The People's Marx: Abridged Popular Edition of the Three Volumes of 'Capital'*, edited by Julian Borchardt and published by International Bookshops Ltd., in 1921 – but in point of fact this book is merely a collection of excerpts from all three volumes of *Capital*, and does not elaborate upon these or provide any further guidance to them.

6 See *Marx and Engels Collected Works* 1991, 45:463, 62n, for a detailed account of Marx's various proposals for the publication of the second and third volumes or *Capital* as a single Vol. II, and the book which is now known as *Theories of Surplus Value* (Marx's notebooks on classical political economy) as *Capital*, Vol. III.

7 Engels himself gave another explanation in the preface to the first German edition of *Capital*, Vol. II, written in May 1884, or just over a year after Marx's death, of why Marx did not complete the publication of *Capital* during his lifetime. 'The mere enumeration of the manuscript material left by Marx for Book II proves the unparalleled conscientiousness and strict self-criticism with which he endeavoured to elaborate his great economic discoveries to the point of utmost completion before he published them. This self-criticism rarely permitted him to adapt his presentation of the subject, in content as

well as in form, to his ever widening horizon, the result of incessant study' (*Capital* Vol. II, 1974b, 2 [1978, 84]).

8 See also a footnote on Nassau Senior and John Stuart Mill (*Capital,* Vol. I., 1974a, 559, 2n [1976, 744, 29n]) in which Marx says: 'John St. Mill, on the contrary, accepts on the one hand Ricardo's theory of profit, and annexes on the other hand Senior's "remuneration of abstinence". He is as much at home in absurd contradictions, as he feels at sea in the Hegelian contradiction, the source of all dialectic. It has never occurred to the vulgar economist to make the simple reflection that every human action may be viewed as 'abstinence' from its opposite. Eating is abstinence from fasting, walking abstinence from standing still, working abstinence from idling, idling abstinence from working etc. These gentlemen would do well to ponder, once in a way, over Spinoza's "Determinatio est Negatio".'

9 As a matter of fact Marx did write one book which has the word 'class' in its title, *The Class Struggle in France, 1848 to 1850,* but since this is in fact little more than a series of articles written during 1850 about the situation in France, after the collapse of the 1848 revolution, although this is still of interest to us as far as Marx's concept of class is concerned, it does not alter the essential point that I am making here in relation to *Capital.* It is not class, but capital, that is the major explanatory variable that Marx is dealing with here and this of course is the reason why his book has the title it does.

Part I: The Development of the Capitalist Mode of Production

1 See Part II, Chapter 5 of this book, for a more detailed discussion of this point.

Part II: The Capitalist Mode of Production

1 I have absolutely no idea at all why Marx extends the scale of the process of production that he considers in this example, other than perhaps because he wished to give a more realistic example of the scale of a genuine capitalist mode of production – the kind of investment that might actually be required at the time he was writing. If that was the case, however, then why not do the same thing in the previous chapter too? Here, it seems as though the extension of the CMP in the example given has already taken place and, in point of fact of course, this detracts from the point that Marx actually wishes to make.

2 On this point see also *Capital,* Vol. II (1974b, 472 [1978, 544]), where Marx argues: 'Foreign trade could help out in either case: in the first case to convert commodities I held in the form of money into articles of consumption, and in the second case to dispose of the commodity surplus. But since foreign trade does not merely replace certain elements (also with regard to value), it only transfers the contradictions to a wider sphere and gives them greater latitude.'

3 The qualification here, that means of production *may* only pass into productive consumption rather than saying that they *must* be so consumed, is added because of the very real possibility that surplus value produced in the form of the means of production, since, as it *cannot* be consumed unproductively, it must be wasted if it cannot be employed in the production process.

4 I say '*approximately* the same' here because it is not entirely clear to me why Marx gives a figure of 376 for the variable capital and surplus value of DII, rather than 375v

and s which would have been an exact quarter of the 1,500c in question. Presumably this is simply a typographical mistake.

5 According to Meghnad Desai (2002, 74) this was actually done – or at least attempted – in the early days of the former Soviet Union.

6 See for example *Capital*, Vol. II (1974b, 454–5 [1978, 526]), where Marx argues: 'the money proceeds realized from the sale of commodities, so far as they turn into money that part of the commodity value which is equal to the wear and tear of fixed capital, are not reconverted into that component part of the productive capital whose diminution in value they cover. They settle down beside the productive capital and persist in the form of money. This *precipitation* of money is repeated, until the period of reproduction consisting of great or small numbers of years has elapsed, during which the fixed element of constant capital continues to function in the process of production in its old bodily form.'

7 No doubt this is why so many books which claim to provide an account of *Capital* only discuss Vol. I, and sometimes Vol. III. One wonders sometimes why Engels bothered to include any of the failed solutions that Marx made in his search for an answer, except, I suppose, that these do at least show the length and the depths that Marx was prepared to go to, to find a solution to the problems he set out to consider in *Capital* as a whole.

Part III: The Underdevelopment of the Capitalist Mode of Production

1 As Marx says on this point in *Capital*, Vol. II (1974b, 50 [1978, 133]), 'The two forms assumed by capital-value at the various stages of its circulation are those of *money-capital* and *commodity-capital*. The form pertaining to the stage of production is that of *productive capital*. The capital which assumes these forms in the course of its total circuit and then discards them and in each of them performs the function corresponding to the particular form, is *industrial capital*, industrial here in the sense that it comprises every branch of industry run on a capitalist basis.'

2 See the General Introduction to the present study, 'A Note on Marx's Method', for more on this point.

3 Marx makes a very similar point to this in *Capital*, Vol. III (1977, 607 [1981, 742]): 'This social character of capital is first promoted and wholly realized through the development of the credit and banking system. On the one hand this goes farther. It places all of the available and even potential capital of society that is not already actively employed at the disposal of the industrial and commercial capitalists so that neither the lenders nor users of this capital are its real owners or producers. It thus does away with the private character of capital and thus contains in itself, *but only in itself*, the abolition of capital itself. By means of the banking system the distribution of capital as *a special business*, a social function, is taken out of the hands of the private capitalists and usurers. But at the same time, banking and credit thus become the most potent means of driving capitalist production beyond its own limits, and one of the most effective vehicles of crisis and swindle' (emphasis added).

4 On this point see Tom Bottomore's introduction to the 1981 English translation of *Das Finanzkapital* (*Finance Capital. A Study of the Latest Phase of Capitalist Development*); see especially 1, for Otto Bauer and Karl Kautsky's comments on this point.

5 The reader who would like to know more about this point might like to look at Georg Simmel's *The Philosophy of Money* (1900; London: Routledge & Kegan Paul, 1978), in which, among other things, Simmel presents an alternative to the labour theory of value.

6 As an ideal-typical construct, the pure case of a rate of profit which did not fall could be used to identify which of the counterbalancing factors were ineffective in the case of an *actual* fall in the rate of profit and, therefore, which of these forces may be said to have actually caused the rate of profit to fall in this particular case.

Part IV: The Value Theory of Labour

1 It is an interesting question to consider here – and I do not know whether this observation has ever been made before – why Marx devoted *quite* so much attention in *Capital*, Vol. I to, and actually named an entire section after, Nassau W. Senior. It is an honour he accords to no one else. Yet elsewhere (*Capital*, 1974a, 559, 2n [1976, 744, 29n]) Marx refers to Senior as a vulgar economist (in order to distinguish him from 'classical economists', i.e. those for whom Marx did have some respect) and seems to hold him in nothing but the very greatest contempt. The answer to this paradox I believe is that Marx derived his entire theory of surplus value – the very thing for which he is now most remembered – from Senior's error. It was because Senior made the mistake of suggesting that all profit derived from the last hour of labour only that gave Marx the clue to the facts and his own theory of surplus value. Because Senior obviously could not be right, something else altogether must be the case. That 'something else' is the difference between profit and surplus value.

2 See Part II, Chapter 5 of the present study for a parallel study of this point in slightly different terms.

3 I have taken this reference from Pilling (1980, 53), but I think his interpretation on this point is incorrect. Marx does not mean that we should abandon the search for an invariable measure of value (i.e. for the concept of value itself) as Pilling seems to think, but that we should try to develop an understanding of the concept of value itself – of what it means to say that something has value – without reducing our understanding of this to something else, e.g. to a measure *of* value. It is the use of the term invariable *measure* of value that I believe Marx is criticizing and not the search for such a concept itself.

4 This is quoted by Marx in *Theories of Surplus Value*, Vol. III (1972, 137), and is attributed by him to one Samuel Bailey. I have taken it from Elson (1979, 154).

5 Marx refers to the cost of reproduction, rather than simply to the cost of production, as the determinant of the value of something, because it is what something *presently* costs to reproduce, not what it originally cost to produce, that determines its present value. 'Aside from all incidental interference, a large part of capital is constantly more or less depreciated in the course of the reproduction process, because the value of commodities is not determined by the labour-time originally expended on their production, but by the labour-time expended in their reproduction, and this decreases continually owing to the development of the social productivity of labour' (*Capital*, Vol. III, Ch. 24, 1977, 398 [1981, 522]).

6 The word 'only' is enclosed in square brackets in this quotation because Lukács includes it in his quotation of this passage from *Capital*, Vol. I. This word *does not* appear in the Lawrence & Wishart/Progress Press 1974 edition of *Capital*. The Penguin edition of *Capital* gives yet another variation of the same passage: 'It is nothing but the definite social relations between men themselves which assumes here' [1976, 165].

7 The reference to 'table turning' here is to a popular form of spiritualism in vogue at the time that Marx was writing in which gullible people would be invited to a meeting in which they were invited to place their hands on a table which would then move violently, allegedly due to the actions of spiritual forces upon it.

BIBLIOGRAPHY

Althusser, L. 1971. *Lenin and Philosophy and Other Essays*. London: Allen Lane.

Althusser, L. and E. Balibar. 1970. *Reading Capital*. London: New Left Books.

Beaud, M. 1974. *A History of Capitalism 1500–1980*. London: Macmillan.

Bottomore, T. 1981. 'Introduction'. In Rudolf Hilferding, *Finance Capital: A Study of the Latest Phase of Capitalist Development*. London: Routledge & Kegan Paul.

Bukharin, N. 1972a. *Imperialism and World Trade*. London: Merlin Press.

_______. 1972b. 'Imperialism and the Accumulation of Capital'. In *Rosa Luxemburg and Nikolai Bukharin: Imperialism and the Accumulation of Capital*. Ed. by Kenneth J. Tarbuck. London: Allen Lane/Penguin Press.

Carchedi, G. 1977. *Of the Economic Identification of Social Classes*. London: Routledge & Kegan Paul.

Desai, Meghnad. 2002, *Marx's Revenge: The Resurgence of Capitalism and the Death of Statist Socialism*. London and New York: Verso Press.

Elson, D. (ed.) 1979. 'The Value Theory of Labour'. In *Value: The Representation of Labour in Capitalism*. London: CSE Books/Humanities Press Inc.

Fine, B. and A. Saad-Filho. 2004. *Marx's Capital*. London: Pluto Press.

Gough, I. 1978. 'Marx's Theory of Productive and Unproductive Labour'. In *Marx: Sociology, Social Change, Capitalism*. Ed. by D. McQuarie. London: Quartet Books.

Hall, S. 1977. 'The "political" and the "economic" in Marx's theory of class'. In *Class and Class Structure*. Ed. by A. Hunt. London: Lawrence & Wishart.

Harvey, D. 2010. *A Companion to Marx's Capital*. London: Verso Press.

Hegel, G. 1956. *The Philosophy of History*. London: Constable and Co.

Hilferding, R. 1981. *Finance Capital: A Study of the Latest Phase of Capitalist Development*. London: Routledge & Kegan Paul.

Hobson, J. A. 1988. *Imperialism: A Study*. London: Unwin Hyman Ltd.

Kay, G. 1975. *Development and Underdevelopment: A Marxist Analysis*. London: Macmillan.

Kemp, T. 1967. *Theories of Imperialism*. London: Dobson Books Ltd.

Kenwood, A. G. and A. L. Lougheed. 1971. *The Growth of the International Economy, 1820–1960*. London: Allen & Unwin.

Korsch, K. 1971. *Three Essays on Marxism*. London: Pluto Press.

Lenin, V. I. 1975. 'Imperialism, the Highest Stage of Capitalism'. In *Selected Works*, Vol. 1. Moscow: Progress Press.

Lukács, G. 1971. *History and Class Consciousness*. London: Merlin Press.

Luxemburg, R. 1963. *The Accumulation of Capital*. London: Routledge & Kegan Paul.

_______. 1972. 'The Accumulation of Capital – An Anti-Critique'. In *Rosa Luxemburg and Nikolai Bukharin: Imperialism and the Accumulation of Capital*. Ed. by Kenneth J. Tarbuck. London: Allen Lane/Penguin Press.

Mandel, E. 1975. *Late Capitalism.* London: Verso Editions.
Markovik, M. 1974. *From Affluence to Praxis.* Ann Arbor: University of Michigan Press.
Marx, K. 1968a. 'The Eighteenth Brumaire of Louis Napoleon'. In *Marx and Engels Selected Works*, Vol. 1. London: Lawrence & Wishart.
______. 1968b. 'The Civil War in France'. In *Marx and Engels Selected Works*, Vol. 1. London: Lawrence & Wishart.
______. 1969a. 'The Class Struggle in France'. In *Marx and Engels Selected Works*, Vol. 1. London: Lawrence & Wishart.
______. 1969b. *The Class Struggle in France 1848–1850.* In *Marx and Engels Selected Works*, Vol. 1. Moscow: Progress Press.
______. 1969c. *The Eighteenth Brumaire of Louis Bonaparte.* In *Marx and Engels Selected Works*, Vol. 1. Moscow: Progress Press.
______. 1969d. *The Civil War in France.* In *Marx and Engels Selected Works*, Vol. 2. Moscow: Progress Press.
______. 1972. *Theories of Surplus Value*, Vols I–III. London: Lawrence & Wishart.
______. 1973. *Grundrisse: Foundations of the Critique of Political Economy (Rough Draft).* London: Penguin Books, in association with New Left Review.
______. 1974a. *Capital*, Vol. I. London: Lawrence & Wishart.
______. 1974b. *Capital*, Vol. II. London: Lawrence & Wishart.
______. 1977. *Capital*, Vol. III. London: Lawrence & Wishart.
Marx, K. and F. Engels. 1936. *Selected Correspondence.* Moscow: Progress Press.
______. 1969. *Marx and Engels Selected Works*, 3 vols. Moscow: Progress Press.
______. 1971. *The Communist Manifesto.* 5th edition. London: Penguin.
______. 1976. *On Colonialism.* 6th edition. Moscow: Progress Press.
______. 1983. *Marx and Engels Collected Works*, Vol. 42. Moscow: Progress Press.
______. 1991. *Marx and Engels Collected Works.* New York: International Publishers.
Mészáros, I. 1970. *Marx's Theory of Alienation.* London: Merlin Press.
Müller, W. and C. Neusüss. 1970/1975. 'The Illusions of State Socialism and the Contradictions Between Wage Labour and Capital'. [Translation of *Die Sozialstaatsillusion und der Widerspruch von Lohnarbeit und Kapital* (1970)]. *Telos* (Winter 1975).
Pilling, G. 1980. *Marx's Capital.* London: Routledge & Kegan Paul.
Poulantzas, N. 1975. *Classes in Contemporary Capitalism.* London: New Left Books.
Ricardo, D. 1971. *Principles of Political Economy and Taxation.* London: Penguin.
Rosdolsky, R. 1980. *The Making of Marx's 'Capital'.* London: Pluto Press.
Schmidt, A. 1971. *The Concept of Nature in Marx*, London: New Left Books.
Schumpeter, J. 1951. *Imperialism and Social Classes.* Oxford: Basil Blackwell.
Smith, A. 1986. *The Wealth of Nations, Books I–III.* Harmondsworth, Middlesex: Penguin.
Smith, K. 2004. 'Marx on the Side of the Market?: Review Essay of Meghnad Desai's *Marx's Revenge*'. *Journal of Classical Sociology* 4, no. 2: 237–54.
Tarbuck, Kenneth J. (ed.) 1972. *Rosa Luxemburg and Nikolai Bukharin: Imperialism and the Accumulation of Capital.* London: Allen Lane/Penguin Press.
Urry, J. 1981. *The Anatomy of Capitalist Societies. The Economy, Civil Society, and the State.* London: Macmillan.
Warren, B. 1973. 'Imperialism and Capitalist Industrialisation'. *New Left Review* 81 (Sept/Oct): 3–44.
______. 1980. *Imperialism, Pioneer of Capitalism.* London: New Left Books/Verso Press.
Weber, Max. 1978. *Economy and Society.* Ed. by Guenther Roth and Claus Wittich. Berkeley: University of California Press.

INDEX